FLYING
AMERICAN
COMBAT AIRCRAFT
OF WWII

D1403322

0 11557 03124 9

FLYING AMERICAN COMBAT AIRCRAFT OF WWII

1939–45

Edited by Robin Higham

STACKPOLE
BOOKS

Library of Congress Cataloging-in-Publication Data

Flying American combat aircraft of WWII : 1939–45 / edited by Robin
Higham.— 1st ed.
    p. cm. — (Stackpole Military history series)
 Articles taken from volumes of Flying combat aircraft of the
USAAF-USAF.
 Includes index.
 ISBN 0-8117-3124-3
 1. Airplanes, Military—United States—History—20th century. 2.
World War, 1939–1945—Aerial operations, American. 3. Air pilots,
Military—United States—Biography. 4. World War, 1939–1945—Personal
narratives, American. I. Higham, Robin D. S. II. Flying combat aircraft
of the USAAF-USAF. III. Series.
UG1243 .F53 2004
940.54'4973'0922—dc22

                                                      2003023081

Table of Contents

Preface

The informative and entertaining pieces presented here are both original documents and fallible memoirs. It is admitted at once that they represent one school of thought only as to the proper way to handle a particular plane. Another pilot in another war theater may have flown the craft quite differently (or thought he did), so no claim is made that these chapters are absolutely reliable guides. We do say each has been prepared both conscientiously and lovingly and has, whenever possible, been checked against an appropriate authoritative manual.

We acknowledge also that an ingredient of flying life is the tendency to "shoot a line." Thus, even though the authors believe some of the stories related here to be completely accurate, they may not be. In any event, we hope readers will find these accounts enlightening, stimulating, and sometimes amusing—all to be recalled, in the case of veterans at least, with fond memories, if not complete agreement.

To include chapters on all combat aircraft was, of course, impossible because of lack of space and the difficulty of finding authors.

Unless otherwise indicated, all photographs are courtesy of the United States Air Force.

R. H. and A. T. S.

Introduction

Robin Higham and Charles D. Bright

A quarter of a century ago, I decided that one of my missions as Editor of the Air Force Historical Foundation's magazine *Aerospace Historian* was to preserve knowledge of how World War II aircraft, as well as others, were flown. I contacted a number of former pilots and asked them to write a piece as if they were talking to me. To help them I sent along this checklist:

> For your contribution to our combat aircraft books would you please try to cover the following points where appropriate:
> 1. First impression
> 2. Getting into the cockpit
> 3. Pilot's and other manuals
> 4. Putting equipment online
> 5. Starting up
> 6. Taxiing
> 7. Pre-take-off drill
> 8. Take-off technique and characteristics, climbing out
> 9. Handling in the air
> 10. Combat handling and idiosyncracies
> 11. Range, endurance, speed
> 12. Bailing out
> 13. Landing procedures and techniques
> 14. Personal experience with the aircraft—love or hate relationship?
> 15. Brief comparison with some other similar type you also flew, either or both contemporary or a piston-jet comparison

16. Any other comment that will help the reader understand
    or appreciate the aircraft; including the effect of special
    equipment
17. Refueling on the ground and in the air

NB. 1. Please do not exceed fourteen to sixteen double-spaced
    typed pages of about 2,000–4,000 words.
2. Please do supply a one-paragraph biography indicating
   where and when you flew the aircraft and a photograph
   of yourself.
3. If you have any good shots of aircraft including the one
   you flew, please lend.
4. Do not hesitate to compare this aircraft to others you
   have flown.

Not all items applied, of course, and not all authors were entirely
successful. Some had to be helped along by requests for clarifications
and more details.

Fortunately, I had myself been trained to fly in 1943–1947 and in
American designed and built machines—the Fairchild PT-26 Cornell, the
Cessna AT-17 Crane, and finally on operations in a Douglas C-47 Dakota.
In addition I trained in blind-landings in the docile Avro Anson and in
Nevil Shute [Norway's] design, the Airspeed Oxford.

Those of us who got our wings (technically, in the RAF, a pilot's
brevet) learned to fly only forty years after the Wright brothers had
launched at Kitty Hawk and only sixteen years after Lindbergh had flown
the Atlantic solo. Flying was still both an escape and an ambition—and
above all a challenge.

The aircraft of World War II were neither as simple as the Wrights'
nor were the flyers as ignorant of their unknown medium as the brothers
were. After all, they were the first to achieve powered flight and the ones
to develop the ability to control a machine in the air.

Progress has been rapid in two important aspects of the subject—the
technical and the instructional. On the technical side, wing warping had
been replaced by ailerons and the elevators in front of the wing, which in
the Wrights' machines had a parachute effect in a stall, by a complete tail
appendage including both a horizontal stabilizer and elevators in addition to the fin and rudder. By 1940 the biplane was being replaced by
monoplanes. I never have flown a biplane but my contemporaries in the
RAF frequently did their Elementary flying training on a De Haviland

Tiger Moth while USAAC/USAAF (the name was changed from the U.S. Army Air Corps to the U.S. Army Air Forces in May 1941) cadets did primary training in the Waco or Stearman PTs. The next step for Service flying training was either on the North American AT-6 Harvard, the Cessna AT-17 Crane, or the Avro Anson. In the USAAC system, cadets went to the Vultee BT-13 "Vibrator" for Basic and then on to either the AT-6 or the AT-17 Bobcat for Advanced. All told, after 150 to 270 hours, cadets got their pilot's brevet in the RAF or wings in the USAAF.

That satisfactory result was achieved rather differently in the two services, and quite differently for Royal Navy Fleet Air Arm pilots and the U.S. Navy aviators trained together at Pensacola on both land planes and flying boats.

In the RAF, the shortage of pilots and the basic concept that cadets with a white flash in their forage caps were potential officers and gentlemen, and extremely costly to train, meant that whether you ended up a sergeant pilot (sixty percent) or an officer, you were too valuable to washout. Every effort was made to try to get you to graduate. In contrast to the high washout rate in the USAAF, supposedly in the name of quality and safety, of my group in 1944, we lost one for a three-point landing on the propeller, wing-tip, and one wheel in a PT-26, and another spun in from a low-level near his girl's house. However, the RAF was anti-colonial, and its potential Coastal Command pilots, who had received their golden wings at Pensacola and even had flown a Consolidated PBY from Bermuda to Scotland, were sent back to Tiger Moth once they reached England.

In the USAAC/USAAF, there was a high washout rate in elaborate pre-flight testing and in all three levels of flight schooling. We know of this primarily from the memoirs of the successful, a number of whom had narrow escapes before someone had the necessary faith and compassion to get them through. The end result was not only a proud, chest-puffing moment but thereafter a gratifying respect from parents and an advantage with girls.

There were some experiential and social factors that influenced events after September 1, 1939, when the U.S. Army Air Corps began what Gen. H. H. "Hap" Arnold called a "vast expansion." The goal was to produce 30,000 new pilots per year. Production from 1919 to then was 300 pilots per year, so the increase was to be at least an incredible 10,000 percent in two years. The U.S. Navy was faced with a similar challenge.

The World War I experience was of value, because the Army had trained 20,000 flyers for it, albeit in simpler times. After demobilization,

18,000 of them returned to civilian life, and many became "barnstormers," bringing the romance of flying to the people.

An even greater social factor was Hollywood. I calculate that the movie industry produced 166 films with aviation a theme or element in the story from 1919 to 1939. Of these, fifty-six, or about one-third, involved the military services. Half of those concerned World War I, two were "blockbusters," with *Wings* winning the first "Best Picture" award from the Motion Picture Academy, and *Hells Angels* containing a pioneering color segment. With Hollywood producing so many films in this period, it is evident that aviation held the public's interest.

Pulp magazines devoted to flying stories became popular in the late 1920s, and this interest lasted until World War II. Popular books included Floyd Gibbons' *The Red Knight of Germany*, James Norman Hall and Charles Nordhoff's *Falcons of France*, and *Hall's High Adventures*.

Building model airplanes "from scratch" or from kits was very popular among boys. In fact, the boys from this generation became flying enthusiasts. It was also an era of real-life spectacular flights by American pilot-heroes such as Charles Lindbergh, Lt. Jimmy Doolittle, Wiley Post, Howard Hughes, and Amelia Earhart. Nevertheless, recruiting would prove to be a problem.

To expand pilot production when the time came, extensive use of civilian schools was contracted for the first phase of training: "Primary." At their peak, the civilian schools for the army numbered fifty-six in May 1943. Before the expansion, cadets had to be at least twenty years of age with at least two years of college. This was eventually cut to eighteen years and high school. The response was so great that recruits had a waiting period before entering active duty because the training facilities could not accommodate so many.

Another step to increase production was to shorten training from a year to seven months. As the army program and instructor pilots became more experienced, more advanced aircraft were used earlier. The advanced single-engine trainer (thus AT-6) was successfully used in Basic Training (which followed Primary), ending use of the Vultee BT-13. By the end of the war the B-25 was used in multi-engined Advanced. It had excellent flying qualities and gave more realistic training than the earlier, simpler aircraft—Cessna AT-17 and UC-78, Beech AT-10 and Curtiss AT-9.

Early in the program a number of types of trainers were used in order to obtain as many as possible: Stearman PT-13 and PT17; Beech AT-7, AT-10, and AT-11; Bellanca AT-21; Cessna AT-8 and AT-17; Vultee BT-15 and AT-19; Fairchild AT-21; Fleet PT-23 and PT-26; Globe AT-10; McDonnell AT-21; Ryan PT-20, PT-21, and PT-25; St. Louis PT-19 and PT-23; and Waco PT-14. By the end of the war, only Stearmans were used in Primary to achieve standardization. Also, the USAAF still had "tail-dragger" aircraft, and it was believed that pilots who mastered the Stearman could land any tail-dragger. The navy trainers were Stearman N2S, Navy Aircraft Factory N3N, and North American SNJ (same as Army AT-6).

The army produced 193,440 pilots between July 1, 1939, and August 31, 1945. It "washed-out" roughly two out of five trainees. Pilot training is expensive, and the elimination rate reflects mainly slow learners rather than an inability to fly. The navy's elimination rate was roughly thirty percent, and for the same reason.

Possibly the pilot training in the last year of the war was the best ever in America, based upon the experience level of the flight instructors.

The RAF and the USAAF also differed in their post-wings approaches. The RAF sent pilots to Advanced flying units to get more time in and generally hone their skills before being posted to a fighter, a bomber, or another specialized Operational Training Unit (OTU). Fighter pilots were then sent to a squadron. Multi-engined pilots upon arriving at an OTU were put in a room full of other aircrew and told to choose a crew. The process was a rather delicate dance in which "the skipper" introduced himself to a navigator, a bomb-aimer, a flight engineer, a wireless-operator (W/Op), and to gunners depending on the type of aircraft—a Wellington needing seven all told. Often, one or two aircrew already knew each other, and a chain-reaction set in. There was a certain hesitation and doubt on both sides since no one knew another's competence or personality. On the whole, with fellows hailing from all over Britain and the Commonwealth, it worked pretty well, especially since RAF Bomber Command flew at night and each crew was on its own from take-off to landing. In Bomber Command, there were also aircrew messes rather than officers', senior NCOs', and airmens'.

In the USAAF, up to thirteen aircrew were assigned to a crew. Given the population of the country, immigrants and all, the variety of accents was as large as in the RAF, and the personalities different. On the whole, the crews clung together pretty well in the air but were more separate on the ground. What was more disruptive was that overseas crews were split up and reformed depending upon deaths, wounds, and the number of missions flown. And the process also varied by theaters.

The RAF treated combat fatigue as Lack of Moral Fibre (LMF), summarily removed the person from flying, stripped them of their brevet, commission, or rank, and gave them a dishonorable discharge (the top righthand corner of their discharge paper being cut off). On the other hand, the flight-surgeon in USAAF units could go to the Commanding Officer (CO) and suggest that a person be relieved from flying. At least in the Pacific, such a compassionate approach was taken on the grounds that such a veteran and his experience was priceless and should be used. Besides, there were always those in rear-area desk jobs eager to get combat experience.

LMF was a hang-over from shell-shock of World War I (1914–1918) and still smacks of the "white feather" of Victorian times, which had to be stopped early in the Battle of Britain when officious persons handed feathers to young men of military age in civilian clothes who turned out to be fighter pilots trying to enjoy a day off. The U.S. experience is detailed in S. A. Stouffer, et al., *The American Soldier*, vol. 2, *Combat and its aftermath* (Princeton, NJ: Princeton University Press, 1949, 1965), 324–410.

The technological revolution in aviation began in the early 1930s and very much affected those learning to fly and conducting operations in the 1941–1945 war. The new items were monoplanes of all-metal construction which called for new manufacturing techniques. These planes were fitted with retractable undercarriages and flaps, with new higher powered engines made possible by high octane fuels. The increased size and weight not only necessitated hydraulic brakes and inflated tires, but also concrete runways at permanent stations and PSP (perforced steel plate or Marston mat) portable runways at temporary airfields and landing grounds. The new aircraft needed bigger generators because of the new electronics, an airborne radar in various forms for IFF (identification friend or foe), to Gee and Loran to enable positions to be plotted, to AI (airborne interception) for night fighters to Rebecca and Eureka homing beacons for dropping paratroopers on a certain DZ (dropping zone). Bomb-aimers began to get computing bombsights to replace the operationally cumbersome Norden. And then there were the jet fighters, a few of whom I saw in England in 1944–1945.

The growth of range, speed, and weight of the USAAF's aircraft can be visualized by Efficiency Ratings. The fighters of 1918 rated about .9, the heavy bombers a bit over 1. By 1939, the fighters were up to about 1.5 and the heavier to 25. By 1945, the P-51D rated a 9.63, the B-17 a 75, the B-24 a 103, and the B-29 rated a 414. Today, the Airbus A-380 is 10,907.

While radio silence except for fighters under sector control was golden, most aircraft in operational theaters were silent until they had something to report or were in distress. Communications were by W/T (wireless using dots and dashes Morse Code) or by voice on VHF or UHF R/T (radio telephone).

Slowly, from Britain, an air/sea rescue (ASR) network developed, coupled to flying control. The first aim was to recover lost aircraft through an elaborate system of having aids from radio bearings to escorting fighters to a triad of searchlights. The ultimate fix was on a ditching position so that ASR teams in planes and high-speed launches could be sent to recover invaluable aircrew who were equipped with inflatable dinghies, Mae West life vests, and signaling apparatus including sea-markers and sustenance. In the Pacific, PBY "Dunbo" flying-boats and eventually submarines did much of the rescue work of USAAF and Allied aircrew.

Learning to fly and going on operations was for many of us a disciplining, exhilarating, life-forming experience never to be forgotten. When on October 28,1944, I got my brevet, it was the proudest moment of my life because for the first time I had done something all by myself without parental guidance.

The Forty, The Spit, and The Jug

John A. C. Andrews

It was July 1943. Parked on the ramp of Sunrise Airport at Tifton, Georgia, was a P-40F painted in wartime camouflage. To a pilot with a total of about 190 hours, all in trainer aircraft, this was an impressive sight. Stories were coming in from North Africa, where American Warhawks and British Kittyhawks of the Desert Air Force were harassing Rommel's army and shooting down German aircraft. The Palm Sunday Massacre had taken place the previous April, when Desert Air Force fighters—mostly P-40s—had shot down sixty-five German aircraft as they desperately attempted to get out of Cape Bon. This was a real warplane, one that I had wanted to fly for four years. My time had come.

I first saw the 400-mile-per-hour Curtiss P-40 at the 1939 New York World's Fair, where the Army Air Corps was displaying this newest fighter. Three years later, I was a second lieutenant on active duty, passing through Philadelphia. Stationed at the municipal airport before deploying to Africa was a squadron of P-40s, and I watched entranced, as they flew landing patterns around the field. I was to report for flying school in a few weeks and here was the airplane that I hoped to fly in combat. (In April 1944 in Italy I was to join this same 315th Squadron of the 324th Fighter Group flying these same P-40s in combat.)

Then, in June 1943, when I was in basic flying school at Shaw Field in Sumter, South Carolina, a combat veteran from Africa came through, flying his P-40 around the country, on a war-bond drive. Of course, the Flying Tigers had in the meantime made a great record with their P-40s against the Zeroes. I had waited a long time, and finally here was my chance.

Fighter pilots are a proud lot—some people say conceited. One of the main reasons is the fact that the pilot can receive instruction only on

---

Opposite page: The P-40F Warhawk in flight.

1

the ground. He has to fly the airplane alone his first time up. Other pilots have several hours of dual time in the air, with an experienced, qualified pilot in their aircraft. So for a student fighter pilot who would not get his wings for more than three more weeks, taking up a brand new kind of airplane was a challenge.

My aircraft was number 55 and had the name *Stinkie* painted on the fuselage. Thirty-five years later, some of the details have been forgotten. However, many impressions remain. The 1,000-horsepower Rolls-Royce Merlin engine was almost twice as much power as I had handled so far.

In the P-40, as well as the Spitfire and the Jug, we would climb on to the trailing edge of the left (port) wing and then into the cockpit. The Spitfire had a horizontally hinged flap on the port side of the cockpit that let down permitting easier entry. The crew chief standing on the left wing would help us with the chute and harness straps after we were seated. There was enough room in the cockpit for a six-footer whose height was in his long legs. It was a comfortable arrangement in there, with good visibility, except straight ahead, where the P-40's long nose blocked the view. My instructor led me through the steps in starting the engine, although I had practiced this several times by myself in simulated cockpit drills. When the engine actually started, I realized that I was on my own.

I have forgotten the exact details of engine start for the three aircraft, and although between them there were minor differences, I am sure nothing stands out in my memory. Aside from the ever-present problem of overheat on the liquid-cooled engine, starting was simple and routine.

The P-40 Warhawk and the Jug had the standard U.S. braking system of individual toe brakes on each rudder. That is, right rudder—right brake, left rudder—left brake. Both had a steerable tailwheel which responded to rudder movement, but most steering was by differential braking. I personally never landed nor took off in a fighter with my heels on the floor; I always put my feet up on the pedals for takeoff and landing, and heels on the floor for taxiing and flying.

Taxiing was not difficult, as we had been taught since our first flight in a primary trainer always to "S" to clear the view dead ahead. But in Italy, we were flying P-40s off dirt strips with a heavy dust problem so the crew chief rode sitting on the leading edge of the left wing astride the pitot tube wearing dust goggles. He would direct our taxiing with hand signals to avoid any chance of collision. As we turned onto the runway, lining up for takeoff, he would jump off, salute us (his pilot), and we would be off. Both in Corsica and France with the P-47, although there was no problem of dust on the hard-packed ground at Istres and on the sod of Amberieu, we kept up the crew chief system of riding the wing. In Africa, in the Spit, we taxied alone.

The pre-takeoff drill in the P-40 of checking propeller controls, magneto, oil pressure and temperature was routine. This liquid-cooled engine on a hot July day in Georgia was quick to overheat and the acrid smell of coolant was one that always seemed present.

The P-40 was a development of the radial-engined P-36. The long liquid-cooled engine placed the propeller several feet farther from the center of gravity than it was on the P-36, so that the torque was greatly increased. On takeoff it was necessary to turn in a good bit of right rudder trim from the control in the cockpit. As the aircraft accelerated along the runway, the effect of torque increased and had to be corrected by proper application of right rudder. The reverse was true in a dive, and it was a standing joke that all P-40 pilots had very highly developed calf muscles as a result of this characteristic.

Having been briefed on all this, a pilot on his first flight was ready, but it was still a difficult thing to control. On takeoff the aircraft would yaw from right to left and back. As the pilot made his corrections, the hot exhaust would blast into the cockpit from six exhaust stacks on each side of the cowling. We took off and landed with the canopy open as a safety measure in case of a crash, and this sudden blast of heat added to the confusion and excitement of a first flight in this fighter. To complicate matters, there was a very strange procedure necessary to raise the gear. The gear handle was placed in the "up" position with the left hand, and at the same time a trigger at the bottom of the pistol grip on the stick was squeezed with the right little finger. (The trigger at the top of the pistol grip squeezed by the index finger fired the six guns!) Next we swapped hands, as it was necessary to check the gear position by pumping the handle of the hydraulic lever located on the right of the cockpit, while controlling the climb with the left hand holding the control stick. Then there was another swap of hands to put the gear lever in the "neutral" position. Then the canopy was cranked shut, with its handle on the right-side canopy track. Once one mastered this technique, the climb was easy, and the aircraft was nice to fly. The rate of climb and the evidence of power were much greater than I had previously experienced and were a great thrill for an aspiring fighter pilot.

Leveling out at 10,000 feet (we were not equipped for using oxygen), this airplane flew beautifully. Slow rolls were particularly easy to do, as the Warhawk just seemed to be designed to roll on the axis of that long nose. Loops also came smoothly, as did the standard chandelles, lazy eights, Immelmans, and Cuban eights. We had been instructed not to spin the aircraft deliberately, but if we got into a spin, neutralizing the controls and releasing them would bring it out easily. About a year later, I was to find this true in the Liri Valley in Italy. In tight turns, if the controls were coordinated, the aircraft would out-turn any fighter (except maybe the early Spitfires), as the Germans in their Me-109s learned when fighting with the Warhawks in the Mediterranean. A bad turn would result in a snap roll, generally to the right.

We were not taught, as the RAF was in Canada, to pull off power. We maintained the same power and pulled into the turn. There was, of course, depending upon the airplane design, the ever-present chance of snapping out; however, this was part of the technique to be learned and practiced.

The P-40 could dive very fast. Our technique in combat when dive-bombing consisted of turning in full left rudder trim at 10,000 to 12,000 feet, making a half roll to the left and then a full-power dive onto the target in as close to a vertical altitude as we could estimate from the cockpit. Using the standard 100-mil gunsight, we would pull the nose up through the target and drop our 1,000-pound bomb just after the target disappeared under the nose. By that time we were down to about 2,000 feet and up to 450 miles per hour. We would leave in the left rudder trim during a zoom back to 10,000 to 12,000 feet, yawing in this climb and confounding the gunners on the ground, who would shoot out in front of our nose but not on our flight path.

One time in the Liri Valley, after dropping the bomb, I popped into clouds which were scattered at about 10,000 feet. But the deck of clouds was much thicker than I had estimated, and I soon found myself in a spin. Neutralizing the rudder trim with the trim tab control wheel I remembered instructions and turned the controls loose. The aircraft came out of the spin and went into a dive. I came out of the bottom of the cloud in a dive, much too low, I thought, to pull out. But I pulled back hard on the stick and went back into the clouds in a coordinated climb. Popping out of the clouds, I thanked the Warhawk and its stability for my life.

After a pilot has been airborne for a while and has put an aircraft through its paces on a first flight, there comes a sense of confidence, even euphoria. Pretty soon, however, the small voice keeps reminding him that he has not landed the aircraft yet (usually the most challenging part of a flight). The P-40 had a narrow landing gear tread, and although the long nose obscured the view dead ahead, I never found it very hard to land. It was heavy and rugged, and although it was not easy to make a perfect landing, it was not any harder to land safely than the primary and advance trainers (PT-17 and AT-6). The procedure for putting the gear down was as complicated as getting it up. Putting the flaps down was just as complicated, but aside from that, I could bring it in safely, sometimes very smoothly.

That successful first flight in a modern high-performance fighter, before even graduating from advanced training and before getting our wings and pilot's rating, was a great thrill to all of us. It was an experiment with our class. Most pilots before this had not flown fighters until they had been graduated and had received a pilot's rating. We continued flying the P-40 for the rest of the week and accumulated about ten hours in eight flights.

The P-40 was about equal in speed to its peers the Spitfire and the Me-109. Although it could not climb as fast as either of them, it could dive and turn just as well. In the hands of experienced pilots it could do better than hold its own. Our 324th Fighter Group, which had fought with the Desert Air Force across North Africa from Egypt to Tunisia and through Sicily and Italy, bested the German Me-109 at a better than two-to-one ratio in victories in air-to-air combat. The aircraft's range and endurance were sufficient for our mission, except for the invasion at Salerno, when our Warhawks, stationed at a distance in Sicily, could only provide very limited beachhead cover. Even though the P-40 had the liquid-cooled engine (considered by most people to be more vulnerable to ground fire than the air-cooled radial engines), it was a rugged sturdy aircraft, a fine combat vehicle.

My dogfighting in combat was very limited. Within these limits we felt that full power was best (the more power the better), especially when we were outmatched as we were in the P-40. In training, to avoid undue wear and tear on engines, we would use less power, maybe forty inches of mercury, rather than cruise or takeoff power. The Spit had comparative pounds boost. Altitude was where it occurred, but only fools would try to climb with an Me-109, and diving was the best course of action, as well as turning.

Flying damaged aircraft in my experience was done on a case-by-case basis. The vital question was whether even to try to fly it. Fine pilots had been killed when, possibly because of pride, they did not bail out. After deciding that a damaged craft could be flown (and this decision was always subject to change), the best general rule was to stay well within the limits of its capability under the circumstances. In other words, never press one's luck—be very conservative. None of these lessons in judgment or common sense are included in a manual.

Bailing out, like so many other facets of air combat, had to be learned by experience. A fellow officer and tentmate had an unsuccessful bailout using a technique that was generally thought to be effective. This consisted of turning the aircraft on its back and dropping out of the cockpit. Unfortunately, the air flowing past the cockpit would hold the pilot in his seat until the nose of the aircraft fell through into a dive. By this time the pilot was usually unable to clear the plane and was hit in the legs by the tail. My friend lost one leg at the knee. Another pilot in our flight tried to pop out of the cockpit by rolling forward full nose-down elevator trim and turning loose the stick. He was thrown upward as he expected by the sudden nose-down maneuver of the aircraft, but not high enough to avoid both legs being virtually cut off at the knees by the canopy. He died before being picked up by rescue craft.

A successful maneuver used by several pilots (including myself) required a certain amount of control of the aircraft. With a dead engine, the canopy was opened and the aircraft put into a shallow climbing turn to the right, holding the airplane in this attitude as long as possible until it was on the verge of a stall. By that time the airflow over the cockpit was not enough to prevent the pilot from climbing out of the cockpit. A dive at the trailing edge of the right wing with the legs tucked up as in a front one-and-a-half somersault off a diving board into a pool, enabled the pilot to clear the aircraft as it went by. Then the chute could be opened.

Landing the P-40 was not any different from landing any other aircraft, although there were variations in landing patterns in the various commands. At flying school, the conventional rectangular pattern was used, but in the operational training unit and at Sarasota, Florida, where we had our combat training, the overhead pattern was standard. The aircraft was flown over the landing runway at 1,500 feet at about 200 miles per hour. As it passed over the upwind end the pilot would pull into a tight 90° turn to the left. In the humid air of Sarasota, this maneuver caused vapor trails to form and stream off the wingtips. This spectacular maneuver became a status symbol of a skilled (and daring) pilot. If this sharp turn was coordinated, there was no danger; but if uncoordinated, the aircraft would snap, often into a spin, deadly at 1,500 feet.

Aside from the chance of a spin this was a good technique for landing. Gear was dropped on the downwind leg of the pattern, flaps on the base leg, and a three-point landing was made at the end of the final approach. As I remember it, the downwind was flown at about 130 miles per hour, base leg at about 120 miles per hour, and final at about 100 miles per hour.

My total time in the P-40 was 225 hours, 123 of which were combat hours, flying seventy-two sorties. We were hard on engines, most of which were rebuilt, and I used up three. My log book, which I am sure does not include all of the small-arms bullet holes, shows five missions in which I was hit badly enough to put the aircraft out of action for at least a day. The worst damage was on June 5, 1944, when I was hit dive-bombing and then strafing German vehicles in their retreat north of Rome. The spinner was more than half shot off, and the resulting vibration made it impossible to use more than a small fraction of available power. However, I was able to make it to our emergency landing strip at Anzio, where repairs were made, and the spinner was replaced. After spending a day at the Anzio strip, I flew my airplane back to our home base. Another bad day for my P-40 required the replacement of the right wing when an 88-millimeter shell went through it without exploding, leaving a hole 88-millimeter in diameter. So the P-40 could take punishment; fortunately, I was never hit by a killing round.

About seventy of my hours in the P-40 were in the K and M models, which were equipped with the Allison engine. The remaining 150 hours, including the ten in flying school and all of my combat time, were in the F and L models with the much better Packard-built Rolls-Royce Merlin engine. On takeoff we had available fifty-four inches of mercury manifold pressure as opposed to forty-eight in the Allison. The Merlin was much more rugged, and even when overheating would deliver full power. The Allison was likely to cut out when it was overheating, and an engine failure on takeoff, the normally hot time, is one of the most dangerous things that can happen to a pilot and his airplane.

All of the P-40s had six 50-caliber machine-guns (the Ls, which normally had four guns, had been converted to the F armament by adding two guns). There was provision for carrying either a seventy-five-gallon auxiliary gasoline tank or a 1,000-pound bomb on a shackle under the fuselage. Under each wing were shackles for three twenty-pound antipersonnel fragmentation bombs.

This aircraft was my first love. I developed a sense of confidence in the P-40 that I never had in any other craft. It always brought me back in combat, and our relationship was like that between a cavalryman and his horse. I felt very sad when I left Number 48, "Old Sixshooter," at Pomigliano Airport at the foot of Mount Vesuvius and went on to Capodicino in Naples to pick up my brand new P-47.

Between the operational training unit and my P-40 squadron, I had a chance to fly Spitfires. Sixty-one fighter pilots who were graduates of the 1943 flying-school classes and operational training units in the P-40 arrived in Morocco in March 1944. All went by train to Bertaux, in Algeria, the Mediterranean Allied Air Force Training Unit, for conversion to the Spitfire. There were two American Fighter Groups in Italy, the 31st and the 52nd, flying Spitfires, and we were to be replacements for these groups after a training month on the Spit in the desert. Plans changed, and we had to draw lots to see which of us would stay and fly the Spitfire and which would go up to Italy to combat units right away. Half of us were to stay for the training in Africa.

Here was our chance to fly the fabulous Spitfire. The aircraft with the lineage of the Supermarine racers—world speed record-holders— and the fame gained in the Battle of Britain (although the Hurricane was the aircraft that was most responsible for that victory over the Germans). We were all excited at the prospect.

Our training program was very informal. Our instructors were fighter pilots who had completed their combat tours and were returning to the United States. They were not anxious to face the hazards of flying formation with us, as green and inexperienced as we were, so their instructions consisted of telling us about the airplane and then having us go up and practice air-to-air combat against each other.

The aircraft we saw on the ramp at Bertaux proved to be a great disappointment. These were war-weary Spitfire Vs from the Desert Air Force. The beautiful Spitfire lines had been ruined by the tropical air filter underneath the spinner. In the air these old airplanes were slow and vibrated badly. Although they could maneuver better than any other current fighters, particularly in a tight turn, and were not too bad in their rate of climb, they were very slow, indicating a cruising speed of only about 175 miles per hour. This was hardly better than the advanced trainer that we flew in flying school!

The British system of brakes required mastering a skill somewhat like rubbing one's stomach in a circular motion with one hand while patting one's head with the other. To apply right brake, unlike the American system of a toe brake on each rudder pedal, the pilot had to push on the rudder bar with his right foot and depress a trigger on the control column with his finger. Like the P-40 method of raising landing gear, this system was fraught with danger, because on the same control column was a button to be depressed by the thumb to fire the eight machine guns! Taxiing this airplane required a good bit of practice. Overheating on the

Spitfire was serious business. Our instructors told us (we had no written pilot's instructions for flying this aircraft) that gray smoke indicated engine overheat, but brown smoke (presumably the next condition) should be followed as soon as possible by the pilot bailing out. We were not impressed by the first Spitfires, but we had only about five hours flying the Mark V before we were reequipped with the Mark VIII. This was a superb airplane. The ones we received were relatively new from the 31st U.S. Fighter Group which was being reequipped with American P-51 Mustangs. The first of these VIIIs that I flew had belonged to Col. Herschel Greene, the Group Commander. It had two-and-one-half black crosses painted on the fuselage, indicating the number of Germans shot down. What a thrill to fly this particular craft!

The Spitfire VIII had more horsepower than the V, although how much I do not know. *Jane's* (1945–1946) shows the FVIII's maximum speed at 408 miles per hour, weight 7,767 pounds, and ceiling 43,000 feet compared to the V's maximum speed of 365 miles per hour, weight 6,600 pounds, and ceiling 38,000 feet. My estimate of the comparison of performance of the two would show a much greater contrast than that shown in *Jane's*, but as mentioned, the Vs we flew were war-weary and the VIIIs were relatively new.

The narrow Spit undercarriage was not a real problem to me. Having had experience in the PT-17, the T-6 (the British called it the Harvard) and the P-40, the Spit was no problem. The V floated because it was light and thus was harder to land than the heavier VIII or P-40. I never experienced any gear failures in any airplane. On my first combat mission in a P-40, I had a flat left tire (unknown to me until I landed), but the dirt runway and some good luck enabled me to keep it straight and on the runway.

The Spitfire VIII had the Merlin engine with a two-stage supercharger. It cruised at 260 miles per hour as opposed to the 175 for the Spit V, and climbed impressively. When passing through 12,000 feet in a climb, the supercharger cut in automatically, giving additional power and increased acceleration. It dived faster than the Warhawk and turned as well as the earlier Spitfires. Its performance was in every way impressive, and it was a joy to fly. It was armed with four 20-millimeter cannon, enough firepower for anyone. It was very stable and was easy to land, due to the elliptical wing which stalled straight ahead without any tendency to snap or drop. It was heavy enough so that it did not float on landing like the V. We had almost nine hours in this craft and found it to be as good an airplane as one could ask for.

Compared to the American P-40, however, I would rather *fly* the Spit but *fight* in the 40. The armor behind the pilot was one-quarter-inch thick in the Spit, but it was three-eighths-inch thick in the Warhawk. I saw many Spit pilots in prison camp with horribly burned faces, because the main fuel tank which was behind the instrument panel (right in front of the pilot's face) had been set on fire by enemy guns. The Warhawk's main fuel tank was under the seat. For fighting, too, I would rather have six fast-firing 50-caliber machine-guns than four slower firing 20-millimeter cannon. However, the Spitfire was a fine aircraft, in my opinion, the best performer of its time—and because I never flew it in combat, I am not a fair judge of its true worth in battle. Plans changed again, and we were all assigned to P-40 units in Italy.

Then, in July 1944, we switched again to P-47s. Soon high over the Mediterranean Alps on August 2, 1944, twelve brand-new silver P-47s of the 315th Fighter Squadron were on a fighter sweep. I was leading Yellow flight, the second of three four-ship flights on this twelve-ship patrol. The mission of a fighter sweep was to clear out all enemy fighters in the area ahead of friendly bombers. Although most of us had only about twenty-five hours in the P-47, we were proud of our new aircraft, confident for the first time that we could outperform the German Me-109s and FW-190s; and we were looking for a fight. We did not have to wait very long.

A pilot in Leader flight (the three flights were Leader, Yellow, and Red) spotted a Ju-88 skimming low over the Alps, and Leader flight dived down to attack. At the same time, four bogies came out of the sun toward Yellow flight, and, like the barroom fights in the Old West when actions showed which were friends or foes, Yellow responded by shooting. As the enemy banked, the unmistakable elliptical wing of the attackers showed them to be Spitfires. Too late—we had hit one of them before I could break off my flight's attack. The Ju-88 turned out to be an American B-25. The 315th did have previous bonafide victories and would have later ones, but this day was a comedy of errors. The Spitfire made it home, damaged, but fortunately, the pilot was unhurt. A few weeks later, a British pilot from this squadron spent the night at our base and when the incident was brought up, described it in typical British fashion as "jolly good shooting."

This was our first combat mission in the P-47 Thunderbolt. We called it the "Jug." We were the last American group in Europe to fly the P-40 in combat and had flown our final P-40 mission on July 18, 1944, from Italy. We had hoped for P-51 Mustangs, but instead received the D-model Thunderbolt, sub-model 27. This was a good aircraft, and we

---

Opposite page: The British Spitfire Mark IX.

soon adjusted to reality and made the best of things, forgetting our disappointment. I was to spend about seventy-five hours in the P-47, about forty-five of them in combat, and fly seventeen combat sorties before being forced to abandon my aircraft over Mulhausen (Mulhouse) in Alsace.

The P-47 was not a difficult aircraft to fly. It had plenty of power (2,000 horsepower), was stable (it had an elliptical wing, somewhat like the Spitfire), and had a widetread landing gear that made a smooth landing easy, especially for us who had been flying the narrow-geared P-40 for so long. The P-47 was much heavier than the P-40, and we brought it down the final approach at about 120 miles per hour, but we learned quickly and soon were very comfortable with this craft. With the P-40 we worried about engine failure (old engines and dust in the intake); the P-47 made us worry about running out of fuel. That 2,000 horsepower engine, although smooth and quiet, burned a lot of gasoline, even with the seventy-five extra gallons it could carry under the belly.

When dive-bombing and strafing, we had to remember that the airplane weighed seven tons and would not pull out of a dive as easily or as quickly as the Warhawk. While I was gone for two days on an administrative trip to Foggia from France, another pilot flew my airplane and crashed into a train that he was strafing. I had a close escape myself once, when I was strafing a field in southern France. On the strafing run, seeing an aircraft in a hangar, I pressed home the attack, concentrating on the target. When I finally pulled up, I barely cleared the hangar roof. Had I been flying the Warhawk, I would have cleared it easily.

Once I was hit by 88-millimeter cannon fire over the beachhead. With a half dozen holes almost the size of my fist, I flew back to Corsica from the Riviera.

The pilot's handbook for the P-47 said that it was not possible to "split-ess" the aircraft from 10,000 feet. This was not true, however, and it could be done with a margin for error. Later versions (D-28 and beyond) had a dorsal fin, because there was a tendency to rudder lock in a slow roll. An inexperienced pilot in our group had this happen when he was performing a victory roll over the field, and he crashed.

The P-47, like the P-40 and the Spitfire, was a fine aircraft. The muffling effect on the engine of the turbosupercharger made it sound like a Cadillac when taxiing. The Spitfire and Warhawk sounded like Indianapolis race cars.

The P-47's cockpit was big and comfortable, and the visibility with the tear-drop canopy was perfect. It had eight 50-caliber machine guns

Opposite page: A P-47.

and could carry a 1,000-pound bomb under each wing and those seventy-five gallons of extra fuel under the belly.

On September 9, 1944, there was a bite of fall in the air. We were based at Amberieux, about twenty miles from Lyon, near the Swiss border. We had just moved out of our tents, in which we had spent the summer, and were happily ensconced in a French chateau. The Group Operations Staff (there were three of us) had our cots in the bathroom, a room about fifteen-by-fifteen feet, with no running water. To use the tub, we had to carry hot water up from the kitchen, but still it was better than the stream on Corsica which served for swimming, bathing, and laundry.

I had changed into a winter woolen shirt and trousers and was comfortable flying the Thunderbolt dressed like that. During the coming weeks, I would be thankful that I had changed. I had scheduled myself for an afternoon strafing mission on September 9 against a German flying field outside Freiburg in the Black Forest, where many German aircraft were reported. This would be my first mission into pre-war Germany.

I led a flight of four, taking off at about two o'clock. The flight to the target was uneventful, as we paralleled the Swiss border. Approaching the target, we encountered some clouds below us so that we had to stay at altitude instead of descending to the deck to find the target. At 12,000 feet, the German radar picked us up and alerted the flak gunners defending the field. We had no bombs, because the southern France beachhead had moved so fast that we had only fuel (carried to us by other fighters) and 50-caliber ammunition. A dive-bombing attack could have put the German gunners down, but when we rolled out onto our strafing run they were waiting for us. I was hit right away in the engine by what appeared to be 37-millimeter antiaircraft cannon fire.

I kept on my strafing run, shot up an enemy aircraft, and then pulled up, figuring that my zoom would help my chute open when I jumped, for it was obvious that jump I must. The cockpit was full of smoke as I undid my belt and shoulder harness in preparation for bailout. When I opened the canopy, the smoke cleared away, and I could see that although I had no oil pressure, the engine seemed to be giving me power enough to climb. Good old rugged Thunderbolt! But I no longer had enough control to fasten my belt, and I knew there was no question of a belly landing. Heading back to the base, I had climbed to about 3,500 feet when the engine froze. I called my flight and gave the other pilots the course home, then jumped out. The P-47 had flown for fifteen minutes without any oil. As the aircraft rolled over and fell away, descending in my chute, I could see its silver bottom all black with oil.

I never flew any of the three aircraft again. But after returning from prison camp, I flew two more fighters, the F-86 and the F-100, though not in combat. Like all pilots, I remain a great enthusiast for those ships I flew in war.

Col. John A. C. Andrews was a fighter pilot in the Twelfth Air Force in Italy and southern France in 1944. He was shot down while strafing a German airfield on his eighty-ninth mission and was held prisoner in Pomerania until May 1945.

B-17 Flying Fortress

James V. Edmundson

As any pilot knows, an airplane is much more than an inanimate collec-tion of metal. It represents the end product of an idea that developed through a complex process of conception, design, test, and production, and it can be measured in terms of performance criteria such as top speed, service ceiling, useful load, range, rate-of-climb, or takeoff and landing speeds.

To those who have flown them, particularly in combat, airplanes have a character, a personality, and an animate being distinctly their own. In many cases, a specific aircraft will have been dominant during an impor-tant part of a pilot's life and will remind him of the crew members who shared so many hours aloft with him, the mechanics who serviced his air-plane between missions, and the squadron mates with whom he lived at the base and with whom he flew in combat. Some of them never returned, but they are not forgotten.

A very few airplanes are of such a special character, so outstanding in design and performance, and so much a part of a particular era that they have a great impact on human awareness, extending far beyond the pilots who flew them. These aircraft can come to represent to a nation, and sometimes to the world, the very essence of the years during which they were dominant in the sky.

Such an airplane was the B-17, the Flying Fortress. For a generation of Americans, British, and Germans, it is impossible to think of the air battles over Europe during World War II without remembering the B-17 as it swarmed aloft by the thousands from English bases, formed up in combat boxes, sometimes escorted by friendly fighters (but more often not), penetrated swarms of hostile fighters and flak "thick enough to walk on," bombed the industrial heartland of the enemy in a succession

Opposite page: Ordnance men at work, with a B-17 in the background.

of daylight missions, and returned to base, often having sustained unbelievable battle damage and bearing wounded and dead crew members.

There were other American bombardment aircraft of that time—B-24s, B-25s, B-26s—I have flown them all and they were all fine birds, but the B-17 was the airplane of that era in a way that no other aircraft can ever be.

There were, of course, many models of the Fortress, starting with the thirteen YB-17s ordered by the Army Air Corps in 1936. One of these was eventually equipped with turbosuperchargers and became the YB-17A. Relatively modest numbers of B-17Bs, Cs, and Ds were procured, each a refinement of its predecessors. Progressively more powerful versions of the Wright R-1820 engines were provided and equipped with superchargers for high-altitude flight. Armament was increased and self-sealing fuel tanks and armor plate were added as the requirements for such improvements were recognized.

In the late summer of 1941, a radically new Flying Fortress appeared, known as the B-17E. It had a more massive vertical fin that housed a tail-gun position with twin .50 caliber machine guns. It also had an upper forward power turret and a "bathtub" belly turret in which the gunner aimed and fired using a mirror in which his target appeared upside down and backwards. In later E models, the "bathtub" was replaced by a Sperry ball turret in the ventral position, greatly enhancing protection against low attacks.

The B-17 was eventually improved through the F and G models, acquiring still more powerful engines to handle the increased weight, "Toyko tanks" in the wingtips to increase range, and a Bendix chin turret to cope with head-on attacks. Boeing's wisdom in building this growth potential into the original design was, indeed, a key factor in the success of the Fortress, and the Army Air Force eventually bought 12,725.

My first view of the B-17 came in the early summer of 1937 when I was a Flying Cadet in training at Randolph Field, Texas. A flight of YB-17s from the 3rd Bombardment Group at Langley Field stopped through Randolph and remained overnight. The entire Cadet Corps went down to "A" Stage and swarmed around and under those huge, beautiful machines that literally filled the hangars. Looking at my photographs of the occasion brings back the feeling of awe and wonder that I shared with my classmates. The thought that some day some of us might fly B-17s was almost too overwhelming to contemplate.

Those of us in the Attack Section at Kelly got some time in B-3s, 4s, and 5s. In the ensuing years, I flew B-10s, B-12s, and B-18s, but I didn't get to meet the B-17 again until the summer of 1941. I was stationed at Hickam Field, Hawaii, in the 31st Squadron of the 5th Bombardment Group flying B-18s when we were designated to convert to B-17s. A group of old friends from the 19th Bomb Group delivered our first air-craft in a mass flight direct from the mainland. This was an impressive display of range in those days, when the Pan American Clippers were the only planes in regular use capable of such a flight. The delivery pilots stayed long enough to check some of us out in the new big birds before they caught the boat for home.

As my checkout progressed, I became increasingly impressed by the capabilities of this remarkable machine. It truly represented a quantum jump over any previous bombers.

To get into the B-17 the pilot climbed through a door on the right-hand rear portion of the waist gunners' compartment and proceeded forward through the radio room and the bomb bay, climbed through the upper power turret, and into the cockpit seats. Navigators and bom-bardiers could enter this way and then go down the crawlway into the nose, but the normal access to their battle stations was through a hatch to the rear of the nose compartment. They chinned themselves and swung their feet up and into the aircraft, then had their parachutes and gear passed up from the ground.

There was really nothing unusual about start-up procedures. Engines were started in normal sequence—3, 4, 2, and 1. Normal engine power controls were the prop controls, turbosupercharger controls, mixture controls, and throttles.

Taxiing the B-17 was not easy. As with most tail-wheel aircraft, it was clumsy and lumbering on the ground. Also, with the big, high fin, taxi-ing in a crosswind was a job because the aircraft tended to weather-cock and it was easy to overheat the upwind brake in attempting to hold a course. The experienced pilot learned to use the tailwheel lock exten-sively in taxiing.

On narrow taxiways, we learned to taxi mostly with the inboards because the outboards would hang over the edge of the paved strip and using them would tend to blow up a lot of dust and gravel. On the other hand, when taxiing on wide taxiways, we used the outboards, primarily because they were higher off the ground and didn't kick up quite as much debris as the inboards.

Prior to takeoff, the engines were run up one at a time, usually in the order in which they had been started, the mags checked, and the tur-bosupercharger set. In spite of this, the turbos would invariably require

adjusting on the takeoff roll to get full power or to avoid excessive manifold pressures.

The tail-wheel lock was a big help on takeoff, and on crosswind takeoffs the tail wheel would be left on the ground as long as possible and the aircraft pulled off from a three-point position in order to avoid weathercocking. On a normal takeoff, the tail wheel was lifted off the ground as soon as the tail would fly, because in this attitude there was less aerodynamic drag and the airplane would gather speed faster and take off shorter. Flaps were normally not used for takeoffs, but a shorter takeoff run could be achieved by using about $\frac{1}{4}$ flaps.

Synchronizing the props was always a chore in the B-17. The pilot could look back through the number 1 and number 2 props and synchronize these two by sight. The copilot would do the same for the number 3 and number 4 props. Then the two sides could be brought into sync aurally.

In those days we knew nothing about weight and balance. Later, when I was faced with computing weight and balance for B-29s, B-47s, B-52s, and B-58s, I wondered how we ever avoided serious trouble with the B-17s. The answer, of course, is that it was a very forgiving airplane. The CG (center of gravity) limits could vary widely and the airplane might feel uncomfortably nose- or tail-heavy, but it seemed to fly well with some highly unusual loading configurations.

Our first aircraft were Cs and Ds, but later we received Es, sturdier and more heavily armed than previous models. Changing to Es brought one surprise to all of us. In the older models, the tail was light and on landing tended to float even with plenty of aft trim. The heavier fin and the additional weight of guns in the tail of the Es tended to bring the tail down firmly, and our first few attempts at three-pointers turned into rather dismal tail-first landings. To counteract this tail-heaviness at low speeds, we never took off or landed with ammunition installed in the tail or with the tail gunner in his combat position. We also never took off or landed with the ball gunner in his turret because he would be trapped in the event of gear failure. Moreover, it was most important that the ball turret be properly stowed prior to landing in order not to damage the gun barrels.

The three-point landing was ideal because getting the locked tail wheel on the ground early gave good stability, particularly in a crosswind. Having landed, and if we were at light weight at the end of the mission, we would usually check the mags as soon as we had cleared the runway

---

Opposite page: A B-17 Flying Fortress bombs a German railroad junction at Munster.

and then shut down either the inboards or the outboards, depending on the taxiing conditions ahead of us.

The B-17 was easy to fly, as are all aircraft, if by flying you mean to take off, bore a hole in the sky, and land. But military flying is much, much more. It consists of operating the subsystems, coordinating the crew within the plane and with other aircraft and crews in the sky, and flying the aircraft to the outer limits of its operating envelope so that the aircraft is able to perform efficiently the military mission for which it was designed.

For example, the F-102 is undoubtedly one of the simplest and easiest airplanes to take off, fly straight and level, and land. Its controls are simple; it doesn't even have flaps. The delta wing gives it maximum stability in flight, and it is almost spin-proof. On the other hand, to operate the radar and infrared systems skillfully and to fly the aircraft within the altitude, speed, attitude, and performance envelope so that the internally carried Falcon missiles can be fired accurately to secure a kill is *not* simple. It is most complex and requires constant and continuing practice.

The B-17 was easy to take off, cruise, and land. However, to a pilot who wanted to give his bombardier the best possible bomb run with minimum deviations in airspeed, elevation, and altitude, to give his navigator a stable platform for his celestial shots and accurately flown double drifts, to teach his gunners to call out attacks quickly and accurately without cluttering up the interphone and to position them within a formation to give them maximum freedom of fire—to such a pilot, flying the B-17 was a demanding job.

The B-17 was a real treat to fly. It handled honestly on takeoffs and landings, it gave a good, clear stall warning, it carried a far more substantial bomb load than any previous bombers, and with its turbosuperchargers it became the first airplane I ever took to 30,000 feet. It was a beautiful formation aircraft, and it had a unique throttle arrangement that assisted immeasurably in flying formation. The four throttles terminated in three pairs of handles, one above the other. The top grip controlled the outboard engines, the bottom grip controlled the inboard engines, and the central grip enabled the pilot to palm all four throttles. Most of us eventually learned to set the outboards and fly formation with the inboards alone, adjusting the outboards only when large power adjustments became necessary.

The normal crew for a B-17 was ten men. The air force traditionally has used two pilots in four-engined bombers such as the B-17 and the B-24 as well as in the far smaller and simpler twin-engined bombers like the B-25 and B-26. This is also true of transport and cargo aircraft such as the C-47, C-46, C-54, and all that followed. I do not know the precise grounds for such policy, but logic leads me to believe there were several reasons:

1. We had sufficient pilots to go first class. We were mounting an Air Force on a much broader manpower base than the British, and we were not forced to crew our aircraft on such an austere basis as the RAF had to.
2. There is no question that one pilot and a sort of flying crew chief in the copilot's seat, who could reach the handles that the pilot couldn't get to, could fly any of these aircraft safely. There is also no question that with a well-coordinated, two-pilot team, the aircraft could be operated with greater military efficiency.
3. There is a built-in training advantage in the pilot/copilot system. The copilot learns from helping the pilot under combat conditions, and when he moves into the left-hand seat he will be a far better pilot than if he just started out by himself in a one-pilot airplane.

   (This, of course, is why the loss rate on green fighter pilots is so high, in spite of giving them extended periods of supervised flight on the wing of more senior pilots. The fact that a fighter is a one-pilot airplane forces us to commit fighter pilots to combat when they are still relatively inexperienced and thus the loss rate is high. Only the lucky and the quick learners survive.)
4. Without a pilot, the aircraft will not get home. Bombardiers, navigators, and gunners can be killed or wounded and the lives of their crew mates are not placed in serious jeopardy, but if the pilot is knocked out, the entire crew is lost. Providing two pilots gives the crew a safety factor. I believe enough bombers returned to base with one or the other pilot dead or disabled to have made this a policy that paid off.

There are other, more complex reasons in favor of two pilots in bombers, but I believe these four reasons are the main ones and that the policy was wise.

Besides the pilot and copilot, there were two other officers, the navigator and bombardier with battle stations in the nose. The B-17 heating system was capable of heating the cockpit to the point where eggs could be fried on the throttle quadrant, but the heat to the nose compartment

was always insufficient. The pilot and copilot would be sweltering in their shirt sleeves while the navigator and bombardier were freezing in their fleece-lined winter flying suits. We used to say the B-17 was like a healthy puppy—it had the coldest nose in town.

Additional crew members included the radio operator, belly gunner, two waist gunners, and a tail gunner. Later we modified our aircraft by adding a twin .50 caliber ring-mount firing out the upper radio compartment hatch, and we added an eleventh man to the crew to spell the radio operator and to man these extra guns. Even later, when some of our aircraft were equipped with rudimentary radar equipment, this man became the radar operator.

For those of us stationed in Hawaii, December 7, 1941, will always be a day of memories. One of mine includes a chapter in the continuing history of the B-17.

On the night of December 6, an element of the 19th Bomb Group under the leadership of Col. Ted Landon had taken off from the mainland for Hawaii on the way to the Philippines. This flight of B-17s arrived in Hawaii on the morning of December 7 just as the Japanese attack was taking place. Some of the crews landed at Hickam in the midst of the uproar and were pretty well shot up by attacking Zeros. Others landed wherever they could. Col. Dick Carmichael landed in the middle of a golf course, as I recall. In an effort to eliminate unnecessary weight, none of the aircraft carried any ammunition for their guns—a commentary on our awareness of the kind of world we were living in.

Shortly after the war began, I was transferred to the 27th Squadron of the 11th Bomb Group, which was commanded by Col. "Blondie" Saunders, one of the truly great combat commanders of World War II. Our B-17s were dispersed throughout the islands and the 26th moved to Wheeler Field, next to Schofield Barracks, where we participated in flying patrols out to the 1,000-mile arc around the Hawaiian Islands.

Our first real action came in June 1942 when all the B-17s were mysteriously ordered to Midway Island. There we were briefed by the navy that they had succeeded in breaking the Japanese code and had forewarning of an attack headed for Midway. The timing was not precisely known, and we cooled our heels for a couple of days while PBYs probed the most likely approach sectors for signs of the coming attack. One evening just about dusk a PBY limped in badly shot up. It had made contact with a Japanese task force and the Battle of Midway was underway. Naval aircraft from our carriers and marine aircraft flying from Midway

Opposite page: New B-17s ready for action.

gave the attacking fleet a warm reception, but I'm sure the biggest surprise for the Nipponese navy was finding itself under attack by B-17s out in the middle of the Pacific Ocean.

Shortly after we returned to Hawaii from Midway, the 11th Group was alerted for a move into the South Pacific and in about ten days, with Colonel Saunders leading the way, we were off. Our route took us first to Christmas Island, where my flying-school classmate, George MacNicol, had a squadron of P-39s, then to Canton Island with its famous lone palm tree, and on to Nandi, a base on Viti Levu, the main island of the Fiji group.

Our first main base was on Efate in the Central New Hebrides Islands, but we soon moved on to a newly constructed base on Espiritu Santo in the Northern New Hebrides. We bombed in support of the marine landings on Guadalcanal, and our targets consisted of Japanese naval units, bases on nearby islands such as Tulagi, and Japanese military formations on Guadalcanal itself.

During these days we literally lived in our aircraft. When we returned from a mission, we would fuel and bomb up our B-17s, often working late into the night. On Efate we had Quonset huts to sleep in, but at Espiritu Santo during the several weeks before our tent camps were erected, we slept with our B-17s as cavalry men slept with their horses. We opened the bomb-bay doors and lowered the flaps to give us some protection against tropical storms and set up our folding cots under the wings, tying our mosquito nets to any convenient part of the airplane.

After the marines had things more or less under control on Guadalcanal, we used Henderson Field as an advance operating base. This forward staging permitted us to search out fleet targets much farther north and to hit bases such as Munda, Gigo, Vella Lavella, Bougainville, and Buin.

The 11th Group was actually attached to the 1st Marine Division (Reinforced) and was included in the Naval Distinguished Unit Citation that went to the 1st Marine Division for its Solomon Islands operation. My citation reached me in 1948 after the air force had become a separate entity. The paperwork accompanying the award originated with the Navy, was transmitted to the Marine Corps for the 1st Division, was then forwarded to the army for award to the army air force units involved, and finally was forwarded to the newly created air force for presentation. To my knowledge, this was the only B-17 unit to be so honored by a sister service.

Aircraft operation was much the same in Europe and the Pacific. Differences were brought about by the varying military requirements of the two theaters. The aircraft were flown heavier in Europe than in the Pacific. This could be done because the operating bases were better and runways were generally hard-surfaced and longer. More time was spent on formation flying in Europe. The form-up for a major strike there could take 1–1 $\frac{1}{2}$ hours. In the Pacific, however, formations were generally smaller, and it was usual for the leader to circle the field once and be on his way, with the others forming up en route.

Missions were generally flown at higher altitude in Europe. Exposure to intense flak for long periods forced operating altitudes up. In the Pacific, however, targets were smaller, sometimes maneuvering surface vessels were targeted, formations were smaller, bomb patterns were less extensive, and bombing had to be done at lower altitudes to give increased accuracy.

The war followed its course. I was privileged to see the magnificent work being done by the British-based 8th Air Force where the B-17 really won its spurs. My own participation in the European air war, however, was cut short. I was called home to take part in the B-29 program, again under General Saunders. This new airplane was destined to see combat in the India-China theater and later in the Marianas, but this is another story. I would only mention as part of the B-17 saga that the vast majority of the key leaders in the early days of the B-29 program were card-carrying members of the B-17 union.

My last contact with the B-17 provides a nostalgic and, in a way, sad touch, but it, too, belongs in this story.

After B-29 combat duty in World War II and in Korea, as well as peacetime tours in B-29s and B-36s in SAC, I found myself during the late 1950s in command of the 36th Air Division at Davis-Monthan Air Force Base near Tucson, Arizona. The division consisted of two wings, the 43rd and the 303rd, both equipped with B-47s.

In 1957, to my surprise and delight, we had a B-17 assigned to the base. It was a museum piece, stripped of all turrets, guns, armor plate, and other combat gear, but it was still a proud B-17. It was actually assigned to the Air Research and Development Command, now known as the Systems Command, and it had been specially instrumented for use in a project to probe and study thunderstorms in conjunction with some air force-sponsored research conducted by the University of Arizona. During June, July, and August, the thunderstorm season, it was a very

busy bird, but for much of the rest of the time it was available for administrative support flights.

I had a requirement to go to Hamilton Air Force Base, California, to give a talk, and I really looked forward to making the trip in the B-17. As I climbed up through the radio compartment and the bomb bay into the cockpit, it was like coming home. Everything seemed to fit, somehow, and although it had been nearly fifteen years since I had been inside a B-17, it all came back to me with a rush. It was a real thrill to start up the engines and taxi out. From that point on I was due for a rude shock.

My B-17 seemed so underpowered. It labored so hard and so long to build up enough speed to stagger into the air. Even after the airplane was cleaned up, the rate of climb was painfully slow. It seemed heavy and sluggish to handle, not at all like the light, responsive bird I remembered, and it took forever to get anywhere. It was noisy and bumpy and rough. I made a lousy landing when we reached Hamilton.

I suppose a man can never step back into the past and find things the way he remembers them. One thousand hours of flying B-47s had altered my sense of values. The B-17 hadn't changed. It was a product of its age and had remained frozen in time while that state of the art had passed by. It was a World War II relic in the jet age. I felt somehow cheated.

Now that I am retired, after thirty-five years of service and 11,000 hours of pilot time, I can look back on many airplanes I have flown and loved. Time has broadened my perspective, and each aircraft takes its place in my memories in its proper time frame. From my vantage point, each bird is a classic in its own time. Comparison of airplanes of different time frames is as impossible and as unnecessary as trying to compare the friends of each era. To me, the tremendous differences between the PT-3, the first airplane I ever flew, and the F-4, in which I flew my last combat mission in Vietnam, do not seem in the least incongruous.

When I think now of the B-17, it is not the old clunker I flew from Davis-Monthan to Hamilton that I remember. My B-17 is the beautiful bird that we lived with in the steaming jungle of the South Pacific. It is the B-17 that took us into combat so many times and brought us safely home. The B-17 I remember was in its day truly the Queen of the Skies.

Lt. Gen. James V. Edmundson flew 107 combat missions during World War II and was credited with sinking one of the first Japanese submarines of the war.

Opposite page: Underside of a B-17.

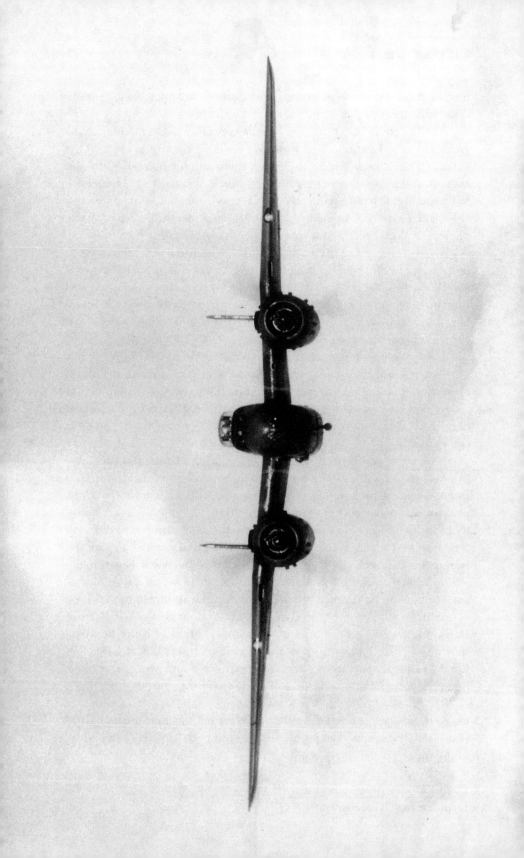

B-25 Mitchell

Keith R. Matzinger

How do you identify an ex-B-25 pilot? Easy: if he doesn't have a hearing aid, he probably needs one.

The combination of the pilot's seat being close to the propeller tips and the individual exhaust stacks made the B-25 one of the noisiest aircraft ever built. But the structural integrity of the pre-World War II design more than made up for the noise.

When the first operational B-25 arrived at Headquarters Squadron of the 17th Bomb Group (M) at McChord Field early in 1941, it created quite a stir. The 17th, not long out of Northrop A-17As, was then equipped with the comfortable, fast Douglas B-23s. The transition from that docile plane with conventional landing gear to the 25 was quite an experience. (Gen. David Jones, in the late 1970s Chief of the Air Force, was among the group.)

The landings were particularly eventful, and it was a tribute to the forgiving nature of the rugged beast that things went as smoothly as they did. There were nose-wheel landings, tail-dragging landings, too-fast landings, and sickeningly slow landings. The atrocious screeching, throw-you-through-the-windshield brakes (early discs) did little for the nerves of the crew who longed for the cozy, quiet, and spacious cabin of the B-23. Radio operators in particular were disenchanted with the change as they moved from the warm front cockpit to the drafty, cold waist compartment. Most felt they had been demoted.

Pilots who have never flown a B-25 cannot realize the amazing flexibility of this bird. Nothing shows that flexibility better than the legendary Colonel Doolittle leading men of the 17th Group off the deck of the carrier *Hornet* in 1942 to bomb Japan. Few people realize that the original plan called for them to land back on the *Hornet*! The fabulous Doolittle

---

Opposite page: The B-25H.

(not exactly a youngster then) characteristically was the first to take off, with less than 400 feet of deck available. Films show that he handled this smoothly and efficiently. Well, for a guy who flew the Gee-Bee maybe it was easy.

During World War II a young pilot in Corsica won a lot of money betting that he could pull a chandelle on takeoff at the end of 5,000-foot runway in a 25. His technique looked daring but actually was relatively easy for someone with the reactions and coordination of a twenty-two-year old.

His method was to pull the control column back into his lap as soon as the throttles were forward. This caused the nose to rise at a sickening angle, and the 25 was ready to fly in just a few hundred feet. He would pull the landing gear just as it was ready to lift, then immediately shove the nose down to stay a few feet off the ground. At this point our young hot dog would dump the flaps, which required raising the nose to offset the sink, then reduce the power to thirty-five inches of mercury and 2,500 revolutions per minute, close the cowl flaps just as he reached the end of the runway at 175 miles per hour indicated, and—*whammo*—he would rack it up into a steep climbing 180, passing the tower at 1,500 feet.

Actually, all he really did was what Colonel Doolittle had done off the *Hornet* two years earlier, but with a few embellishments.

The arguments still rage among old B-25 pilots over pulling it off the ground or running till the end of the runway on takeoff. The bad booze consumed over that discussion would float the *Hornet*, but few will argue over the amazing flight characteristics of the 25 or its basic structural strength.

One day over the Anzio beachhead, a wing man, flying on a rookie flight leader, slipped his engines into high supercharger ratio (in defiance of operating rules) because he felt the leader might peel off and dive too fast after the bombs were dropped. The wing man decided he would need all the power available to stay in close for protection against the FW-190s that were circling the beachhead, and that is exactly what happened. In the ensuing wild dive, the wing man ran the manifold pressure past the end of the gauges (fifty-five inches of mercury) and later estimated he was doing well over 400 miles per hour as they went from 12,000 feet to the deck in six miles (VNE was 340 miles per hour). As a matter of interest, he was the only one in the formation who stayed with the leader and came out with only a few flak holes. Three others were shot down, and heavy damage was inflicted on the rest.

Opposite page: Underside view of a B-25 Mitchell medium bomber, showing the 75-mm cannon and dual 50-caliber machine guns in the nose.

A B-25 was fairly easy to fly without a copilot except for raising and lowering the landing gear. That necessitated diving below the level of the instrument panel to reach the gear control on the floor. In fact, the H models, with the 75-millimeter cannon, had only one set of controls, and the cannoneer-navigator or flight engineer rode in the right seat.

The G and H models with the cannon were, to say the least, an unusual experience when they were first sent to Columbia, South Carolina, to train crews. The cannon was installed in what had been the tunnel to the bombardier's compartment, with the breech extending into the navigator's compartment. The cannoneer-navigator (most were formerly bombardier-navigators) was the loader, and he stood in an almost windowless compartment where the more than thirty-pound shells hung in clip racks on the wall.

It was no fun, in a bouncing airplane, to grab a shell off the wall, slam it into the breech, then jump back to await the firing by the pilot while holding onto a handle on the wall, the only support. When the gun was fired, the breech opened, smoke and dirt flew back into the compartment, and the heavy brass shell case ejected against a piece of plywood, thence to roll around on the floor. The cannoneer was soon ankle deep in shell cases. It took a strong stomach to cope with being down in that hole, with no outside reference, while the exuberant young pilots threw the airplane around at tree-top level.

Nightly, the cannoneer-navigators sat in the bar wishing they had been sent to B-17s. They were probably the only commissioned cannon loaders in the history of the U.S. Army.

The more venturesome student pilots had a picnic with the G and H models, as buzzing was not only legal, it was part of the program. All practice missions, even cross-country, were flown at tree-top level, and firing that cannon was great sport.

Early in 1944 it was determined that the low-level cannon missions in Europe were not practical because of the relatively low speed of the aircraft in face of intense ground fire, so the cannon ships were sent off to the Pacific and the Orient where their success, particularly against shipping, was legendary.

The durability of the 25 is well exemplified by one C model that went from North Africa to Sicily to Italy to Corsica with the 321st Group. By 1945 this particular ship had flown more than 300 missions and had been bellied-in four or five times. The bottom of the fuselage resembled the surface of the moon. Painted a desert tan for camouflage, this old bird had been cared for by a crew chief with a macabre sense of humor.

Each time he patched a flak hole, he painted the patch with bright yellow zinc chromate. By 1944, the ship had been named *Patches*, and its venerable hide carried over 400 bright yellow blotches. By then it had been bent so many times that it flew with 8° of left aileron trim and 6° of right rudder.

Thus trimmed, *Patches* flew with a pronounced bias. Finally, the bias became so severe that the old bird had to be retired from combat because in formation the sideways flight caused everyone following to trim up on a crab. It was pretty ridiculous to see the first six aircraft in a flight flying straight and the last six flying sideways. When the war ended, old *Patches* was still merrily rumbling along sideways, carrying booze and vegetables from Sicily.

B-25 pilots were often mixed groups. Some came from B-26s, some from fighters (half of one class at Williams Field, a P-38 school, were sent to B-25s, to their chagrin), and the result was often a mixture of hot-rod types with the most conservative characters. Just after releasing his bombs over San Stefano, Italy, one of the Williams Field group, was hit by flak that severed the rudder trim-tab cable. The tab was flopping back and forth, causing violent rudder oscillation. It was obvious that the aircraft would soon shake itself to pieces. The engines were rocking severely and the instruments banged on the limits of their shock mounts. The pilot was unable to remain in formation and was left alone some 300 miles north of the base near Naples. Because the rudder trim control spun loosely, the pilot deduced the source of the trouble and instructed the tail gunner to attempt to shoot the trim off with his .50 caliber machine gun.

Unable to pivot his .50 far enough, the gunner took his .45 pistol, knocked a hole in the Plexiglas, and with his arm thrust into the slipstream fired seven shots, the last of which hit the trim-tab hinge, jamming the tab, and stopping the vibration. With both pilots holding right rudder to keep it straight, the no-longer-shaking 25 limped home safely at 140 miles per hour through 300 miles of fighter-infested territory. The gunner was decorated for his part in the incident.

Single-engine operation was no problem unless the aircraft was extremely heavily loaded. One not-too-brilliant pilot, returning to Corsica from Rome with a nonpilot in the right seat and fifteen returning rest-campers scattered throughout the ship (a violation of the eight-man maximum rule), stupidly chose the half way point, 1,000 feet over the Mediterranean, to show the nonpilot how to feather an engine. Naturally, the prop stuck in the full-feathered position. Adding power to the good engine, he easily climbed to 2,000 feet and cruised on into an uneventful landing. His only problem was trying to explain to the operations officer why he had feathered it in the first place.

The B-25 was never accorded the recognition or acclaim that was given, for example, the B-17. Some believe that was because the 25 was used in less glamorous theaters, but its contribution to the World War II effort was far greater than most people realize. The 57th Bomb Wing flew more than 60,000 sorties in the Mediterranean area.

The B-25 wasn't glamorous, nor was it beautiful; in fact, it was somewhat ungainly looking. It was noisy, drafty, and cold. Heavy on the controls, flying was work, particularly in formation for four or five hours; but it was undoubtedly used in more different fashions, in as many different places, as any other World War II aircraft.

If you want two or three hours of war stories, just ask an ex-B-25 pilot about flying. But be sure to speak loudly, clearly, and distinctly.

Keith R. Matzinger was a radio operator gunner from 1940–1941 in A-17As, B-18s, B-23s, and B-25s. He was a B-25 pilot in the Mediterranean Theater from 1943–1945.

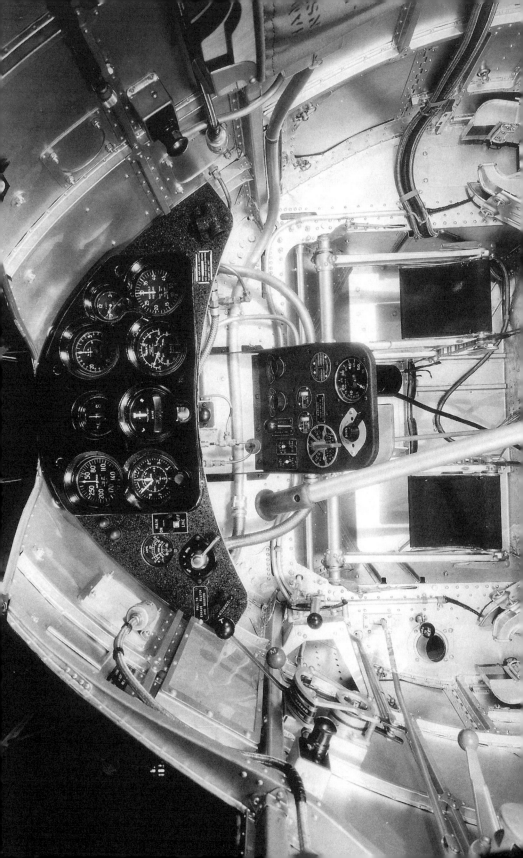

P-26 Peashooter

Ross G. Hoyt

I reported for duty at Barksdale Field, Shreveport, Louisiana, in September 1937 after my second four-year tour in the Office of the Chief of the Air Corps and was assigned to command the 20th Fighter Group. It was equipped with P-26s and retained them throughout the remainder of 1937, and during the 1938 Air Corps Exercises based at Roosevelt Field, Long Island, New York, until they were replaced by P-36s in late 1938 and early 1939.

The P-26, designed and built by the Boeing Aircraft Company, Seattle, Washington, was a low-winged, open-cockpit monoplane of metal construction with faired, fixed landing gear, swiveling tail wheel, horizontal stabilizer adjustable on the ground only, elevator trim tabs adjustable from the cockpit, left aileron and rudder trim tabs adjustable on the ground for roll and yaw, toe brakes, hydraulic shock absorbers, hand-operated landing flaps, and a fifty-two-gallon main fuel tank in the fuselage with a twenty-gallon reserve standpipe and two twenty-six-gallon tanks, one in each wing. A small bomb rack could be attached, but was rarely used except for magnesium flares for emergency night landings. Power was provided by a Pratt & Whitney R 1340-27 engine in the first one hundred eleven aircraft.

Of the final twenty-five aircraft, the first two had R 1340-33 engines with fuel injection and were designated P-26B. The remaining aircraft were completed with the original R1340-33 engine without fuel injection and were designated P-26C, differing only in minor control changes from the P-26A. The delivery of P-26Cs began in February 1936; they were all later converted to P-26Bs.

A two-bladed, fixed-pitch propeller was used. The engine was fitted with a ring cowling and was started by a hand-energized inertia starter

---

Opposite page: Cockpit of the P-26.

with removable crank inserted on the left-hand side. Streamlined brace wires ran from a few feet inboard on the top of the wing to the fuselage and from the bottom of the wing to the landing gear. Streamlined cross brace-wires ran from a few feet inboard of the top of the wing to the fuselage and from the bottom of the wing to the landing gear. Streamlined cross brace wires ran between landing-gear struts. This increased strength, but it also increased parasitic resistance. With the fixed landing gear and other parasitic drag, the top speed was considerably reduced.

Armament, in the first several P-26s, consisted of two .30 caliber fixed machine guns, cocked from the cockpit, synchronized to fire through the propeller, aimed by an exterior sight mounted in front of the windshield, and fired by pistol grip on the control stick. In further production, armament was changed to one .30 caliber and one .50 caliber gun. Synchronization reduced the rate of fire about fifty percent. With bomb rack, the P-26, with a stretch of imagination, might be considered a forerunner of the fighter-bomber.

Communication was provided by an SCR 183 radio with seven watts output on phone, MCW, and CW.

The instrument board included oil pressure and temperature gauges, tachometer, fuel pressure gauge, fuel gauge (quantity—main tank only), altimeter, compass, rate-of-climb indicator, bank-and-turn indicator, turn indicator (gyro), ammunition counter, and manifold pressure gauge.

With the addition of an improvised cockpit hood, instrument flying training could be conducted with a second plane trailing with the pilot acting as an instructor, giving warning of any dangerous situation.

The first time I saw a P-26, I thought, "Well, here is the big brother of the Sperry Messenger," which, for the benefit of those who don't know or remember, was a little toy-sized, low-wing monoplane powered by a small, three-cylinder radial engine produced experimentally for use by the ground forces for the purpose its name indicates.

A short-coupled, sturdy, low-winged monoplane, the P-26 was the nearest in appearance to a fighter pilot's conception of what a fighter aircraft should look like at the time of its introduction into the inventory of the Air Corps.

Getting into the cockpit of the P-26 entailed placing the right foot on the left wing next to the fuselage, grasping the rear edge of the cockpit, hauling oneself up onto the wing, and stepping into the open cockpit through a longitudinally hinged door which dropped down to facilitate the process. After being seated in the cockpit, you lifted, shut, and latched the door.

Opposite page: P-26B with flaps down.

The engine was started by a mechanic standing on the left wing to hand-energize the inertia starter by means of a crank inserted into the starter shaft. When the starter was "wound up" sufficiently, the pilot turned on the ignition switch and engaged the starter. If good luck prevailed, the engine started on the first try.

Because of its short coupling, brakes, and swiveling tail wheel, the airplane was very easily maneuvered on the ground. However, because of the sensitivity of the hydraulic landing gear, a wing would go down on turns. As a result, the plane gained the sobriquet "limber legs." It was also known jocularly as the "peashooter."

After taxiing to takeoff position, the brakes were applied and the throttle opened to maximum allowable manifold pressure at sea level. The throttle quadrant had a "gate" that could be set for maximum allowable manifold pressure so that it was not necessary to look at the manifold pressure gauge each takeoff. After checking engine operation and condition, the throttle was closed, brakes released, and throttle opened gradually until flying speed was attained. It was important that the throttle was opened slowly. As stated earlier, the airplane was equipped with hydraulic shock absorbers. If the throttle was advanced too rapidly, the engine and propeller torque might compress the left shock absorber to the extent that the left horizontal stabilizer could strike the ground, causing an abrupt turn. This situation was to be avoided at any time, but especially on takeoff in formation, when collision would probably occur. One such minor accident occurred in the 20th Fighter Group during my tenure of command.

Visibility in flight was good up, to the right and left, and to the rear. Visibility down was obscured through a wide angle by the wings. Visibility forward in level flight was good.

The P-26 responded readily to the controls and was capable of performing all the aerobatic maneuvers, but it was not stable in flight to the extent that it could be flown "hands off."

Landing flaps were used habitually in the 20th Fighter Group for formation landings. Sideslips were employed in individual landings if desired but were barred in formation landings, obviously.

I am informed that, because of its tapered wing (in both thickness and form), the P-26 had a dangerous stalling characteristic. Fortunately, I did not encounter that trait. But if pulled up into a stall, the P-26 would slip back down tail first and then fall into a dive with little or no tendency to spin. This trait proved helpful in shaking an enemy off one's tail in combat.

Opposite page: P-26As in combat formation.

As Air Force Representative on the American Military Mission to China, I was at Toungoo, Burma, from October 9 to 20, 1941, for a conference with Claire Chennault, commanding officer of the American Volunteer Group, to determine, in detail, the situation pertaining to personnel, training, and materiel in the group and to obtain his recommendations and conclusions. During the course of the conference, my notes show Chennault stated that in 1937 the Chinese air force had three fighter groups: one equipped with Curtiss Hawk-3 biplanes, one equipped with Curtiss Hawk-2 biplanes, and one equipped with two squadrons of Fiats and one squadron of P-26s. There is also a note stating that the P-26 proved excellent in combat.

Although compared to present-day aircraft the P-26 was deficient in armament, it made a good showing in combat with contemporary aircraft—that is, the pre-Japanese Zero.

Performance data and specifications for the P-26 were obtained from the Headquarters, United States Air Force, United States Air Force History Division, as follows:

Landing speed	73 miles per hour
Maximum speed	234 miles per hour
Cruising speed	199 miles per hour
Range	360 statute miles
Rate of climb	2,360 feet per minute
Service ceiling	27,400 feet
Wingspan	27 feet 11 $\frac{1}{2}$ inches
Length	23 feet 10 inches
Height	10 feet 5 inches
Engine	500-horsepower Pratt & Whitney

Landing procedure was simple. If planes were in formation, the landing area (usually a grass field) would be circled in a counterclockwise direction at about gliding distance from the airport to allow all pilots to obtain a view of the area. Landing then could be made individually, by elements (three planes), flights (two elements), or squadron (three flights). Modern airports with runways would probably restrict landings to formations no larger than an element.

Approaching crosswind on the downwind side of the landing area about gliding distance away, a turn into the wind could be made, throttle closed, landing flaps placed down, and flying speed maintained to set down. There was no tendency to ground loop during landing roll. It was, therefore, a safe airplane to land in formation and to use in training newly rated pilots.

In the hundreds of hours of formation and individual flying in a P-26, it was never necessary for me to bail out. However, I often contemplated what the best procedure might be for abandoning ship if the occasion arose.

If the pilot had control, he could roll over on his back, unfasten his safety belt, and fall out. If not, he could stand up, and while grasping windshield and headrest, step out onto the wing, fall prone, and slide off. He could stand up and jump to the side, hoping he would clear the vertical fin and horizontal stabilizer.

I led the 20th Fighter Group, equipped with a total of forty-eight P-26s, from Barksdale Field, Louisiana, to Roosevelt Field, Long Island, New York, participated in the extensive Air Corps Exercises of 1938, and returned with all forty-eight airplanes to home station with only routine maintenance of engine and airplane performed by the crew chief of each plane. For ease of maintenance, no better evidence than that of the above performance exists.

The P-26 was, I believe, the first low-winged monoplane fighter aircraft procured by the air corps and the last fighter plane with fixed landing gear.

It was a good interim airplane for use in all-around training: individual and formation flying, aerobatics, simulated combat, gunnery, navigation, and instrument flying. It was employed on extensive and widespread Air Corps maneuvers in conjunction with ground forces.

I enjoyed flying the P-26 and appreciated its performance, but I always looked forward to the day of closed cockpit, retractable landing gear, free-firing guns of larger caliber, cannon, and engines of greater horsepower with resultant increase in fighter performance. All these came in the late 1930s and during the 1940s.

Brig. Gen. Ross G. Hoyt was active in military aviation since 1918, commanding fighter units in peace and war. Between duty in the southwest Pacific and the United Kingdom during World War II, he commanded the Single-Engine Advanced Flying School at Luke Field, Arizona—the largest in the world.

Flying the North American O-47 and the Curtiss-Wright O-52

Rick Glasebrook

World War I gave birth to the practical use of heavier-than-air machines for military aviation, and in the cauldron of combat the roles and tactics to be employed by these new weapons of war were developed. Observation was one of the most important roles, and eighteen of the forty-five U.S. squadrons to see combat action on the Western Front prior to November 11, 1918, were comprised of observation aircraft operating in direct support of ground troops. The primary missions of the observation squadrons were artillery adjustment and visual and photographic reconnaissance of enemy front line ground action and the support areas immediately to the rear.

The most common survivable aircraft configuration consisted of a pilot and an observer. The pilot flew the plane and operated one or more forward firing machine-guns. The observer was equally busy. While watching enemy ground activity, recording his observations, or adjusting friendly artillery fire with his key-operated wireless, he also had to keep the "eyes in the back of his head" trained on unfriendly skies to the east for Boche fighters who intended to destroy these spies in the sky. He was most vulnerable when hunched over the camera photographing through a hole in the cockpit floor. When attacked, he immediately turned his full attention to manning the flexible rear firing machine-gun. Meanwhile, the pilot put the plane into a dive toward his own lines and methodically (frantically?) kicked the rudder, throwing the tail from side to side. This made the blind spot under the tail less vulnerable, and the observer could fire at the attacker without shooting off his own empennage.[1] This operational philosophy continued into the late 1930s, and in

---

Opposite page: O-47A with float gear attached.

47

air matters, our primary strategic concerns were the determination of air requirements for hemisphere defense and the development of sufficient balanced forces and support elements to assure the destruction of any invader who attempted to reach our shores by air, land, or sea. Thus, observation squadrons were an important adjunct to the military installations located along our coasts and on our overseas bases in allowing the ground commanders to see "beyond the horizon."[2]

It was against these requirements that the O-47 and the O-52 were designed, produced, and introduced into the army air corps. However, by the time the U.S. entered the shooting war, these aircraft were obsolete and the majority remained stateside performing training or utility roles. Those overseas in the combat areas were quickly destroyed, and those in the less threatened backwaters lived on to perform support missions, freeing the newer, better performing aircraft for combat.

You can imagine the shock of eleven second lieutenant fighter pilots undergoing P-47 training—snatched from their bunks in the middle of the night at Dale Mabry Field, Tallahassee, Florida, bundled into a C-46 bound for a classified overseas destination, then four hours out of Miami, opened their sealed orders and found they had been assigned to the 4th Tactical Reconnaissance Squadron, APO 485, NY, NY.

As dawn broke, we landed at a tropical island base, Borinquen Field, Puerto Rico, to be greeted by the motliest group of aircraft ever assembled on one ramp: war-weary P-39Ns and Qs, B-18s and B-25s, O-47s and O-52s, L-1s, L-4s, and one UC-78. Slowly the residual glow of the booze we had managed to sneak aboard the Curtiss Commando carrying us off to combat and glory faded away to be replaced by a sinking sour mass in the pit of our stomachs as we realized that THIS WAS THE "4TH TAC RECON." In subsequent years it had been claimed in some quarters that I didn't always exhibit the proper respect for aircraft I was flying. I deny this. But if my id harbored some hidden resentment, it was born at that moment.

Being the "new boys," naturally we got the choice sorties. In my case, being short "4 for pay" with the month rapidly drawing to a close, a quick checkout in the O-47 was ordained. In those days we didn't have long involved ground schools and checklists to confuse the mind and boggle the senses. You found someone who had successfully flown the bird to give you a blindfold cockpit check, show you how to start the engine, operate the gear and flaps, and then back smartly away from the aircraft so that he wouldn't be associated with it if you did something stupid or embarrassing in the next hour or so.

Sitting on the ramp on its conventional two main gear and steerable tail wheel, the O-47 looked like a debauched AT-6 that had been put in a family way by some Grumman mongrel. As you approached it, you checked visually to see if there were any large wet spots underneath and if the wings were roughly parallel to the ground. Occasionally, one of the air-oil main gear struts would stick down on a high speed turn into the ramp requiring the crew chief to walk out to the tip of the high side wing and jump up and down to free it. If the condition was uncorrected between flights, one suspected the crew chief was not around supervising and more serious problems might be in the offing. The crew chief owned the airplane, was responsible for its condition, and merely suffered the pilots who occasionally borrowed and abused it. There was an unwritten but well understood rule that "the crew chiefs wouldn't fly the airplane if the pilots wouldn't do anything else but." It worked very well for all concerned. If the underside of the airplane was sparkly clean, you knew it had not flown that day. Wright engines have always been notoriously "wet" engines and the Cyclone was a spitting example. After every flight the helper would grab a wad of waste, a bucket of gas, and start swabbing down the underside of the entire aircraft so the pilots wouldn't start asking dumb questions about where all that oil came from. At the end of the flying day he broke out a mop and a couple buckets of gas and did a thorough cleanup. His workday ended when the chief decided "his" airplane was ready for another day's flying.

Mounting the beast was the most difficult part of flying it. On the first flight I clawed my way up the left wing from the rear and bracing the left hand on top of the wind screen and the right on top of the rearward sliding hatch, swung both feet smartly over the cockpit combing. Unfortunately, the throttle quadrant stuck up sufficiently high to catch my left foot and I ended up on my knees in the cockpit with the underside of my bare right forearm resting on the exhaust stack that ran the full length of the cockpit down the right side of the fuselage. It was still hot from the preflight, but the resulting burn healed in less than two weeks and didn't leave a permanent scar. I quickly learned not to dangle my right arm out of the cockpit on that airplane.

Much of the AT-6 and BC-1 engineering was immediately recognizable in the cockpit, and the new items were mostly connected with the communications, anti-icing, and de-icing systems. After adjusting the seat and strapping in, I took about five minutes to finger my way around the cockpit alternately closing my eyes, feeling for the switch I wanted, and then opening them to make sure I had the right one. Many items in a cockpit have a distinctive feel—but like young girls in the back seat of a parked car, switches and gauges feel very much alike. It was several years later before standardized handles with a distinctive feel were developed.

Soon my instructor pilot arrived and after assuring him I was ready, he borrowed a rag from the crew chief, blindfolded me, and then told me to "walk" the cockpit from left to right. Immediately off the left elbow on the side panel is the hydraulic power control. You selected the desired gear or flap position with their individual control handles after pushing the power control button, and the system was actuated. The button had to be actuated for each operating cycle. Forward and inboard was the fuel tank selector. There were four positions on the "A" model: off, left wing, right wing (each holding forty-five gallons), and main (sixty gallons including a twenty-nine-gallon standpipe reserve). The "B" had front and rear fuselage tanks that overloaded to sixty gallons each. If you didn't get a positive click when a small ball dropped into a hole at each position—or if you twisted the handle off of its stem—fuel feed problems developed shortly thereafter. Next came the flap control handle which gave a choice of up, down, neutral, or could be locked in any intermediate position. I never had occasion to use the flaps, except while dog fighting with the P-39s, when cracking in about one-quarter of the all metal trailing edge, split-type flaps gave a superior, tight radius of turn. All of our runways were over 2,000 feet and the O-47 easily landed and took off clean without having to overly concern yourself with crosswind techniques involving the use of flaps.

Off the left knee from inboard were the emergency hand pump, the wobble pump (hand fuel pump for starting and in case of failure of the engine driven fuel-pump—for you late arrivals), an easy-to-grab elevator trim tab, and the landing-gear control handle. The latter had a plunger on top which had to be pulled out before you could operate the gear handle to the UP or DOWN position.

Forward of this group were the rudder trim tab (a knurled wheel lying horizontally), the carburetor heat control, and the elevator trim tab (identical to the rudder trim tab except positioned vertically—turn left to drop the left wing and right to drop the right wing). The ailerons, rudder, and elevators were fabric covered, dynamically balanced, and could be trimmed from the cockpit.

Above the gear handle was the control quadrant containing the fuel mixture control, the propellor control for the Hamilton Standard three-blade hydro-controllable constant-speed propeller, and the throttle. As mentioned earlier, the quadrant was positioned too high on the cockpit wall for either comfortable formation flying or for easy cockpit ingress/egress.

The instrument panel was well laid out and lighted, and I never felt uncomfortable flying on instruments either under the hood or at night. Unlike the later practice of grouping all the flight instruments in the center and squeezing the miniaturized engine instruments into any inaccessible remaining space not occupied by radio or radar controls, the directional gyro and artificial horizon were in the center flanked on the left by the altimeter and rate of climb indicator and on the right by the "whiskey" compass with the needle and ball immediately below the primary flight instruments. The engine instruments—tachometer, manifold pressure, and fuel and oil pressure gauges—were grouped on the next tier down. The ignition switch was located in the upper left corner of the panel with the electrical panel just below it.

The central panel contained primary equipment such as the landing gear indicator which showed gear travel from UP to DOWN and all the intermediate positions; the vacuum selector switch providing vacuum from either the engine-driven vacuum pump (or as an alternate source the carburetor venturi); and the parking brake handle. The engine primer was located in the upper right-hand corner of the instrument panel. The engine was primed by turning the handle to the left to unlock it, pulling it out to fill the primer chamber, and pushing it back in, driving a charge of fuel into the primer lines connected through a manifold to the cylinders. The right-hand cockpit console was used for the cold weather gear such as wing de-icers, propeller anti-icer fluid, cockpit heat and ventilator controls, forward-firing gun charging control, oxygen regulator, radio control panels, and flare release controls. As we were operating in a tropical climate, all of the icing equipment was wired off. Nor did we use the forward-firing gun, as all of the pilots received their gunnery qualification, both ground and air, in the P-39. We normally flew between 4,000 and 8,000 feet, so the ventilator control was frozen in the full cold position and no oxygen equipment was installed. The standard "joy stick" contained a trigger for the forward-firing gun and a button for a throat mike. The radio equipment consisted of an SCR-238 short-range liaison set mounted in the center cockpit and a four-button VHF command communications radio. The engine starter was a two-position teeter-totter switch mounted on the right-hand floor board.

Having passed my blindfold cockpit check, the IP stood on the wing while I started the engine. Inhaling a lung full of the cockpit vapors of that era (a mixture of high octane gas and hydraulic oil which produced a euphoric high that today's odor of burnt kerosene can't begin to approach), I bellowed a thunderous CLEAR! alerting everyone in northwestern Puerto Rico that an engine was about to be started. Mixture control—IDLE CUT-OFF, propeller control aft to the full DECREASE RPM position, throttle cracked one-half inch—battery switch-ON, unlock the primer—one shot of prime (the engine was warm), build up fuel pressure with the wobble pump, back on the starter switch with the heel of the right foot to energize—magneto switch on BOTH, down on the toe of the right foot to engage the starter—when the engine coughs, mixture control full forward. Normally this would start the engine, and in my initial trial I was most fortunate and it caught immediately. The cardinal sin in starting the engine was to pump the throttle, which on occasion would either backfire the engine (highly irritating the crew chief) or create a stack fire covering the tail gunner in the third, or most aft, cockpit position with a rolling, noxious sheet of flame. We had one tail gunner (they were a temperamental lot as I will discuss later) who refused to fly with one of the pilots after twice having his eye lashes and eye brows singed from stack fires.

Once the engine was running smoothly, the propeller control was advanced to the full forward or HIGH RPM position. I gave the chocks-out signal by raising both arms in a V and simultaneously rotating the extended thumbs from clinched fists in a rolling outward motion. Then the ground crew displayed the chocks and pitot cover I released the brakes, taking taxi signals from the ground crewman, and cleared the ramp. We normally taxied with the throttle set at 800 revolutions per minute and maintained directional control by differential braking, slowly S-ing through the other parked aircraft. The nose was not inordinately above the sight line of the cockpit, and taxiing was not the chore that it was in the P-40 and the P-47. As our ambient temperature rarely fell below 60° F, oil temperature was not a problem. Our local procedure was to call the tower as we cleared the squadron ramp prior to entering the main taxiway. Radio malfunctions were not uncommon and a green light from the "bisquit gun" was just as effective—once you got their attention. The airplane was turned into the wind on the run-up pad, brakes set, stick pulled full back into the belly, throttle run up to forty-two inches of mercury, and the left and right magneto checked individually. If the magneto drop was 125 revolutions per minute or less, the throttle was reduced to 1,000 revolutions per minute (to prevent fouling the plugs)—then tower clearance obtained, a quick check made of the base leg and final approach, and you took the runway. When I was a Kaydet in advanced, a friend of mine made a sloppy traffic check one night, and a landing AT-6 chewed its way right up to the point where the prop cut his backpack chute off his back. To this day, I always do a 360° scan for traffic.

We normally took off with all canopies in the open position and made a quick check on interphone with the other crew members. Solo, I lined up the airplane and gingerly started the takeoff roll by slowly advancing the throttle. We usually used only thirty-six inches of mercury as we had over 10,000 feet of runway and our prime concern was extended engine life. Initially, I tended to stick in too much right rudder to compensate for engine torque as a carryover from my P-40 and P-47 experience. However, I soon learned to overcome this tendency and by presetting about $1\frac{1}{2}°$ of right rudder trim prior to takeoff, very little right rudder lead was required in the O-47A or B.

As the airplane came through sixty miles per hour you could feel the stick forces start to lighten, and by easing off slightly on the back pressure, the tail wheel came off the ground and you became airborne around seventy miles per hour IAS holding a slight tail low altitude. When I felt the airplane positively airborne I hit the hydraulic power button, pressurizing the system, and pulled the gear handle to the up position. As the gears retracted inward into their wells, I reduced rpm to 2,200 and trimmed the airplane for climb. We maintained thirty-six inches and 1,920 revolutions per minute, which in the "B" bird gave about 190 miles per hour True Air Speed at 8,000 feet and an 800 mile range. I was surprised to find that the airplane handled more comfortably than its ungainly appearance indicated that it might. It was a little heavier and more solid than the AT-6 but had the rapid aileron response associated with all North American single-engine aircraft. The majority of our missions were practice tracking exercises for the anti-aircraft batteries to enable them to calibrate their guns. A secondary function was towing targets for P-39 air-to-air gunnery. Although the aircraft was primarily designed to perform photographic missions, we rarely used it as a photographic platform because the squadron B-25s provided much more latitude and flexibility in the selection of cameras and the altitude cones for these cameras.

The center cockpit was designed for the observer/photographer. But it also could be used as an auxiliary pilot position with a folding seat, detachable control stick, throttle quadrant, and the bare minimum of instruments required to fly safely and land the airplane. A pilot in the center cockpit had only two choices of mixture—full rich or full lean—but could otherwise operate the engine controls in a normal manner. He also could operate the gear and flaps and communicate with the outside world. A crew member performing primary duty as an observer/photographer could deploy another folding seat, open a set of doors in the bottom of the fuselage, and operate the K-3B aerial camera with either the 8 1/4-inch or the twelve-inch cones. For spotting missions, a K-10 camera could be mounted; for tactical mapping missions, the T-3A camera; and for night photographic missions, the K-12 camera, employing 8x10-inch cut film holders. Each of the other cameras used preloaded magazines. For night photography, four flashlight bombs were carried in the forward center section of the gunner station in the rear cockpit. There were intervalometers mounted in both the front and the center cockpits so that the cameras could be operated automatically from either position. One of the fun games pilots enjoyed playing on new photographers was to instruct them to open the two camera doors, and, as the belly of the airplane extended about a foot below the propeller blades, buzz the ocean giving the observer a salt water bath. The observer and the gunner usually did not appreciate this, and the crew chief got downright apoplectic about it because after the mission the aircraft had to be hosed down with freshwater to inhibit corrosion.

As we didn't have a real war to occupy our time we thought up various other ways to kill ourselves, some of which succeeded. Tow-target missions were the most unpopular as they required a little more skill and technique in execution. The pilot would taxi into a position at the end of the runway and hold while about 300 feet of cable was unwound from a reel mounted in the aft gunner's compartment. This was hauled down the runway and connected to the target or "rag" attached to a six-foot steel bar. When the ground crew indicated that all connections were secure and the tow-target operator gave the signal that the tow reel was locked, the pilot applied full throttle and after the takeoff roll started, pushed the stick forward to get a tail-high attitude as rapidly as possible. If you were quick enough, you felt the jolt of the target being snatched off the ground; if you were skillful enough, you were airborne without either cutting off an elevator with the tow cable or snagging the "rag" on some fixed ground object.

For gunnery missions we usually operated at 10,000 to 12,000 feet, cruising back and forth on a predetermined course in an assigned gunnery area prohibited to all other aircraft and shipping. Once the tow plane was established he would call the P-39 flight leader and clear him to start making gunnery passes. Usually as a courtesy to the tow plane operator, the first passes were dry runs so that the P-39 pilots could get a "picture" of the rag in relation to the tow plane and so that the tow plane operators could get a confidence factor for the pilots who would soon be shooting at them. In our air-to-air gunnery with live ammunition, we only used the high side approach where the gunnery flight would fly parallel to the tow ship and slightly above. On the signal of the gunnery flight leader, each aircraft would peel down and toward the target and then roll into a pursuit curve as it drew into firing range. Normally, the pilot drew his lead on the rag by lining up on the O-47 tow ship. As we all took turns flying the tow ship, this usually did not bother the tow pilot, but occasionally a green P-39 pilot would extend his base leg out too far and end up in a stern chase on the rag which would then include the tow ship in its lethal cone of fire.

As we loaded one tracer to every four rounds of ball ammunition, this proved very disconcerting to the tow operator, and one of these fellows, whom I remember most vividly because of his luxurious shock of flaming red hair, always carried a spare cable cutter in his flying suit pocket. On those occasions when the P-39 flattened out his lead angle to the point where Red felt threatened, he would cut the cable and as the rag fluttered down into the sea he would come up with a terse "dammit, Lieutenant, he shot the rag off the cable."

According to the "Bird Book," the aircraft was prohibited from loops, rolls, spins, full stalls, and anything else that might be fun for a young fighter pilot whose juices were still flowing freely. In practice, one was liable to be bounced by a P-39 at any time and then it was "Katy-bar-the-gate." The O-47 could out-turn the P-39, but the most serious disadvantage came from its inferior redline speed of about 290 miles per hour versus the P-39's 525 miles per hour. If a P-39 could make a pass unobserved you were dead. However, once you were engaged, the only way a P-39 could make a destructive pass was from head on or by using his superior speed in a yo-yo maneuver, i.e., vertical passes from above and below. This advantage was reduced by getting the O-47 quickly on the deck World War I style to restrict the P-39's maneuver area. In turn, once a P-39 decided to stay and fight, you could get a lead on him in about two orbits of a Lufberry circle. When he saw your nose coming inside his radius of turn, his options were fairly limited as his speed had been killed off sufficiently to deny any effective climbing maneuver. If he tried a vertical reverse, an aggressive O-47 pilot could stay with him, although the maneuver was not the "headcracker against the canopy" associated with the AT-6. If he split-S'd with anything less than a smartly executed maneuver, an aileron roll in the direction of his turn would hold any lead you already had built in until about midway through the roll. After that, you had best continue to roll as a nose-down attitude quickly exceeded the redline speed. Apparently, the G forces in the gunner's position were pretty vicious. One day after a particularly spirited engagement with my roommate, my rear gunner marched up to the Ops Officer, threw his gunner's wings down on the desk, and announced that he was through flying. I felt badly about this as I have always admired the courage of any aircrew member who was not in possession of a set of controls, yet had to fly with any pilot issued to him by Operations.

My experience with the O-52 was less extensive. Our O-52s had been put into flyable storage and transferred to the Puerto Rican Air Depot. However, being a time-hungry second lieutenant flight test maintenance officer, I was able to get scheduled for the less desirable test flights. The O-52 was a contemporary of the O-47 but had many more advanced aerodynamic features, such as leading edge wing slats for improved slow flight and "Fowler" type flaps, which further improved handling characteristics at lower flying speeds than the O-47 could achieve. When the flaps were lowered 60°, the ailerons also drooped 15°, increasing drag and lift. The slats would extend first when the flaps were pumped down and in turn would stay extended until the flaps were raised, except when the aerodynamic loads caused them to retract. I first experienced wing slats on the L-1, but it still produced an eerie feeling to watch them slide in and out in slow flight. Another interesting feature was that the elevator trim tabs acted as aerodynamic balances, thereby reducing stick forces.

An all-metal, two-place, high-wing monoplane, it had much better downward pilot visibility than the O-47, making it admirably suited for visual reconnaissance, but the view upward and to the rear gave the same uncomfortable vulnerable blind feeling I had flying the Piper J-3 Cub. However, the major detractor in flying the O-52 was the hydraulic system. The landing gear and wing flaps had to be manually pumped up and down through a gear-driven chain. The gear UP or DOWN cockpit indicators operated independently, but the arm-weary pilot really knew the gear was at full travel down when one of the chain links on each side which had been painted yellow came to the top of the drive gear. A pilot flying the P-80 for the first time could be identified by his waggling wing tips from the time he broke ground until he disappeared from sight; the virgin pilot in the O-52 showed inexperience by porpoising down the runway in a tight sine curve after becoming airborne and pumping the hydraulic pump and the control stick in unison. It took about twenty to thirty strokes to get the gear full up. There was also a

Opposite page: The Curtiss O-52.

provision for raising the gear and flaps simultaneously, which I never had the curiosity or stamina to try.

Entry to the pilot's cabin was made through an access door on the right side of the fuselage which was hinged to the top of the wing root. For a six-foot 185 pounder, getting in was a real Chinese fire drill. As the pilot's seat rotated 90° to the right, my method was to place my chute in the seat first, then back into it. Once seated you could tuck your knees under your chin, rotate the seat to face forward, have it secured, and then buckle in. Shorter fellows who ordered their drinks at the bar in a voice with a touch of soprano were observed to climb in left leg first, dragging the rest of their body after it. Instrumentation and location of the controls in the front cockpit was almost the same as in the O-47. However, the observer's position contained only the barest of emergency flight controls. It also had camera doors in the bottom of the fuselage and a rear firing flexible machine-gun which was streamlined by a folding turtleback when the gun was stowed. Camera selection was limited to the K-3B or K-7C cameras.

The starting procedures for the Wright R-1340-51 Wasp engine were practically the same as for the Cyclone in the O-47. Minor differences were that the battery switch was incorporated in the magneto switch and once airborne, engine temperature could be controlled through the adjustment of hydraulically actuated cowl flaps.

The airplane taxied like most narrow-geared high-wing monoplanes with the attendant problems in the peripheral edges of the visual spectrum and difficulty with cross winds. The tail wheel was steerable to 30° on either side, and then it became a swivel.

Takeoffs, as mentioned, were a physical chore. Once airborne and tidied up, the O-52 handled nicely and was a comfortable airplane to fly. Although the only prohibited maneuvers within its 270 miles per hour redline limitation were such exotic things as outside loops, inverted spins, or spins of more than three turns, I never really wrung it out like I did the O-47. Perhaps because when sitting in the cockpit the raw, unfinished interior gave the appearance of an all-metal kite. The O-47 just looked and felt more solid and gave one a feeling of confidence in its structural integrity.

I never had the desire or the occasion to bail out of either aircraft, but I feel it would have been easier in the O-47. Just slide the canopy back, and as the old saw goes, "tidy up the cockpit and step smartly over the LEFT side." Had I been required to part company with the O-52 in flight, I planned to "blow" the door by stomping on a foot pedal which pulled the hinge pins and then go head first through the resultant hole in the fuselage.

Both the O-52 and the O-47 were good cross-country aircraft as they had ample room to store all the twelve-dollar-a-case Scotch whiskey a second lieutenant could buy on the R&R trips to Barbados or Trinidad. In addition, the 800-mile range that the O-52 and the O-47B would achieve with a full fuel overload was sufficient to go where the action was.

I don't know why the decision was made to retain the O-47 in our squadron's active inventory and retire the O-52, but I assumed it was primarily a logistical problem as it was the only aircraft in the Caribbean Air Command using the Pratt & Whitney R-1340 engine. Secondarily, despite its many innovative features it didn't provide the operational flexibility required by the 4th Tac Recon's mission.

Both airplanes with their .30-caliber machine-guns were undergunned, and with all the experience Curtiss-Wright had with the Wasp engine (it was first flight tested in the Curtiss Hawk airframe[3], I never could understand why they didn't insist on its having an engine-driven hydraulic pump. It sure would have made it an easier aircraft to fly. However, to its credit, many of its aerodynamic features were incorporated in highly successful later generation aircraft.

In today's tight budgetary climate I doubt if the O-52 would have survived a fly-off competition with the O-47. But, in the political atmosphere of the late 1930s, the construction of 164 O-47As, 740 B models by North American, and 203 O-52s by Curtiss Wright[4] was a vital shot in the arm to a flagging aircraft industry. Because of this infusion, however, when President Franklin D. Roosevelt decreed in a fireside chat in 1940 that America would build 50,000 airplanes to meet the Nazi challenge, the industry had the knowhow, facilities, and trained manpower to meet adequately the challenge. And that's what it's all about.

Col. Rick Glasebrook flew the P-38, P-39, and P-80 during World War II.

1. 1st Lt. Lawrence L. Smart, *The Hawks That Guided the Guns* (135 Aero Sqd USAS, 3510 Mancopa St., Apt. 410, Torrance, CA 90503, privately printed), 37-42.
2. Maj. Gen. H. H. Arnold and Col. Ira C. Eaker, *Winged Warfare* (New York: Harper Bros., 1941).
3. Cdr. Eugene E. Wilson, USN (Ret.), *Slipstream: The Autobiography of an Aircraftsman* (Literary Investment Guild, Ltd., Palm Beach, FL 33480), 73, 74.
4. James C. Fahey, *U.S. Army Aircraft, 1908-1946* (Ships & Aircraft, P.O. Box 48, Falls Church, VA 22045), 31.

P-38 Lightning

Royal D. Frey

A soft muffled sigh drifted across the Santa Ana Army Air Base preflight center. Rushing from my tent, I saw for the first time that intriguing and mysterious airplane about which I had so often read, the Lockheed P-38 Lightning. It not only looked different from any other airplane I had ever seen—it even sounded different. The preflight center was located only a couple of miles west of Santa Ana Army Airfield; at the time I reported as an aviation cadet for classification and preflight training (August 1942) a squadron of P-38s was based on the field. Nearly every day we cadets could see P-38s taking off and later buzzing the runway prior to landing. Even in my wildest dreams I never imagined I would ever be so fortunate as to fly one of them.

While I was at Basic Flying School at Pecos, Texas, in February 1943, the famous long-distance civilian pilot Jimmy Mattern brought in a P-38 for flight demonstration. Upon seeing him roll it off the deck into a dead engine, I was convinced that this was the plane for me. I ran across the ramp to my instructor and pleaded my case—the P-38 was what I really wanted to fly. The crocodile tears in my eyes must have turned the trick, for I was next sent to Williams Field near Phoenix—the AAF's twin-engine fighter school.

After getting seventy hours in the AT-17, six hours dual gunnery in the AT-6, and ten hours in the AT-9 (if you can fly the AT-9 without getting killed, you can fly anything!), I was scheduled for checkout in the RP-322. The RP-322 was known as the "castrated P-38" because it lacked turbo-superchargers. It also lacked guns, armor plate, and standard P-38 communications equipment. It had evolved from the Lightnings originally purchased by the British and subsequently taken over by the AAF for training purposes.

Opposite page: The P-38 Lightning.

Although the RP-322 lacked much of the P-38's equipment, it also lacked much of the P-38's weight. As a result, at full throttle on the deck it scooted like a scalded deer. However, at 15,000 feet it became a dud, not even able to hold its own against antiquated P-40s from Luke Field on the other side of Phoenix.

After getting ten hours in the RP-322, I was awarded my wings on May 20, 1943, and sent to Operational Training Unit (OTU) at Muroc Army Air Base (now Edwards AFB). Here began the most exciting and carefree period of my life—my brief career as a P-38 pilot. It came to an abrupt end less than nine months later when I was forced to bail out over Germany.

With its tricycle gear, counterrotating props, and inherent stability the P-38 was extremely easy to fly. Once trimmed for straight and level flight, it was a hands-off airplane. If you put it into an unusual attitude (within reasonable limits) and then got off the controls, it would slowly waddle and oscillate around in the air and eventually return to straight and level flight. This was because its center of lift was above its center of gravity—i.e., most of the mass of the airplane was slung under a wing having a large amount of dihedral. Other fighters of the era with their low wings (and the consequential lower center of lift) tended to drop off on one wing or the other, since the center of lift would always tend to seek a position above the center of gravity. In the P-38 this feature was built in.

Another excellent feature built into the P-38 was its stall characteristic—it stalled from the center section outward to the tips. As a result, in a panic break with an enemy plane behind you, you could pull the P-38 into such a tight turn that it would begin to buffet, but you would still have remarkable aileron control.

One day in July 1943, while landing at Portland, Oregon, on my first cross-country in a P-38, I learned how completely forgiving was the Lightning. Flying No. 2 on the break, I got much too low on the final turn. The runway at Portland somehow completely disrupted my perspective. (I later learned it was covered with tar and wooden chips and was much wider than normal—to me at the time it appeared almost as wide as it was long.) In any case, there I was on the treetops off the approach end of the runway, needing to tighten my left turn in order to line up for landing, but much too low to steepen my bank without dragging my left wing tip through the top of someone's house. So I gradually began to feed in more and more left rudder. Suddenly, without any warning, the rudder pedals shook violently several times and then the left rudder pedal slammed my foot backward to the full rear position—a complete

---

Opposite page: P-38s in formation.

rudder stall. I immediately poured on the throttles for a few seconds to increase my airspeed slightly, and the rudder pedals returned to neutral. I dumped full-flaps, chopped throttles, and still made a normal routine landing. My buddy flying No. 3 a short distance behind me never noticed anything unusual. Had we been in single-engine fighters, he would probably have seen my plane flip into the trees and explode.

With its inherent stability, counterrotating props, muffled engine exhausts through the turbos, and fairly heavy weight, the P-38 was a sheer delight on takeoff. You would take the runway, line up and brake to a full stop, and advance the throttles to at least forty-four inches of manifold pressure to where the turbos would cut in. The nose would gradually drop as the increasing pull of the props forced the nose strut to compress, and the whole plane would shake and vibrate, waiting to be released from the bonds that held it. A quick glance across the instrument panel and off the brakes. Up popped the nose and you bounded forward like a racehorse from the starting gate.

As you gathered speed down the runway, the heavy weight of the plane deadened any bumps, and you felt as if you were in a Cadillac. At the same time the turbo exhausts made the engines sound extremely muffled as if you were in a high-powered pleasure boat: no loud crackling or roar so usual in those days of reciprocating engines. No torque to swing the nose, and beautiful visibility down the runway from the level attitude of the tricycle gear. At seventy miles per hour you gently eased back on the control yoke, and at 95–100 miles per hour the plane lifted softly into the air. What complete comfort for a combat plane!

One of the greatest bugaboos of the P-38 was engine failure on takeoff. Consequently we had drilled into us critical single-engine speed on takeoff—130 miles per hour. Even before God, Motherhood, and Country came that 130 miles per hour as soon as possible after your wheels left the runway. As a result, as soon as the plane broke ground, you dropped your nose to maintain level flight five to ten feet off the runway. You always added ten miles per hour for next-of-kin and another ten miles per hour or so as a fudge factor. Then you gradually lifted the nose for optimum climb speed of 160 miles per hour. If in a populated area, the tendency was to hold the plane on the deck and build up as much speed as possible before beginning your climb—it was much more impressive to the taxpayer who might be driving his auto down a street off the end of the runway when your props cut through the air within a hair of his head. We all knew it was legalized buzzing but defended it fervently; we had to get that safe single-engine speed or die!

I do not personally recall anyone ever losing an engine or prop on takeoff. I do remember hearing of a few instances of a runaway prop, but many of them might have been caused by the pilot taking off with one of his Curtiss electric props locked in fixed pitch.

My only personal experience with this type of difficulty on takeoff resulted from an oil cap coming loose while taxiing along the rough grass runway at Wittering RAF Station in England. On liftoff I noticed oil pouring along the cowling of my right engine. I first hit the right feather switch and then trimmed in left rudder and left aileron after pulling the mixture control to idle-cutoff. I do not remember my exact airspeed as I crossed the boundary at the far end of the field, but I could not have been doing more than 135–140 miles per hour. At this fairly low speed, the plane was anything but the snarling, uncontrollable monster I had been led to believe.

Landing the P-38 was as smooth and pleasant an operation as take-off. We would dive onto the field, buzz the runway at about ten feet, and peel up into a steep climbing turn. With no torque there was no neces-sity for constantly cranking in rudder trim, and the nose did not wander all over the sky as airspeed dropped off. While on top of the peel-up, in a vertical bank almost on our back, we chopped throttles and moved the flap handle into half-flap position (maneuver flaps). With no power and so much increased lift, plus the great stability of the plane, we could pull it around onto the final approach as tightly as was required in order to line up with the runway. In fact, we soon got to be such "hot pilots" that we would still be in a steep diving turn as we crossed the boundary of the field, as full flaps came down, rolling out just before the main wheels touched the ground.

The P-38 was an excellent gun platform, although it was more diffi-cult than in a P-47 or P-51 to get strikes on a target because the four .50 caliber guns and 20-millimeter cannon were grouped so closely together in the nose. However, if we got any strikes at all, we had a much better chance of getting a victory; those five weapons put out such a heavy col-umn of projectiles that they bored a large hole through anything they hit.

The P-38 had the famous Fowler flap, which, at half-extended posi-tion, greatly decreased turn radius at altitude at the expense of very little additional drag. This feature, incorporated in the P-38 for combat, was given the name "maneuver flaps." With maneuver flaps I actually turned with late-model Spitfires during "rat races" over England and turned inside FW-190s in action over Europe.

There was a poor design feature associated with the maneuver flaps, however—namely the control lever, located on the right side of the cockpit. Since the P-38 was flown with the left hand on the throttles and the right hand on the control wheel, any use of maneuver flaps required the pilot to keep his right hand dancing from the wheel to the lever while at the same time moving his left hand from the throttles to the wheel every time he took his right hand off the wheel to move the flap lever. Whoever gave the final approval for the location of the flap handle in the P-38 certainly must not have given any thought to its use in combat.

Although the P-38 could turn very tightly once it got into a bank, getting it into the bank was another matter. Late K series and L series Lightnings had aileron boost, but this feature came too late for those few of us who took on the Luftwaffe deep inside Germany in those grim days of late 1943 and early 1944. Because of the weight of the plane and the poor leverage of a control wheel compared to that of a control stick, the plane's roll rate approximated that of a pregnant whale. If we ever got behind a single-engine fighter in a tight turn, all the other pilot had to do was flip into an opposite turn and dive; by the time we had banked and turned after him, he was practically out of sight.

One day on a local flight over England, I noticed that by jamming in quite a lot of rudder a second or two before trying to bank, I was apparently able to speed up the plane's roll response by lessening the force needed to turn the wheel. Whether it actually had any effect or not is a good question, but it did a lot for my mental attitude.

One trick I once used (other P-38 pilots may also have used it at times) when a German plane got close behind me in a tight left turn was to chop right throttle and kick full right rudder along with right aileron. I seemed to snap up and over to the right, and although I am certain I never approached a spin, I do not know to this day exactly what maneuver the plane executed. However, the German plane could not follow me through it, and that was the important factor. I never needed to try this trick in a right bank, but the resulting maneuver probably would have been the same though in the opposite direction.

The P-38 had a combat tactic that was very effective against German fighters but not taught to or known by many P-38 pilots. Luckily I was one of the exceptions. On January 4, 1944, the 8th Air Force bombed Kiel. That evening while reading the intelligence TWX (teletype printout) of the mission, I noticed a statement by a pilot of the 55th Fighter Group who reported that he had escaped from a German fighter by pouring on full throttle and going into a steep corkscrew climb to the right.

Inside a Lightning's cockpit.

The next day the 8th went back to Kiel, and this time I went along on escort. My flight of four P-38s was bounced by twenty-five to thirty FW-190s of the yellow-nose variety from Abbeville. A string of six or more of them got in behind me before I noticed them, and just as No. 1 began to fire, I rolled into a right climbing turn and went to war emergency of sixty inches manifold pressure. As we went round and round in our corkscrew climb, I could see over my right shoulder the various FW-190 pilots booting right rudder attempting to control their torque at 150 miles per hour and full throttle, but one by one they flipped over to the left and spun out. Incidentally, although I had been told in the States that it was not possible, I could actually see tracer bullets leave their barrels and zip toward me!

Upon landing back in England, I was told that my plane whistled as I circled for landing. There was good reason—the left wing outside the boom was shot so full of holes that it had to be replaced. Those FW-190 pilots had been able to get sufficient lead to hit my left wing, but none had been able to get that little extra bit of lead needed to knock out my left engine or put a burst of fire into the cockpit.

In addition to an agonizingly slow roll rate, the P-38s I flew in combat had two other very limiting features—restricted dive and cockpit temperature. It was suicide to put the P-38 into a near-vertical dive at high altitude; all we P-38 pilots knew it, and I believe all the Luftwaffe pilots knew it, for they usually used the vertical dive to escape from us. You could "split-S" and do other vertical-type maneuvers at high altitude; and as long as you continued to pull the nose through the vertical, you always held your airspeed within limits. But let the nose stay in the vertical position for more than a few seconds and you reached what was termed "compressibility" in those days. The nose would actually "tuck under" beyond the vertical position, and it would be impossible to recover the plane from its dive. The only salvation was to pop the canopy, release your seat belt, and hope you would clear the plane as you were sucked from the cockpit. The 20th Group lost two P-38s in vertical dives over England before we went operational, but both pilots bailed out successfully (although one of them almost killed himself when he popped his chute too soon).

According to a Lockheed tech rep who once visited us, theoretically the air was sufficiently dense at 1,500 feet *below* sea level for the P-38 to *begin* pulling out of a high-speed vertical dive. Such a statement did little to bolster my confidence. Later Lightnings had dive brakes under the wings to correct this problem, but they were too late to be of value to me.

The other limiting feature, cockpit temperature, would be more correctly identified as "paralyzing." Cockpit heat from the engine manifolds was nonexistent. When you were at 30,000 feet on bomber escort and the air temperature was —55° F outside the cockpit, it was —55° F inside the cockpit. After thirty minutes or so at such a temperature, a pilot became so numb that he was too miserable to be of any real value; to make matters worse, he did not particularly care. Only his head and neck exposed to the direct rays of the sun retained any warmth.

Not only did the numbness seriously decrease a pilot's efficiency, but the balky clothing he wore further restricted his efforts. For example, I wore double-thickness silk gloves, then heavy chamois gloves, and topped these with heavy leather gauntlets (all British issue). Inside all these layers were fingers almost frozen stiff and completely without feeling. Flipping a single electrical switch required deep concentration, skill, and luck, and the P-38 cockpit was loaded with electrical switches. How we envied the P-47 and P-51 pilots with a heat-producing engine in front of them to maintain a decent cockpit temperature.

The greatest problem of all with the P-38 over Europe in 1943–44 was its engines, or rather its engine installation. When the AAF decided to add more internal fuel to the P-38 and thereby increase its range, the only place more tankage could be placed was in the leading edges of the wings where the intercoolers were located. So leading edge tanks for about one hour's additional endurance were installed, and the intercooler radiators were moved to the lower noses of the booms under the prop spinners.

The intercoolers worked fine in this position, but the adjacent oil coolers were now much too efficient. We would put up a Group strength of forty-eight planes, and if thirty got to the target, we considered ourselves fortunate. On every mission plane after plane would turn back for England once we had reached high altitude, primarily because of an engine that had blown up or a turbosupercharger that had "run away"— i.e., uncontrollable over-speeding.

A couple of months after my left engine had blown up while I was flying deep inside Germany (an event that led to my capture), Col. Mark Hubbard, 20th Group CO, arrived at Stalag Luft I, my POW camp on the Baltic Sea north of Berlin. In a conversation one day he remarked that during the first three months the 20th Group was on operations, it had the equivalent of a complete turnover in pilots—seventy percent of which could be attributed either directly or indirectly to engine trouble. What a needless waste of highly trained men to the enemy!

A Lockheed tech rep explained that at the tremendously low air temperatures in which we were flying, the oil in the radiators cooled to such an extent that its viscosity resembled that of molasses. It simply refused to flow sufficiently, and the engines would eventually explode or the oil-type turboregulators would malfunction.

The P-38 had a horrible reputation when it came to a pilot bailing out. The horizontal empennage, which we dubbed "the cheese knife," was considered a menace. In reality it was less of a threat than the stabilizers on the P-47 and P-51, simply because it was located farther to the rear from the P-38 cockpit, thereby providing more chance for a pilot to clear it on bailout. In addition the P-38 did not have a fin and rudder directly behind the cockpit which the pilot had to avoid. The only fighter pilot I knew in POW camp to strike the tail of his plane was a fellow who bailed out of a P-51D. When I was forced to bail out over Germany, I rolled my P-38 onto its back and dropped clear without any difficulty.

The experience that led to my capture in February 1944 sheds light on the performance of the P-38 in combat. Five Lightnings dove on four Me-410s and two Me-110s in a combat over Germany, and the Luftwaffe pilots scattered in all directions. I decided that if I were going to have to chase one of the German planes, I might as well be heading toward England, so I selected an Me-110 scooting westward on top of the cloud deck. Having had a right engine shot out by an Me-110 rear gunner over Frankfort two weeks previously, I had developed quite a healthy respect for any rear gunner. Therefore, I lined up behind the German plane and dropped into the cloud deck, holding a steady compass course. When I slowly pulled up from the cloud layer, the Me-110 was slightly above me at a range of less than 200 feet. I took careful aim at its belly through my gunsight and let it have all four .50 caliber guns and the 20-millimeter cannon. The Me-110 flamed so rapidly that the crew probably never had time to realize what had happened to them.

Quite elated, I pushed my prop pitches forward to 3,000 revolutions per minute and any throttles to fifty-four inches of manifold pressure, maximum allowable military power. Although the P-38 handbook allowed fifteen minutes of operation at military power, my left engine blew up after only three minutes. The Allison "time bomb" had once again held true to its reputation.

I feathered the left prop immediately and headed westward as before, hoping to reach England more than 300 miles away. However, the P-38J-10-LO had a design feature none of its pilots could ever quite fathom: it had only one generator, and it was on the left engine. (Later

---

Opposite page: A P-38 in flight.

series J airplanes were produced with a generator on each engine.) Normally this would not have been a problem, but the cross-feed on the P-38 was electrical, and a pilot had to have electrical power to transfer his fuel from the tanks on one side of the plane to the engine on the other side. Even though I had turned off all electrical equipment immediately upon losing the left engine, I realized my cross-feed would probably drain my battery before my right engine had time to burn all the fuel in my two left tanks. I determined to stay on cross-feed until the battery went dead and then switch to my right tanks. This would probably never get me across the North Sea to England, but it should get me to Holland, where I had a chance of being picked up by the underground.

After flying on instruments for almost an hour, I broke through the western edge of the cloud layer into clear air; suddenly I saw five bursts of light flak walking in on me from the right side, exactly at my altitude. Then, to my utter horror, I heard the sixth one somewhere from below my plane. My mind flashed back to the bars in London in those days before I began flying ops when the bomber boys used to quip, "If you ever hear it, it's got you."

Their words were prophetic, for within a few seconds my right engine began smoking. To get away from the flak battery as rapidly as possible, I dove for the deck and leveled off on the treetops. I sped across forests and open fields with the smoke rapidly getting more intense. Before long I began to smell it as it seeped through the wing into the cockpit. It did not take much debate for me to decide I should not attempt to belly-land a smoking plane. Besides, the Germans, to the best of my knowledge, had not yet received a J series P-38 in any respectable condition worthy of close technical examination.

As I approached another forest, I decided to use the remaining "excess" speed from my dive for a zoom to sufficient height for bailout. As I reached the other side of the forest, I pulled up into a climb, leveled off, cranked in full-down nose trim, rolled the plane on its back, pulled the canopy release, and unlatched my safety belt. With flames now coming into the cockpit from around the right window, all these motions were performed almost as one, and I next felt myself drop into the rushing airstream.

Admittedly, the P-38 was outperformed by the P-47 and P-51 in the skies over Europe, but many of its difficulties were the result of unnecessary design deficiencies and the slow pace of both the AAF and Lockheed in correcting them. One can only ponder about how much more rapidly the troubles would have been remedied if the slide-rule types had been flying the plane in combat against the Luftwaffe. But I will always remember the P-38 with the greatest fondness. Even with all her idiosyncrasies, she was a real dream to fly.

Lt. Col. Royal D. Frey flew P-38s over Europe on long-range escort missions.

The Vultee BT-13A

Al Strunk with Robin Higham

There I was as a twenty-four-year old hanging by my straps looking up at the California countryside whirling over my head. The wind whipped my face around the goggles. The cloth helmet kept my ears safe. But otherwise I could really relish the freedom of flying in an open cockpit biplane in the good old days. That was in March 1941. I was a cadet in the old USAAF flying training program on my way to earning my wings. This was Primary, and I was flying the Stearman PT-13.

In those days it all started with primary school where we were taught on the Stearman PT-13, a 220 horsepower bi-wing airplane. About 100 air cadets arrived at Tex Rankin School at Tulare, California, around March 15, 1941. The school was still in the process of being built, so we lived at hotels in town and flew off the municipal airport for about three to four weeks before moving into our new location.

The Stearman had an open cockpit. We had done about ten hours each before soloing, followed by twelve hours of circuits and landings and another thirty-eight hours on climbs, glides, stalls, S turns across a road, forced landings, spins, and a few cross-countries. With a total of sixty hours under our belts, we were then transferred to Moffett Field, California, where the skies were filled with blue and yellow BT-13As. What a pretty sight! In those days trainers in the USAAF were painted for real visibility, as well they need to be with many as 100 to 200 aircraft in the air at any time. The wings were yellow with big red, white, and blue roundels with a red center and a white star, enclosed in a blue circle. The fuselages were blue, but the tail was yellow with a vertical blue stripe on the forward edge of the rudder and horizontal red and white stripes on the rest of it.

To us fledglings, the BT-13A was a *big* bird. When you walked out to her, parked in those great long rows on the flight line, she stood there

Opposite page: The BT-13.

glistening in her multicolored paint with that great big Pratt and Whitney, nine-cylinder, radial, air-cooled, direct-drive engine that developed 450 horsepower at sea level. The propeller was a Hamilton standard two-blade hydro-controllable two-position type, nine feet in diameter—low pitch 12.5° and high pitch 18°. It looked a bit small, but it worked. And the combination of engine and propeller produced not only adequate power, but a most satisfying noise, especially on the takeoff—not only for those on the ground, but for those in the aircraft, as the exhaust manifold pipe ended about four feet forward of the cockpit. More than this, the crate seemed big because its wings were cantilever type, symmetrical airfoil, internally braced, covered with semi-stressed skin and with sixty-gallon gas tanks built in each wing.

After we had arrived at the aircraft all hot and puffing from lugging the twenty-five-pound parachute over our shoulders, we would walk quickly around the machine looking superficially for any damage, kick the tires, and come around again to the left-hand side to mount up. There was no particular reason for this except that somehow the traditional way to mount a horse just naturally carried over into aircraft when people stopped sitting on the forward edge of the wings as the Wright Brothers had.

At this point, after the completion of the visual check, cadet and instructor stopped, slung their parachutes properly over their shoulders so that the top straps hung down their chest, stuck them into the quick-release gear attached to the D-ring, and reached through their legs and gathered the two bottom straps which had meanwhile been clinking on the ground and brought them up and snapped them into the quick-release also. Then we were ready to climb aboard. The cadet always went into the forward seat, unless practicing instrument flying, and the instructor into the rear. To get into either cockpit necessitated putting the right foot on the catwalk, not on the flaps or on the wings, grabbing the hand hold in the main fuselage, and then pulling your left leg onto the little walkway on the left lower mainplane. You then operated the handles to open and close the forward canopy, which, like the rear one, had emergency exit locks from inside and outside. Getting into the rear seat involved putting your left foot onto the step and then swinging on into the cockpit.

Once seated on your parachute, you grasped the two shoulder straps of the Sutton harness and pulled them down to your belly, then pulled up the other two lap straps placing the left one underneath, as it had a large pin attached to it over which grommets in the other three fitted. Once this collection was assembled, a special pin with a ring on it fixed to the righthand lap belt was inserted. In the event of an emergency, this pin could be pulled and you could leap out of the cockpit if on the ground or fall out or climb out if in the air. The quick-release gear on the parachute operated in a somewhat similar fashion to grant you your freedom, only in its case, it took a half-turn twist to place it in the quick-release position. Then when your feet touched the ground or the water, you thumped it with your fist and the chute would quickly drift away from you to prevent you from either being dragged across the ground through the sage brush or drowned by the chute landing on top of you in the pond. Or, at least, so we were told.

At this point we settled in the cockpit, adjusted the seat up or down, and made the following checks: rudder trim tab controls neutralized by feel—until the bolt in the spoke of the wheel was uppermost; flaps up one turn of the crank (equalled) approximately 2° of flaps; we were told the flaps should never be down when the airspeed exceeded 120 miles per hour; control lock firmly clipped down when the controls were unlocked or it would snap up and jam the controls inflight; parking brakes set before the airplane was started and when it was parked—remembering to release them before taxiing; and be sure headset was not hanging near the instrument panel because the instruments would become magnetized and would not function properly.

Some of the precautions that were stressed before starting the engine were: (1) never pump or prime with the throttle as this could cause gas to leak out of the carburetor into the cowl and catch fire; (2) have mixture control all the way forward. Pulling mixture control partially back leaned the mixture and could cause detonation, loss of power, and overheating. When it was all the way back the engine would stop immediately because it was equipped with an "idle cut off"; (3) have the propeller control back for starting, forward for warm-up, high rpm, and quick power. All three controls in the throttle quadrant had to be in the full forward position for maximum quick power; (4) be sure you can feel the "click" to know the pointer is in the right position for unrestricted gas flow and be sure the pointer and not the handle is on the desired tank; (5) be sure you always lock the primer immediately after priming; otherwise fuel could leak and create a fire hazard; (6) if on starting fire should pour out of the exhaust, keep the starter engaged and smoothly open the throttle, and when the engine starts it will blow out the fire.

The things that were stressed before starting the engine were:

1. Check Form 1A. Fill out Form 1 (Time on the airplane)
2. Set parking brake. Unlock controls and secure control lock in floor clip
3. Carburetor heat cold
4. Oil cooler shutter open
5. Battery disconnect and generator switch ON
6. Ignition switch OFF
7. Mixture control FULL RICH
8. Propeller control back (low revolutions per minute)
9. Throttle set $\frac{3}{4}$ inches OPEN
10. Check fuel supply selector valve on RESERVE

A further glance around to ensure that everyone was clear—the crew chief gave a thumbs up—and we were ready to start up. You gave a couple of pumps on the wobble pump to get a fuel pressure of three or four pounds, primed the engine a few squirts with the priming pump, and then turned the ignition switch ON. Fuel pressure was maintained with the wobble pump until the engine started.

After the oil gauge indicated pressure, the engine was run at 600 to 800 revolutions per minute. If oil pressure did not indicate within thirty seconds, the engine was stopped. If that was no problem, you moved the propeller control forward (high rpm) after sixty pounds pressure was indicated and warmed up the engine at 1,000 revolutions per minute. Oil pressure started at seventy-five to ninety pounds when idling and then dropped to fifteen pounds. Oil temperature was 50° to 70° C, fuel pressure three to four pounds. You then checked engine and magneto at 1,500 revolutions per minute. If on either magneto there was a drop of more than 100 revolutions per minute, you shut the engine off and got a mechanic. Next you checked the generator and the electric switches, the volt meter and the ammeter, and tuned the radio to the tower frequency with the volume up.

Once everything checked out all right, you waived the chocks away, when you could catch the mechanic's eye, looked carefully to either side, blipped the engine up enough to start taxiing, weaved a bit from side to side to make sure no one was passing across that great big blind spot hidden by the great blue cowling ahead of you, and left the line. Once you could see your way clear, you opened up to 1,200 revolutions per minute to keep the gyros from toppling and began to roll weaving lazily from side to side to be sure no one was in your way.

The BT-13 was easy to taxi with its toe brakes, and the slipstream was refreshingly cool in summer, but icy in winter. Though taxiing was easy, there was almost always heavy traffic on the ground at Moffett Field. Aircraft were constantly moving to the takeoff point, and frequently a line developed. In this case you watched the wing tips and tail of the aircraft ahead and as long as they stayed ahead, you knew you would not chew its tail off. At night this was more difficult, as wingtip lights were not so clearly visible. Near the runway, those who were just taxiing out for the first flight in a cold aircraft would swing off to the right and park at 45° to the traffic to run up their engines, first on one magneto and then on the other, watching always for a tell-tale drop of more than 100 revolutions per minute, which would mean that something was wrong and a return to the flight line was required.

The basic pre-takeoff drill was:

1. check controls for free movement '
2. engine controls: mixture full rich, oil cooler shutter open, carburetor heat as required, propeller control forward (high rpm), check gasoline quantity and select tank fuel lines
3. engine run up to full rpm. Check the gauge readings. Oil pressure, 75-90. Minimum oil temperatures, 30° C. Fuel pressure, three to four pounds.
4. set rudder and elevator tabs at 0°
5. flaps down ten turns to 20°

Once you got the green light from the caravan at the end of the runway, you swung on, and began your roll. You could always tell new pilots because they stopped, got organized mentally, and then opened the throttle for takeoff. Once you pushed that throttle slowly but firmly all the way to the stop, that big radial really wound up to its full 2,300 revolutions per minute and the whole aircraft leaped forward. This took a lot of right rudder to control, though once you got used to it, rudder and throttle went together so that you got a straight takeoff. Until the tail came up at about 40 miles per hour indicated, you could still not see straight ahead, and thus you had to watch the construction lines in the concrete to keep going straight, especially in a cross-wind. But once that tail came up, what a difference. You could see the whole airfield boundary and the ribbon of concrete stretching ahead, but not for long. It took no time or distance, perhaps only 300 feet, to reach takeoff, when the plane flew itself off the ground and climbed away. Full throttle to 300 feet (no noise abatement then), then cut back to 2,100 revolutions per minute and at 500 feet turn

left and then turn right out of pattern and go about your business. If you had an engine failure before reaching 500 feet, under no circumstances—repeat, no circumstances—were you to try to turn downwind and to get back to the field. There were two very good reasons for this. First, you would lose so much altitude in the turn made off a low climbing speed that you were unlikely to reach the field again anyway; and second, whether or not you made the field, you would be landing downwind into the crowd taking off. Unfortunately, every now and then someone tried it. There really was no sense in turning because all around ahead were fields you could land in.

Each student had to demonstrate a reasonable degree of proficiency in the following before he was allowed to solo:

1. use of cockpit checklist
2. altimeter setting
3. use of trim tabs
4. use of propeller control
5. fuel procedures and changing fuel tanks
6. taxiing
7. use of flap control
8. takeoffs
9. torque correction
10. climbing turns
11. leveling off
12. medium turns
13. gliding turns
14. clearing the engine
15. traffic patterns
16. landings
17. undershooting or overshooting procedure
18. clearing the area
19. recovery from stalls
20. recovery from spins
21. forced landings
22. radio
23. blindfold cockpit test

After about forty hours of flying time, we would normally climb to 5,000 feet to practice our aerobatics unless we were to do lazy eights around some inverted pylons (in which case we stayed at about 1,500

Opposite page: A field of BT-13s.

feet) or if we were to practice forced landings at one of the designated satellite fields.

The BT-13 was a great acrobatic aircraft. We normally did loops, slow rolls, snap rolls, Immelmans, and other exciting exercises. To do a loop, you climbed to 6,000 feet, cleared the area with exceptional care, and chose a road, section line, or fence line for orientation. You dove your airplane down your reference line and when you attained 165 miles per hour used considerable back pressure to start your arc of a circle. You maintained the arc with a steady pressure increasing your throttle to a position of maximum power. Gradually, you relaxed the back pressure as speed decreased or you would stall before you reached the inverted position at the top of the loop. As the airplane approached the inverted position; you threw your head back to pick up your reference line and make corrections in altitude, excessive rpm, and excessive speed. As the airplane reached the horizon, you used full throttle and climbed to gain altitude. When you slowed down to cruising airspeed, you resumed level flight and adjusted throttle.

To do a slow roll, you cleared the area and established a speed of 115 miles per hour and raised the nose approximately 20° above the horizon in line with a reference point. You built up positive back stick and rudder pressures simultaneously in the direction of the snap. When these pressures reached a given point, the airplane suddenly stalled and entered the snap roll. You didn't increase your back pressure after the stall occurred because you wanted to avoid a violent stall. When about one half of the way around, you relaxed the rudder pressure used to enter the snap and smoothly applied opposite rudder. At approximately three fourths of the way around, if the timing was correct, the rotation would begin to slow down. You then moved the rudder smoothly toward the neutral position. When the wings rolled out level, you held only sufficient rudder pressure to correct for torque. This was the most difficult part of the maneuver and required good timing and considerable practice to stop the wings in a level position with the nose on the reference point.

A slow roll is a maneuver that is accurately described by its name. It is a slow, complete rotation of the airplane around its longitudinal axis. It gives one practice in analyzing the use of controls in a continuously changing and unfamiliar attitude. Slow rolls also overcome the natural aversion to inverted flight and develop one's ability to orient oneself.

I never had to bail out of a BT-13, but we were always told that the procedure was to open the cockpit canopy or, if necessary, the emergency exit—slow the airplane as much as possible, disconnect the radio headset, release the safety belt and shoulder harness, and dive out and down. Often you could go out flat, onto the wind, and slide head first off the trailing edge. Once in space, you had to be sure to keep your eyes open and look around and, if you had enough altitude, wait at least five to ten seconds before pulling the ripcord.

In our basic course we received instrument training, night flying, cross country work, and formation flying.

Coming back in to land we always flew over the field at about 1,500 to see the tee and observe other airplanes, then let down and joined the pattern from the downwind side at 700 feet above ground at about 100 miles per hour, keeping a side lookout for other aircraft. The downwind leg largely consisted of figuring out how far ahead the next aircraft was and how wide a pattern would be needed for landing. Mixture was returned to rich, the fuel tanks checked to see which one was the fullest and the selector put on it, and 20° of flap was rolled down. When the downwind end of the runway passed behind the trailing edge of the port wing, you swung left onto the crosswind leg with the throttle back to 120 miles per hour. As the runway came up through the wingtips, you executed another fine bank to port, chopped the throttle, and settled down into a nice glide at 85 miles per hour, watching the air speed and the runway in order not to stall by stretching your glide. Then with the engine just ticking over nicely, you gave the throttle one blip to make sure that it was idling freely and would start again in case you had to go around. Then you slid over the end of the runway, flared just above it, and eased her back with a gentle hand and slightly wiggling rudder until suddenly she either slid onto the runway in a perfect three-pointer, or more often suddenly lost flying speed and settled on plonk. Then it was open canopy and head out the side of the cockpit while you rolled her along and slowed, turning off at the first available exit and either back around for another circuit or back to the line to hear what your instructor had to say.

One feature of the BT-13 on approaches was its ability to side-slip, done in this case with dropping the wing and holding it down at the proper angle with ailerons. Hold parallel to the landing lane with the rudder. Just before contacting the ground, raise the wing to level position with the ailerons and keep the airplane lined up with the lane with rudder control.

How you liked the BT-13 rather depended upon your empathy with your instructor. Mine was very good. He could break a maneuver down so that we could understand it and in the air tap the rudder or stick to tell us when to shift emphasis. He had patience and was always enthusiastic. He was a stickler for discipline, and we could appreciate that for our safety.

The airplane radio was brand new to us. It was a mysterious device until it was adequately explained—then it was relatively simple. We were told always to check the radio before takeoff to be sure it was working and properly tuned to the tower. We were advised always to think what we were going to say beforehand and always listen before squeezing the microphone button so we would not interrupt another transmission. Call letters were always given for identification before each transmission: "Moffet Tower, this is M-Four Two." And every transmission ended with "over" if a response was expected and "out" if no response was desired or needed. "Roger" meant "I received your last message." "Wilco" meant "I received your message and will comply with it." And we always kept earphones on and tuned to the tower and used the radio on every flight, or so the manual said!

Well, those were the good old days. I got seventy hours in the BT-13 as a student and another 2,146 as an instructor. Those were great carefree days, and that was a wonderful aircraft. After graduating from Basic, a number of us went to Luke Field at Phoenix, Arizona, where we flew the AT-6 in advanced school. We graduated October 31, 1941, as second lieutenants and received our pilots' wings. I was then assigned to Bakersfield, California, as a Basic Instructor in BT-13s.

Al Strunk was a BT-13 pilot and instructor.

B-24 Liberator

Carl H. Fritsche

The four-engined B-24 Liberator of World War II was a "truck." It looked like a truck, it hauled a big load like a truck, and it flew like a truck. But trucks were needed at that time of the war, and over 18,000 of the B-24s were built. I am proud to say that I was a "truck driver" and that I flew the B-24 over the world's highest mountains and crossed some of its seas at fifty feet above the waves. It was a good plane for its time in history, but it was not the shapely, romantic beauty some of its contemporaries were. In the air it was like a fat lady doing a ballet—I was always amazed at how beautiful it looked in spite of its bulk as it turned and circled trying its best to be the star of the show. It was never a star. It was an excellent truck.

At Riverside, California, during the winter of 1943–1944, the newspapers reported a tragic B-24 accident. The plane had crashed into an Army barracks and had caused a heavy loss of life. Not too far from Riverside was March Air Force Base. My new crew remarked about the accident as I was leading them out to the ramp for their first look at a B-24. My flight engineer and I were the only two trained on the B-24. Of my total of 325 flying hours, 105 were accumulated in learning how to fly the B-24 at Tarrant Field, Fort Worth, Texas. My copilot was just out of flying school and had never flown a multiengined airplane. As we made our ground inspection, he was impressed by the 110-foot long wing spread, the sixty-seven-foot long fuselage, and the four R-1830-65 Pratt & Whitney engines. I went to the right side of the plane, pulled the small hydraulic lever, and the bomb-bay doors rolled up so that we could climb to the flight deck. My navigator and bombardier crawled under the flight deck up to the nose of the craft for an inspection of their stations and

---

Opposite page: Amid bursting flak, B-24 Liberators bomb an oil refinery at Ploesti, Romania.

then returned to the flight deck about the same time I had completed my twenty-one items on the preflight list. Because my engineer was well trained, we had few problems with our checklist, but I knew that my new copilot was overwhelmed with all the instruments and levers. After the four gunners, radioman, bombardier, and navigator had crowded on the flight deck, my engineer started the small gasoline auxiliary power "put-put" unit located under the flight deck. He left the unit running and took his position between the pilot's and copilot's seats so that we could begin the starting of the engines.

Because the plane's hydraulic system was operated from a pump located on number 3 engine, we were trained to start that engine first, followed by number 4, number 2, and number 1. The ground crew fire guard moved from engine to engine with a hand-held CO_2 extinguisher during the starting procedure. I told my copilot to turn the ignition switches to "both on," and then turn each electric fuel booster pump on as each engine was started. The fuel pressure gauge would register approximately eight pounds pressure before each engine was primed with the electric priming switch. I had set all four throttles to $1/3$-open position and then energized the number 3 engine. After about twelve seconds of energizing the engine, I flipped the same little switch to the "mesh" position and the engine turned over quickly and started. I moved the mix control to the "auto lean" position and made certain the oil pressure came up to normal within thirty seconds. After I had throttled the engine to about 1,000 revolutions per minute, I turned off the booster pump for that particular engine and started the remaining engines. As the engines idled, I checked the flight indicator for rapid erection. Vacuum pumps for these instruments were located on number 1 and number 2 engines, so I switched the selector valve to each engine to make sure that the pressure was $4-4\frac{1}{2}$ pounds at 1,000 revolutions per minute. Quickly I scanned the instrument panel checking the oil pressure, oil temperature, engine-head temperature, fuel pressure, carburetor air temperature, free-air pressure, tachometers, manifold pressure, hydraulic pressures, magnetic compass, landing gear warning light, and finally, clock. I called the tower for the altimeter setting and was pleased to find that my altimeter registered the field elevation. I released the hydraulic brakes and started to taxi out for takeoff.

The B-24 was an easy plane to taxi. By using the outboard engines and the hydraulic foot brakes, I could turn the plane with ease. The tricycle landing gear supported the plane in a level position, giving me an excellent view of its left side. There was a blind spot where the nose turret blocked the view, but my copilot had good visibility on his side of the

Liberators conduct a low-altitude raid at Ploesti, Romania.

plane, so it was his duty to warn me of obstacles. As I grew more experienced with the B-24, I found that I could taxi the plane without excessive use of the brakes. We didn't have to fishtail the plane as we taxied, so on some combat fields where a turnaround was required after the landing roll, we taxied the plane at 40–50 miles per hour.

About thirty planes were ready for takeoff that morning, and my B-24 was the fourth in line. Near the runway we turned our planes 45° to the taxi ramp for engine run-up. I put the mixture control in "auto rich" position. I then ran the props to a full "low" position to check for maximum rpm-drop, then back to "high" for maximum rpm-gain, and then returned the turbos to the "off" position. I reduced the throttles to 1,200 revolutions per minute and returned the mix to "auto lean." Each engine was then checked in the following order: 4, 3, 2, and 1. I set the mix for the number 4 engine to "auto rich" and opened the throttle to 2,000 revolutions per minute. I had my copilot check the mags. He turned to "left mag" and back to "both," then he turned to "right mag" and back to "both" so that we could check the rpm-drop and also see the roughness of the engine nacelle vibration as a visual check of the ignition operation. After checking all the mags, I then advanced the throttle to full "open" position and checked the engine instruments for proper readings. I advanced the turbo and set it carefully to forty-seven inches and stopped at 2,700 revolutions per minute. Slowly I reduced the number 4 engine throttle to 1,200 revolutions per minute and the mix to "auto lean" and repeated, in sequence, the run-up of the other three engines. My directional gyro was set to correspond to the magnetic compass, the wing flaps were extended to 20° down, and I signaled my engineer to turn on all four generators and turn off the gasoline auxiliary "put-put" power unit. Quickly I moved the gang switch to high rpm for the props and saw that the four green lights came on. I set my trim tabs 3° right rudder, 0° aileron, and 0° elevator. While I checked my surface controls, I told my copilot to place the mix controls into the "auto rich" position and directed my engineer to turn off the electric auxiliary hydraulic pump, close the bomb doors and hatches, and make sure the other crew members were seated on the flight deck in a safe position. All the pilots finished their checklists and lined up ready to roll with the tower's permission.

The first B-24 started down the runway for takeoff, then the second started before the first was in the air. The third B-24 moved out, and then it was my turn. As I pushed the four throttles open to increase speed, I could see the explosions and black clouds of smoke ahead of me where the first two B-24s had crashed on takeoff. The third B-24 was off the ground and in the black smoke. I lifted the nosewheel at about 70 miles per hour and at about 130 miles per hour was off the ground and burrowing through the black smoke and fire. Seconds later I was out of the smoke and climbing with the landing gear swinging up into the wheel wells. I reduced the manifold pressure from forty-nine inches to forty-five inches and had my copilot reduce the props from 2,700 to 2,550 revolutions per minute and move the props into synchronization. At 800 feet above the terrain I reduced the flaps to 5° for stability and continued to climb.

With two planes down and twenty men lost, the tower called us and told us the field was closed for investigation and for us to come back and land. I was having problems, too. The main gear would swing up, but the nosewheel of the tricycle landing gear was stuck crossways in the wheel well and would not go up or down. My crew was getting initiated to the B-24, and they didn't like what they saw. The other B-24 in the air circled and landed while I tried every trick I knew to get my gear either up or down.

Climbing to 4,000 feet, I snapped my fuel booster pumps off and started to cruise over the field at about 200 miles per hour. I reduced the manifold pressure to thirty inches and the revolutions to 2,000 per minute. With the flaps up I made a quick check: mixture control in "auto lean" position, oil temperature less than 75° C redline, oil pressure 80 pounds per square inch, cylinder head temperature well below the 232° C maximum, fuel pressure 15 pounds per square inch, and cowl flaps closed. The plane was in good shape, with the exception of the nosewheel. I reported my problem to the tower and then told my copilot to fly it straight and level while I went down for a look.

My engineer and I crawled under the flight deck and up to the nosewheel, fighting a tornadolike wind coming in the open wheel-well door. No amount of prying would turn it, as it was wedged at a 90° angle in the door. When I returned to the pilot's seat there was a suggestion from the tower that we might have to go over the Pacific and jump. I asked for another suggestion. After consultation they told me to try a crash landing at San Bernardino repair depot, which had been alerted to my problem. Flying over San Bernardino, I could see the fire wagons and "meat" wagons lined up by the runway and a crowd of people out to watch the landing. My crew wasn't too happy about their first B-24 flight. I told them I would make a normal landing but that the main gear touching the runway was their signal to run to the tail of the plane, lie down, and hang on. On the downwind leg I slowed the plane to an airspeed of 155 and put down the main gear. The revolutions were raised to 2,550 and the flaps lowered to 20°. We went through the rest of the checklist and on the final approach lowered the flaps to 40° for landing. The plane touched down at about 110 airspeed and all the crew, including the copilot, ran to the rear. As I fought to hold the nose of the plane off the runway, I could hear the fire sirens screeching from the many trucks following me down the landing strip. I had slowed to about 40 miles per hour before the wings of the plane completely lost "lift" and the plane tilted forward allowing the partially retracted nosewheel to strike the runway and skid along sideways. The B-24 then whipped to the right. I slammed left brake, then right, and we slid to a stop with very little damage.

The air force's answer to the B-24 accidents came in the form of a tough little captain with a "fruit salad" on his chest. His ramrod straight posture and confidence indicated that he had the world by the tail and wasn't going to let it go. In no uncertain terms he told us that the B-24 was an excellent plane but that the pilot had to fly it. The three accidents, he said, were all caused by pilot error. Investigation had proved that the pilot who had crashed into the army barracks had become confused at night and had thought the main street of the army camp was the runway. He had landed on the street killing the crew and others in the camp. The two planes had crashed on takeoff because the pilots were not used to flying with 91 octane gas. They had trained with 100 octane gas, so instead of ramming the throttles through the instrument panel when they saw they were in trouble the pilots just sat there and took their crews to their death. The number 3 aircraft and I had both gotten off the ground with plenty of runway to spare so we had no cause for alarm. We had trained in Texas where we were instructed on both types of gasoline.

Later the captain complimented me on the way I had landed my damaged plane. He also assigned me to the lead ship in about a 100-plane formation over the city of Los Angeles. Fighter pilots from area fields were to make mock passes at us as we flew over the city. With the captain in the right seat, me in the left, and that long "train" of planes out behind, I felt as safe as though I was in my mother's cradle at home.

As training continued, our confidence in the B-24 increased. The tower called us one day and told us to scatter! A ferry pilot had run out of gas over the field. I was at 8,000 feet when I saw this new B-24, with all four engines feathered, pass me on his way down to the field. My copilot said, "There goes another dead man!" After we were cleared to land I went over to see the "wreckage." The pilot had made a perfect belly landing with no power. I didn't think it was possible to land with so little damage to the belly of the craft. The ground crew jacked the plane up; the wheels were pumped down; and a tow motor pulled it away for repairs.

With our training complete, crews were given brand new B-24Js, and on June 7, 1944, we left California and headed east. I had 513 flying hours—293 of that in B-24s. In addition I had about fifty-three hours Link trainer or "hood" time. Because none of the pilots of the transit crews had ever been in actual instrument weather, we were required to fly CAVU (clear air, visibility unlimited). We flew under an overcast to the islands of the Azores, over the top, until we found CAVU near the coast of Africa, and from Africa to India, it was CAVU all the way. After assignment delays in Karachi, it was on July 29, 1944 that about ten new B-24s rolled to a stop on the runway at Dacca, India. We had been assigned to the 492nd Bomb Squadron, 7th Bomb Group, of the 10th AF.

The 7th Bomb Group had temporarily been ordered to aid the 14th AF in China by supplying gasoline carried in bomb-bay tanks of combat B-24s. Single planes flew across 500 miles of enemy territory. It was an emergency measure and the enemy planes, weather, and mountains made it dangerous. The Hump, as it was called, was littered with more than 900 crashed planes—most downed by weather. As newly trained bomber pilots, most of us had never made an actual instrument let down, nor had we ever been in a storm cloud. On August 14, 1944, I made my first trip to China as a copilot so I could learn the route. The Hump was "asleep," and we just had a few fair-weather clouds to pass. On the next flight I took my own crew, and when I approached the Burma foothills, I saw a solid line of black thunderheads reaching thousands of feet into the air. My last time in a Link trainer had been in April, so I had to make a couple of circles to build up my courage. I knew I couldn't stay there forever, so I headed straight into the boiling mass. Somehow I got through and when I came out on the other side, I saw a buddy of mine, on his way back in another 24, circling to get up his courage. He radioed, "If you can make it then I can too!" The Hump made you an instrument pilot or a casualty.

The B-24 was an excellent instrument ship. I think this was partly due to its weight of 36,000 pounds empty and 65,000 pounds loaded. Some planes were even loaded up over 70,000 pounds. In fact, it was the heavily loaded takeoff and landing that was the grim reaper rather than the difficult weather on the Hump. Most of the pilots soon learned that the B-24 was just an overgrown Link trainer with a built-in fatality factor if they made a mistake. The controls of the plane were hard to move, reducing the pilot's chance of overcontrolling in the clouds—even if his knees were shaking.

To take off from a hot runway in India with a heavily loaded B-24 was always a challenge. The bamboo trees at the end of the 6,000-foot runway were too close, and many a B-24 had pinched bamboo limbs into the

wheel wells and carried them flapping in the breeze all the way to China. If there was an accident with a gasoline-loaded plane on takeoff or landing, there never were any survivors. Once the plane was in the air, you could parachute out if you got into trouble. I talked to two crews that did parachute out of their B-24s. One crew walked into Kunming, and the other parachuted into the Burma jungle and came back to India by elephant. Both crews agreed that the best way to leave a 24 was to dive out the bomb bays. One pilot told me that the worst ordeal was not bailing out of the plane but eating roast monkey with the natives in Burma. He said, "As hungry as I was, there was just no way that I could eat those little hands and feet!"

Icing was always a serious problem on the Hump. De-icing boots had been removed from all our combat planes because most of the boots had small flak holes in them. Without the boots the pilot's only defense was to get out of the icing layer. You could do this in an overcast but not in the violence of a Hump storm. On one flight I had a two-inch layer of ice all around the pilot's windows, and my flight instruments froze and tumbled. The ice must have bridged the pitot tube because the heater did no good. I let the autopilot have it, and we bounced around in the terrible up and down drafts for about an hour before we got out. We had unloaded our gas in China so the lighter weight did help the plane carry the great load of ice. When the ice started to melt in the warm air of India, I chipped a hole big enough to look out at the engine nacelles and wings. I was amazed that the B-24 would stay in the air with so much ice welded to it. Once the ice melted, the flight instruments erected and the two vacuum pumps worked normally. After I landed, I crawled out the upper hatch and checked the pitot tube. It was so hot you couldn't touch it. By the time a few of the B-24s with thermal deicers came into the theater, we were off the Hump flights and didn't get to test them.

The 492nd and the 493rd Bomb Squadrons each had about 100 flying officers. With four officers to a crew (plus six enlisted men), each squadron usually had eighteen to twenty combat-armed B-24s on the Hump gas haul each day. Most of the pilots made twenty-five to thirty round trips to China with gas before the units were returned to bombardment work.

Several crews from the 492nd and 493rd were sent to China to haul gas and help evacuate the eastern air bases. We not only had to fly on instruments; we also had "hitch-hikers." The Flying Tigers would bring their fighter planes in on us for a free, no-think ride down through the

---

Opposite page: The B-24 was considered an "ugly duckling"; the narrow Davis wing was the only part critics thought beautiful.

overcast. I would turn on my wing lights and these jockeys would grab hold of my hip pockets—one behind each wing and sometimes one above or below for a "hen and chickens" letdown through several thousand feet of solid overcast. At Suichuan, China, we had to make two 180s on letdown with the fighters because of the high mountains. The B-24 could hold a good rate of descent and make standard turns easily. But it was not a fun way to fly. The fighters were usually very low on gas and had to get down as fast as they could.

I was always concerned with the weight and balance of the plane, especially when we were hauling gas to the eastern China bases. The four big bomb-bay gas tanks were heavy and caused problems getting off the ground. In addition the ground crews would back a truck up to the waist windows and dump in a large quantity of materials.

At Luliang, China, which has an altitude of 6,000 feet, I complained bitterly about this practice. But the situation in the East was critical, so I was given a pat on the shoulder and told to get flying. My plane was already overloaded when I started to taxi out, so when I was flagged down and six fighter pilots climbed aboard I was furious. My gunners had to go to the rear of the plane, causing the plane's tail skid to drag the ground like a ruptured goose. The fighter pilots, a "gung ho" gang with a lot of energy and chatter, were just in from the States to ferry planes back from the eastern China bases. The flight deck was crawling with people.

Luliang's gravel runway was 10,000 feet long and built high in the mountains. The hundreds of Chinese who maintained the runway had a custom of running across as a plane took off so that when it passed close behind them, it would cut off the evil spirits they believed followed them. The closer the plane came to them, the more evil spirits were cut off. From a standing start I rammed the throttles forward, released the brakes, and started to roll. The Chinese saw us coming and huge numbers started running. Several men with water buffalo and carts plodded across and made it just as number 4 prop passed over them. The fighter pilots had never seen any thing like this, so they were having the time of their lives.

I wasn't laughing! We were down the field and not near the speed we should have been. The fighter pilots kept laughing and shouted, "Pull'er off into a good chandelle!" As we closed in on the end of the runway, I took a quick look over my shoulder. The chatter had stopped, and all I could see was a bunch of pale-faced pilots with eyes about twice the size they ought to be. My engineer kicked the gear handle when we ran off the 10,000-foot runway. As the gear started up, I could feel the plane settle off the end of the runway and into a ravine down the mountain. I had dropped below the level of the runway, and the tower kept calling to ask if I was in trouble. Ever so carefully I followed the ravine until I felt secure enough to try to climb. When we were finally out of danger, the fighter pilots were no longer jovial. One of them shook my hand and said, "They ought to give you boys the Distinguished Flying Cross every time you take off in one of these SOBs!"

Later in the year when I flew bombing missions, it was the ground engineering officer's duty to figure the weight and balance of the plane. With bombs loaded according to the design of the plane, getting off the ground was much easier. When the plane was used for a "moving van," the ground crews filled it full without regard for the balance.

When the whiskey ration came in the first of the month, I flew from China to Calcutta, India, to pick it up in my B-24. My hometown is Westerville, Ohio, the home of the Anti-Saloon League and the "Dry Capital of the World." Speakers and literature were sent all over the world from Westerville for the "dry" cause. The 18th Amendment to the U.S. Constitution was engineered from Westerville. I knew the leaders of the dry movement and had taken the dry pledge from Dr. Howard Hyde Russell himself. In China I was told that a lot of whiskey was being lost on the black market so they were giving me—the "Drytowner"—the booze run. Several times my B-24 was piled full of cartons of whiskey, and with all gun turrets manned, I skimmed across 500 miles of enemy territory so that the Flying Tigers could have a "happy hour." I never lost a bottle nor had one explode from too high an altitude.

When those of us who had served with the 14th AF in China returned to India, we found that the 492nd Squadron had moved from Dacca, India, to a base called Madhaiganj near Asansol. Living conditions were good at our new base and the pilots breathed a sigh of relief when they saw that there were no trees hugging the end of the runway. From this new base we flew in a forty-plane formation to bomb from high level the rail yards at Mandalay, Burma. Most of our missions from this base were flown at cruising speeds of about 225 miles per hour, and they lasted from seven to about eighteen hours. By adding the two bomb-bay tanks again and filling the rear bays with bombs, the B-24 had a range of about 3,000 miles. Strikes were made from India against the shipping and the docks at Bangkok, Thailand.

To fly formation for several hours in a B-24 required endurance. The controls took so much strength to move that you didn't have to worry about getting to sleep after a long mission. At the close of my tour of duty, I did get to fly on two missions the model of the 24 that had the hydraulic booster controls. It was extremely easy to fly.

Although the B-24 carried ten .50 caliber machine guns and could put up a good fight, it could be shot down if you attended the right social gathering. It didn't take a 24 pilot long to discover that he was riding a "slow horse" and that his best insurance was to stay in formation. The J model of the 24 had twin-gun nose, top, and tail hydraulic turrets plus the Sperry ball turret and two waist flexible guns of the same .50 caliber. The flight engineer operated the top turret and the four gunners operated the rest. Most of the gun turrets were equipped with electric flight suits to keep the gunners comfortable at high altitudes. These thin suits worked well in the plane, but they were extremely poor protection if you had to bail out onto the high snow-covered mountains. Very few of our flight deck heaters worked satisfactorily, so most of the crews wore heavy clothing and forgot the turret suits.

Enemy fighter planes had been thinned down in Burma by March 1945. Small B-24 formations, in combinations of three, were sent against targets. Ack-ack fire was still extremely heavy over most targets. In a large formation you never really knew who they were shooting at, but in a small formation you got the full concentration of fire in one direction. Over the rail yards of a large city we might have six three-plane formations coming in on the target from different directions and at proper intervals. My navigator would get us to the target I.P. (initial point) and on the proper heading. I would put the plane on autopilot and then my bombardier would guide the plane with the combination autopilot and the Norden bomb sight until "bombs away." At that point I would snap off the autopilot and try evasive action with the plane until we got out of the range of the ack-ack.

My copilot was a Golden Gloves boxing champion—tough and intelligent—with very little use for religion. I had attended a small country community church. My bombardier was a devout Roman Catholic, and my navigator was a cantor in the Syrian Orthodox Church. We had some interesting conversations. When Rangoon was still a very "hot" target, I led one of the three-plane formations over that city. The navigator shouted, "We're picking up heavy ack-ack!" Just then the sky was black with explosions. In awe I exclaimed, "Oh my God!" The bombardier, who was still on the flight deck, dropped to his knees with his rosary in his hand. The blood drained out of my copilot's face as explosions bracketed the plane. In panic he looked around the flight deck and saw the bombardier on his knees with the rosary. In a pleading voice he said,

"Leonard, you better give those beads hell! Things look terrible up here!" In spite of our great danger, all three of us laughed almost hysterically, for we knew that a reluctant believer had just uttered his first prayer.

Our first effort at low-level bombing of bridges with B-24s ended in disaster. In single file, six planes were flying down a narrow Burma mountain valley toward a large railroad bridge. We were to fly over the bridge at 50-100 feet and let the bombardier "guess" where to toggle out the bombs. I was flying the second plane and I noticed that beyond the bridge the railroad made a sharp bend around a cliff. As low as we were, I didn't think a B-24 could make that turn. We were flying into a box canyon! I grabbed the radio mike and warned everyone to pull up. The first plane kept right on going and crashed into the cliff. All the other planes followed me in a frantic climb to get over the mountains. My navigator, who was looking out the nose window and watching the rocks go by kept shouting, "Pull 'er up! We're going to crash!" I reached to the left side of the pilot's seat and grabbed the bomb salvo lever. The five tons of bombs dropped and the plane went up like an elevator, dusting off the top of the mountain as we flew by.

Back at our home base a practice bridge was built. The abutments were made of fifty-gallon oil drums. A single-bomb release button was put on the pilot's control wheel. Bombardiers were not carried on the B-24s for these practice missions. Each pilot was given twelve sand-filled bombs to practice his technique on the bridge. Because the nose of the plane obstructed the view on a low-level flight, we were forced to use a diving approach to the target. We flew in a circle at an altitude of 500–1,000 feet and then dived the plane at a speed of about 300 miles per hour toward the bridge. The pilot pulled out of his gradual dive at 50–100 feet above the bridge and pressed the special bomb release button on the control column. It was all guesswork, for there was no bombsight; the pilot dropped the bomb where he thought it might be effective. I noticed a row of rivets in front of my seat extending out across the nose of the plane. This was my bombsight. As that row of rivets seemed to scoop over the bridge abutment, I released the bomb. In twelve runs I got eleven bombs right on the target, winning for my flight engineer a case of beer from the ground crew. Other pilots had similar success. With delayed-action 500-pound bombs and the diving attack with the B-24, the railroad bridges of Burma fell with astounding success.

We flew overwater flights twelve to eighteen hours long against targets on the Malay Peninsula. At fifty feet above the water we would fly down the Bay of Bengal, cross the Andaman Sea, and bomb the railroad

bridges in single-plane attacks. On heavily defended, multispan bridges, with Allied prisoners of war forced to camp around the land abutments, we used a decoy plane to draw ack-ack fire while six B-24s flew up the river and dropped bombs on the abutments built in the water. We used this method on two missions, and I flew the decoy on both.

Although our decoy 24s had self-sealing wing tanks, the bomb-bay tanks were extremely vulnerable to any kind of enemy action. If we had not needed the tanks to fly back home, we could have dropped them out the bomb-bay doors. As it was, we dodged flak for thirty minutes before diving for the Andaman Sea. Halfway back to India there was usually a PBY flying boat cruising around to pick up any of the crews in trouble.

Most crews avoided ditching a B-24. Most of us felt it was much safer to dump the life rafts out and have a few crew members try to parachute close to the raft. We learned this lesson after flying search missions over water. The B-24 apparently broke apart rapidly (just aft of the bomb bay) upon ditching and sank before crew members could get out. On the search missions I flew, only oil slicks were found.

The four Pratt & Whitney engines were extremely reliable, but even if only three engines were going, the B-24 flew well (but slower). I have flown alongside pilots who had to fly all the way home from a bombing mission on three engines—a distance of 1,000 miles. During the evacuation of the air bases in eastern China, I saw B-24s take off on three engines and fly to safety. I never witnessed anyone who flew very far on two engines. Some landings were made that way, but they were few. In training I flew a 24 on one engine to see what happened. It had a pretty fast rate of descent. Even empty, with no gun turrets, you were on your way down if you tried one-engine operation.

The B-24 had a definite vibration when it stalled, but it recovered easily with the addition of power. With rudders used properly, the plane would fall straight down with no tendency to drop a wing even though one prop might be feathered. I never put the plane into a full spin, but in training we did try recovery from $1/4$- to $1/2$-turn spins. The plane would recover in a very tight spiral which could lead to trouble if the pilot was not able to recognize a high-speed stall. In spite of the increased speed, the pilot still had to push the control column forward to recover. On the landing approach, the plane would stall out gently, allowing the pilot to "grease" the plane down onto the runway.

The plane was considered an "ugly duckling" in design; the narrow, high-speed Davis wing was the only part critics thought beautiful. Some

Opposite page: The B-24 looked like a truck, hauled like a truck, and flew like a truck.

pilots remarked that the designers simply hung a bucket on the Davis wing. Considering the designs of foreign planes of the same era, I never felt the B-24 designers had to hang their heads in shame. The Davis wing was designed with Fowler flaps that slid back and down from the trailing edge to give greater area for better landing stability at lower speeds. Even though designers considered the wing beautiful, the pilots knew it was designed to be "alive," because it would really flap when we bounced around inside the Hump thunderstorms.

Because the B-24 was not a pressurized plane, it was necessary for all crew members to wear face-type oxygen masks. When we ran out of oxygen in China, I flew the lower Hump twice without oxygen. I did notice my depth perception was off when I started to land, and thus I had a tendency to drag the plane in and feel for the ground.

After fifty missions in the CBI my crew was given R & R, but I was kept on in the squadron to fly new crews on their first bombing mission. When I had completed nine more missions, I was retired and given the job of flight-testing planes and flying damaged planes from our base at Asansol to the depot at Bangalore, India, for repair or junk.

What do I think of the B-24? Let me answer with one more story. When Suichuan (China) air base was under daily attack, I led some P-51s into that base at night with my B-24 loaded with gas. With no radio contact the tower gave me the green light to land—even though some of the runway lights had been bombed out in a recent raid. The 51s landed and then I lined up on what lights I could see through the mist and light rain. With a heavy load and on a bad night I touched down between the first two lights at about 150 miles per hour and was still rolling about 80 miles per hour when I saw the end of the runway. I knew I wasn't going to make it. I also knew that at the end of the runway was a big drop-off. So I turned the plane toward a bomb hole and a pile of dirt, and we plowed to a stop. The B-24 stood on its nose over an embankment. The miracle of the whole thing was that the Chinese had just the day before gathered that big pile of loose dirt dug from trenches they were making to defend the field. At any other time it wouldn't have been there. If the dirt hadn't been loose, the plane probably would have exploded, as most gas carriers did on impact. We pumped the gas to the P-51s and they took off at dawn. Because there wasn't a bulldozer for thousands of miles around, I figured my crew and I had a 500-mile walk. Early the next morning hundreds of Chinese came to the runway, each carrying a small grapevine. They wound the vines into a rope, tied it to my B-24, and dragged the plane back to the runway. The plane shook badly as I started down the runway, but as I passed that long line of Chinese, they gave me the "thumbs-up" salute and shouted *Ding Hao* (Chinese for "OK"). And when I saw the old B-24 at the Air Force Museum I gave it a very respectful thumbs-up salute and said *Ding Hao*—it really was OK!

Carl H. Fritsche was a B-24 pilot in the China-Burma-India Theater during World War II.

The P-39 Airacobra in Europe

James J. Hudson

Our flight of P-39 Airacobras wheeled sharply to the right as it approached the French coast at Cape Camarat. For the next few minutes the Airacobras, flying at deck level, raced on up the coast past St. Tropez toward the resort town of Cannes.

The mission that gloomy December afternoon, described in the 345th Fighter Squadron Mission Report as a "sea patrol," had originated an hour earlier, at 1350 hours, at Alghero-Fertilla in Northern Sardinia. The ceiling was a bare 1,500 feet, but it made little difference for we had been flying at less than twenty feet since passing Ajaccio on the Corsican coast some 125 miles to the south. In fact, the "prop blast" of Lt. Len Nelson, my element leader, was actually leaving a wake in the glassy smooth Mediterranean. My position on his wing, normally a little lower and a few feet behind, left me at a low altitude indeed, for at the end of the mission, my crew chief discovered the gun camera lens in the leading edge of my Airacobra's right wing was coated with salt from the sea spray.

Despite the excellent forward and downward visibility from the cockpit of the P-39, this kind of flying required great concentration and was nerve-straining if continued for a long time. Yet such an approach was necessary if we hoped to reach the French coast undetected by German radar crews. For safety sake I trimmed my fighter to climb slightly rather than to crash into the sea should I be momentarily distracted in my search for a target of opportunity.

At first no worthwhile target appeared, and I wondered to myself if the Flight Commander, Lt. Marland Marshall, would "allow us to stray" a few miles inland toward a supposed enemy airfield recently reported by intelligence sources. Suddenly, my radio crackled with "two Bogies at 12 o'clock low!" In his excitement, the speaker had forgotten the squadron's

---

Opposite page: The Bell YP-39C.

105

call word, but it mattered little for all six pairs of eyes were now pinned on two single-engine twin float type aircraft circling in the haze some 800 yards dead ahead. Were they enemy? Probably so, for no American single-engine seaplanes were operating in that part of the Mediterranean, and the British Walrus amphibian flying-boat was a single hull aircraft.

Anticipating the possibility of combat, I quickly reached down with my left hand and switched the fuel-selector valve from "Aux" (belly tank) to one of the main tanks. Then, almost in the same motion, I pulled the belly tank release handle and lifted the fighter gently away from the falling tank by easing back slightly on the stick with the right hand. In the next few seconds, I turned on the electric gun sight, snapped on the gun switches for both the machineguns and the 37-millimeter cannon, adjusted the fuel-mixture control to "full rich," and shoved the throttle forward "to the wire."

As the P-39s rapidly closed the distance, all doubt regarding the nationality of the seaplanes, later identified as Arado 196s, was removed when their rear gunners opened fire. Nelson's plane leaped ahead of mine, and he was already blasting away at the Arado on the left. The other Airacobra pilots also had entered the battle. Although tracer fire from the enemy gunners probed dangerously close, my chief fear of the moment was that I would not be able to get in my licks before my squadron mates sent the enemy planes crashing into the sea. Then, anticipating that the Jerries might attempt to turn toward the little village a few hundred yards to the left, I banked in that direction. Fortunately, I guessed right for one of the Arado 196s, already trailing a column of black smoke but still firing, turned directly into my sights. From 250 yards I squeezed the machine-gun trigger in the front of the hand grip on the control stick and pressed the cannon firing button on top of the stick. Fascinated, I watched the machine-gun and cannon fire rip the enemy plane from tail to nose. Almost simultaneously the Arado, burning brightly, crashed into the sea. Moments later the second German aircraft plunged into the water. The battle was over in a few seconds, but smoke bursts from the six 37-millimeter cannons, like small flak explosions, continued to fill the air as we surveyed the situation.

After one quick circle of the downed enemy planes, we turned southward toward our home base in Sardinia some 250 miles away. Within a few minutes, however, we were directed to land at Ajaccio in Corsica. The high rate of fuel consumption in the fight plus the possibility of bad weather in the Straits of Bonifacio, between Corsica and Sardinia, dictated the change in plans. Certainly, one of the real weaknesses of the Airacobra was its relatively short cruising range.

The P-39, along with the P-40 and the P-38, was to carry the burden of America's fighter effort during the first two years of the war. However, the Airacobra was never a popular aircraft with the U.S. Army Air Force. Its short cruising range and its comparatively poor performance above 15,000 feet (due to the failure to fit a turbo-supercharger engine on the production models) severely limited the P-39 as an escort fighter for bomber operations. It was variously described as "disappointing," of no use for operations "except in an emergency," "suited for wide, low and slow circles," and the "widow maker" by pilots and historians of the army air force. The latter remark probably stemmed from the airplane's reputation for flat spining and tumbling end over end out of stalled situations. Undoubtedly, the evil reputation of the P-39's flying characteristics was somewhat exaggerated.

In something over 600 hours of flying time in the P-39 (with perhaps 250 hours in operational missions), I never once had the aircraft tumble or fall into any other unorthodox spin situation. True, it was extremely sensitive to controls and seldom gave much warning before it stalled. Consequently, the wise pilot avoided low-speed turns at low altitudes. Needless to say, tricky stall characteristics tend to inhibit fighter pilots in low-level dogfights. Even so, on many occasions experienced P-39 pilots scored significant victories over the Luftwaffe. For example, on April 6, 1944 six Airacobra pilots from the 350th Fighter Group destroyed no less than six ME-109s and FW-190s in a tree-top level dogfight near Leghorn, Italy, without the loss of a single P-39.

In the words of one historian, "If the performance of the aircraft is analyzed, it appears the Airacobra may have been the most underestimated aircraft of the Second World War." Obviously the P-39 cannot be compared favorably with the P-47, P-38, or P-51, but in the dark days of 1942 and early 1943, neither the Thunderbolt, the Lightning, nor the Mustang were available in sufficient numbers to serve the needs of the army air force. Therefore, the P-39 must be compared to the only other fighter available in sufficiently large numbers, the P-40. In tests arranged by the Australian Department of the Air, the P-39D was faster and climbed faster than its contemporary P-40E at any altitude between sea level and 30,000 feet. In the official U.S. Army Air Force tests, the P-39 compared favorably with the War Hawk. Why then did the Airacobra suffer such a "bad press" when compared with the P-40?

Rather than technical difficulties, the P-39 was beset with psychological misgivings on the part of the average pilot who disliked knowing that the heavy Allison engine, mounted just behind the cockpit, was poised behind him ready to crush him in case of a belly landing. This fear, although understandable, was not borne out by facts, as the fighter proved to be exceptionally sturdy. Indeed, the Airacobra was an extremely easy aircraft to belly land because it had few obstructions on its bottom surfaces to impede the slide. I never saw an engine break loose and crush the pilot except in "straight in" crashes where the pilot would have been killed in any type of fighter.

Perhaps the chief reason for the Airacobra's "killer" reputation was the sizable number of accidents resulting from failure to recover from spins and from stalls on the landing approach. Because the P-39's elevator controls were extremely sensitive, it was easy for an inexperienced pilot to allow his airspeed to drop below flying speed while his attention was focused on lowering the landing gear and wing flaps and on making proper power adjustments. This type of accident was confined pretty much to training situations in the United States. The veteran fighter pilot, respecting the P-39's idiosyncrasies, kept one eye on the airspeed indicator and found it an easy plane to land. In nearly eighteen months of combat service in the Mediterranean Theater of Operation, I don't believe I witnessed a single landing approach accident due to a stall—I did witness with horror a mid-air collision on the peel off for a landing from an echelon formation.

On some of the early models of the P-39, the mixed armament (one 37-millimeter cannon firing through the propeller hub, two fuselage-mounted .50-caliber machine-guns, and four wing-mounted .30-caliber machine-guns) created both ballistic and maintenance problems. These problems were reduced with the P-39Q which was armed with the cannon and two fuselage- and two wing-mounted .50-caliber machine-guns. The long extension shaft, which proved highly reliable (there is some evidence that the V-1710 engine lasted longer in the P-39 than in the P40), vibrated and caused unnecessary fatigue for pilots, and the howl of the gear box may have left many of us with ear damage.

Despite its short range, mediocre speed (approximately 385 miles per hour at 10,000 feet), limited ceiling, and relatively poor turning characteristics, some of us had a great affection for the Bell P-39 Airacobra. For me it may have been my near-fatal attraction for buzzing under bridges and hedge-hopping over the landscape at deck level and the fact the P-39 with its excellent visibility forward and below performed that work well. In addition, the Airacobra was the first fighter plane I ever flew—and one does not forget his first love easily. Shortly after arrival at the Fighter Pilot Replacement Center near Casablanca in late spring of

1943, I was given the opportunity to transfer to Spitfire Vs but decided to go to the front in the Airacobra.

The P-39 was unusual for its engine location as well as for a retractable tricycle landing gear and automobile-type entrance doors on either side of the tiny and shoulder-width cockpit instead of the more conventional sliding canopy. Because either of the doors could be released by a simple pull of a handle, the pilot had no real difficulty in bailing out in emergencies. The only problem, and it was not serious, was that the pilot sometimes received minor burns if the slipstream pushed him against the hot exhaust stacks located immediately behind the cockpit. There was no difficulty in avoiding the horizontal stabilizer as was experienced in bailing out of the P-38 and some other fighters.

Because of the position of the throttle quadrant on the left side, normally the cockpit was entered through the right door. The seat-type parachute used by P-39 pilots acted as a cushion, and the cockpit, although quite snug, was reasonably comfortable. All frequently used controls and switches were within easy reach of the pilot even with the lap belt and shoulder harness firmly latched.

Because the first flight in a single-seat fighter is always a solo flight, the fledgling pilot is normally required to run through the cockpit check many times—until the location and function of every switch, control, and dial is burned into his mind and reflexes—before he is allowed to take off. Memories of thirty years ago came flooding back when I recently tried to reconstruct the starting and takeoff procedures on the Airacobra (memories later confirmed by a quick glance at the *Pilots' Flight Instructions for the P-39*).

The first action of the pilot after properly fastening his safety belt was to see that ignition, fuselage gun, wing gun, and cannon switches were off. Then a check was made to be certain that the landing gear clutch handle was set for electric operation. The flap control switch was checked for OFF and the generator switch for ON. The parking brakes were set by depressing the brake pedals and pulling out on the parking brake handle. At this point the rudder pedals were adjusted to a comfortable length for the individual pilot. By moving the rudder pedals and the control stick, the free movement of rudder, elevator, and aileron was tested. In addition, the oxygen control valve and oxygen supply was checked, even though flight above 12,000 feet might not be anticipated.

Starting the in-line, liquid-cooled engine was quite simple (on the P-39 Q-1 this was the Allison V-1710-85)—especially in the Mediterranean-type climate. With the airplane ignition switch off, the three-blade propeller (an AeroProducts prop on the P-39Q) was turned over two or three complete revolutions by hand. Then the battery switch was turned on and the ignition switch was turned to BOTH. The fuel selector valve was placed on RESERVE, the fuel mixture control was adjusted to the IDLE CUT-OFF, and the throttle was opened about one inch. At this stage the fuel booster pump was turned on and the engine primed two or three strokes (when the engine was cold). Then the booster pump was turned off. With the engine properly primed, the pilot then energized the starter by pressing the starter pedal downward with his heel until the inertia flywheel sounded as though it had reached maximum rpm. The starter was engaged by tipping the pedal forward with the toe. When the engine started, the mixture control handle was pushed forward to AUTOMATIC RICH.

The engine warm-up on the P-39 was conducted at about 1400 revolutions per minute or a little less. Meanwhile, the pilot checked air and coolant temperature gauges and the air pressure gauge. Because of the P-39's tendency to overheat quickly, the coolant and oil shutters were usually fully open until takeoff. If everything registered in the green portion of the dial, the parking brakes were released and with appropriate radio permission from the control tower the plane was taxied to a takeoff position. Indeed, the P-39, like most tricycle-gear fighters was a dream to handle on the ground. No S-ing back and forth was necessary, as in the case of the P-47 and the P-51, and the plane could be taxied at a high rate of speed with safety.

Before lining up for the takeoff run, the propeller-pitch control, located on the engine-control quadrant, was moved back and forth to check for proper operation. After the propeller check was completed, the magnetos were tested at engine speeds of approximately 2,300 revolutions per minute with the prop in full low or takeoff pitch and the mixture control in AUTOMATIC RICH. It was normal f or the right mag to drop off 80 revolutions per minute and the left mag to decrease about 60 revolutions per minute. A loss of 100 revolutions per minute generally indicated faulty ignition or spark plugs, and the plane was usually returned to the flight line for inspection.

With the cockpit check completed and takeoff instruction received, the fighter was taxied onto the runway. (In North Africa, Sardinia, and Corsica, the runway was typically a steel mat or in some cases only a grass or dirt strip). For the takeoff run, the mixture control was advanced to FULL RICH and the rudder, elevator, and aileron trim tabs were checked.

Then the throttle was advanced to obtain takeoff power. (A maximum of 3,000 revolutions per minute and 50 inches of manifold pressure was allowed at sea level on the P-39Q). As takeoff power was applied, there was a strong tendency to pull to the left, but this could be corrected by application of right rudder. (The tremendous torque on a propeller-driven single-engine fighter is always the biggest surprise for the pilot moving up from trainers for the first time).

Because of the tricycle landing gear, it was a good practice to ease the ship from the ground when an indicated airspeed of 100 miles per hour was attained. As soon as the aircraft had gained a few feet of altitude, the landing gear switch was flipped to the UP position. When the wheels were fully retracted, the landing gear switch was placed in the OFF position, and the throttle was reduced to approximately 35 inches of manifold pressure and 2,600 revolutions per minute. Perhaps the best climbing speed for the Airacobra was at 160 miles per hour, at which speed it would reach 15,000 feet in 4.5 minutes. After reaching cruising altitude, the power was reduced to 2,400 revolutions per minute and twenty-eight inches of manifold pressure.

In the Mediterranean Theater the P-39s were used frequently as fighter-bombers and with adequate fighter cover were quite effective in that role. The Airacobra could carry a 500-pound bomb without difficulty, and once the bomb had been dropped, the fighter proved an excellent gun platform for strafing operations against railroad and highway traffic. Its good deck-level speed and fine straight-ahead visibility enabled the P-39 pilot to approach his target with little warning. The .50-caliber machine-guns were effective against most highway vehicles, and the 37-millimeter cannon, firing armor-piercing and high-explosive shells through the propeller hub, was utterly devastating. On two occasions in particular, I had opportunity to witness the destructive power of the cannon. The first was March 8, 1944, when two of us flying P-39Ns acted as escort for a RAF Air-Sea Rescue Boat engaged in an effort to pick up the crew from a disabled Walrus flying-boat a few hundred yards off the Island of Elba. Despite heavy coastal gunfire, the rescue was made without casualty. However, when it appeared that the Germans were attempting to seize the British plane, we were ordered to destroy it. I remember hitting the Walrus with a single 37-millimeter round from approximately 400 yards and was startled to see the seaplane blow up in a cloud of flames and smoke. The second occasion of spectacular result from a single cannon shot happened only three days after the seaplane episode. On the afternoon of March 11, about eight P-39s of the 345th Fighter

Squadron skip-bombed a military barracks complex just outside the city limits of Grosseto, Italy, and then proceeded to seek targets of opportunity along the highway and railroad running northward toward Livorno (Leghorn). Several trucks and two locomotives were left disabled and smoking. Near the little town of Fallonica, I spotted a German staff car carrying four soldiers racing southward on an open stretch of highway. Once again disdaining use of the Airacobra's full fire power, I fired a single round with the cannon. The high explosive shell hit the small automobile with such force that it cartwheeled several times into an open field and burst into flames. Rumors had it that the recoil from the big gun would slow the P-39's speed by some 15 miles per hour. I do not know whether this was true, for I never had time to look at the airspeed indicator whenever I had occasion to use the 37-millimeter weapon for any sustained fire.

In addition to its fighter-bomber role in the Mediterranean Theater, the P-39 was used extensively in convoy-patrol work. If the Airacobra was not fast enough to cope with the Messerschmitt 109 or the Focke-Wulf 190, it could, at least, beat off the Luftwaffe's Junkers 88, Heinkel 111, and Focke-Wulf 200 bombing planes that might attack Allied shipping. Although the task of protecting troop ships, tankers, and supply vessels was, indeed, important, many fighter pilots found the duty boring and longed for the hot strafing runs or the dogfights with enemy fighters. Consequently, most P-39 pilots waited impatiently for the long-promised P-63 King Cobra or the P-47 Thunderbolt. When the 350th Fighter Group was finally equipped with the latter in the spring and summer of 1944, we looked forward to a change in our basic mission. As it turned out, dive-bombing, strafing, and tactical type escort work continued to be our principal responsibility.

Convinced that much of the Airacobra's "killer" reputation was a psychological problem, I immediately set out to prove to myself that the P-47 Thunderbolt (the "Jug") was safe and predictable. On my second flight in the Thunderbolt, I climbed the big radial-engine fighter to 10,000 feet and for the next hour put it through every aerobatic maneuver I could conjure up. Although a little heavier on the controls than the P-39, the Jug responded as honestly as a primary trainer. I even forced the big fighter into a spin and was pleased to find that it recovered quickly when the opposite rudder was applied and the stick was pushed forward. Loops, rolls, and Immelmann turns were quite predictable. The P-39 had to be held in power dive because it had an inherent tendency to level out. The P-47, on the other hand, would dive forever unless back pressure was exerted on the control stick. In fact, it was rather easy to reach a point of compressibility (the speed of sound) if the P-47 was allowed to dive at a steep angle. Because we knew little about this phenomenon during World War II, this could be a problem to the fighter pilot who was not alert to the rapid build-up of speed. On the other hand, a Thunderbolt pilot could easily dive away from any pursuer provided he had sufficient altitude to exercise that option.

The one plane that the large majority of the P-39 pilots in North Africa and Italy really hoped for was the P-63 King Cobra. Bell Aircraft Company Technical Representatives had been singing its praises for months, and the word was that it retained all the P-39's good qualities while remedying its weaknesses. But the plane never appeared in American combat squadrons, though a few were delivered to the Russians late in the war. Nonetheless, I did eventually have the opportunity to fly the King Cobra. After returning to the United States from a combat tour in the Mediterranean, I was able to win an assignment to a Flying Circus outfit equipped with P-63s, then engaged in making simulated attacks on B-29 crews preparing for duty against Japan. The P-63, without a doubt, was the sweetest flying fighter plane I ever climbed into. Because of a more powerful supercharged engine, modification in wing structure, taller vertical stabilizer, and over-all better balance, the King Cobra did solve all the P-39's problems—except its relatively short range. It was basically an interceptor. The P-63 was fast (well over 400 miles per hour), "climbed like a homesick angel" (over 5,000 feet per minute which was much better than the P-47, P-38, and P-51), and could turn with the best. Its stall characteristics were as honest as those of the Thunderbolt. The P-63 was so completely responsive to every mood of its pilot that John Gillespie MacGee's magnificent poem "High Flight" would have fitted the King Cobra perfectly:

> Oh, I have slipped the surly bonds of Earth,
> And danced the skies on laughter-silvered wings:
> Sunward I've climbed and joined the tumbling mirth
> Of sun-split clouds—and done a hundred things
> You have not dreamed of—wheeled and soared and swung
> High in the sunlit silence. Hov'ring there,
> I've chased the shouting wind along and flung
> My eager craft through footless halls of air.
> Up, up the long delirious, burning blue
> I've topped the wind-swept heights with easy grace,

Where never lark, or even eagle flew;
And while with silent lifting mind I've trod
The high untrespassed sanctity of Space,
Put out my hand, and touched the face of God.

Perhaps no pilot was ever quite so enthusiastic about the Bell P-39 Airacobra, but it could be effective in the hands of the experienced fighter pilot (several of the top Russian aces flew the P-39 in combat). And last but not least, it was in the army air force's inventory when America badly needed fighter aircraft.

Dr. James Hudson served with the 345th Fighter Squadron of the 350th Fighter Group in the Mediterranean Theater. He flew 191 operational missions in P-38, P-39, and P-47 aircraft. After returning to the United States in late 1944, he was assigned to a P-3 King Cobra outfit.

The B-18—A Reminiscence

Winton R. Close

"Ninety, eighty-five, seventy-eight, seventy-eight, seventy-eight."

I was on the final approach to the Don Q Rum Company airstrip just outside of Ponce, Puerto Rico, and the copilot was calling out the airspeed. I went over the fence at about six feet, hanging on the props. I cut the throttles and landed slightly tailwheel first, straight out of the glide with no flare. We rolled about 900 feet. The dirt strip was 1,200 feet long.

The time was early 1941, and the airplane was a B-18A. The B-18 was a bomber manufactured by Douglas, most of them in 1938. The wings, empennage, and the landing gear were similar to those of the DC-2. It had a wing span of eighty-seven feet, an over-all length of fifty-seven feet, a height of fifteen feet, and a wing area of 965 square feet. The book said that its gross weight was 28,000 pounds. But the book said a lot of things that we didn't buy. For example, its cruising speed. Contrary to what the book said, the B-18 flew at 135 miles per hour indicated. It is not much of an exaggeration to say that the B-18 embraced that speed with complete indifference to altitude, gross weight, or power setting. The fact of the matter was that it simply liked to fly at 135; it did not like to fly at any other airspeed.

The B-18 was not an exciting airplane, but it was reliable. It looked sturdy and squatty, and was. It had an honest stall with a polite amount of warning. In 1,000 hours, I never lost an engine. The two engines were Wright 1820s developing 1,000 horsepower each, and except that they were always a little oily on the outside, they were great. They did not, however, provide us with breath-taking performance. But on the other hand, we were not sure that the airframe was up to a breathtaking performance, anyway, so it all came out even.

Opposite page: B-18s in formation.

117

The test pilot, who in describing the performance of a new airplane, said, "It takes off like a scalded cat and climbs like a homesick angel," was not describing the B-18. On the contrary, the B-18 seemed to have a strong affection for the ground. When we had to take off with a heavy load from a short strip, we would stick its tail between the fence posts, hold the brakes, and open the throttles wide. When all the parts seemed to be shaking at the right frequency, and all the noises were at the proper resonance, and the two seemed to be in a reasonably harmonious relationship, we would release the brakes. Nothing would happen for a while. But then, pretty soon, the aircraft would start to move.

This performance, or lack of it, tended to alarm passengers not familiar with the plane. But it didn't alarm us because we knew that no matter what, it would get off the ground in time to clear the trees at the far end of the strip. It always had, and it always would. It simply would bump slowly down the field, and then at the last possible moment, when those of little faith would be looking somewhat drawn, it would lurch into the air and soar triumphantly over the trees, not without, I may add, a certain grace.

The B-18's affection for the ground was demonstrated again when it landed. As it touched the ground, transferring its weight from its wings to its landing gear, it would emit an audible little sigh, much like a fat lady sitting down in a soft chair.

We didn't pay any attention to the max gross weight listed in the tech order. As a matter of fact, I don't think we knew what it was. We simply loaded the aircraft with anything we wanted to, having regard only for a proper center of gravity. The way we established the proper center of gravity was by saying, "Chief, better move some of those cases farther forward."

The B-18 always climbed at the same rate—350 feet per minute—and there was nothing we could do about that either. Once we had leveled off at cruising altitude, we could trim it so that it would fly almost hands-off. That was nice, because the auto pilot never worked properly anyway. The armament people to whom this problem would be referred would always blame the whole thing on "dirty dashpots." We apparently accepted this explanation and never thought to pursue the subject farther. To this day, I am not quite up on dashpots or why they couldn't be kept clean.

At this point you may be asking what a couple of nice second lieutenants like us were doing flying this somewhat pot-bellied airplane into a scrubby airstrip in Puerto Rico. This gives me the opportunity to tell you that we were assigned to the Tenth Squadron of the Twenty-Fifth

---

Opposite page: A B-18A—with an extended turret for the bombardier.

Bomb Group stationed at Borinquen Field, Puerto Rico. We had been there since November 1940, when we had brought the whole outfit down from Langley Field, Virginia. We had flown from Langley to Miami, to Camaguey, Cuba, to Borinquen, with overnight stops at Miami and Camaguey. This doesn't sound like a very big deal in 1980, but in 1940, it was pretty exciting, especially for second lieutenants.

But to get back to what we were doing on this day—what we were doing was flying the mail run. The mail run was a general term covering the carrying of supplies, mail, and people between Borinquen, Ponce, San Juan, St. Croix, and St. Thomas. At that time, fighter strips were being constructed at Ponce and St. Croix, and we were the supply line to those places. San Juan was on the list because it was the site of the headquarters of the Puerto Rican Department, the army organization with over-all command of Puerto Rico. As we were under the control of the Puerto Rican Department, we responded to their requests for aerial transportation for their senior officers with reasonably good grace, particularly when one wanted to go to St. Thomas on an inspection trip.

The landing strip at St. Thomas was a fairway of a golf course. This was the home base of a squadron of dive bombers. These antiquated, fabric-covered, open-cockpit biplanes were flown with panache by a bunch of friendly Marines who did not seem over-awed by our sleek, all-metal, low-wing monoplanes with two engines. Even when we pointed out to them that we didn't have to wear helmets and goggles to fly our airplanes, they remained friendly, but unimpressed.

Good things happened to you if you flew B-18s. For example, one day in St. Thomas when I had burned out an engine starter—one of the few mechanical problems I had ever had with a B-18—the marine line chief, a venerable old master sergeant, volunteered to start the engine without a starter. In a few minutes he showed up in a truck with two men and a thirty-foot length of shock cord. To one end of the cord was attached a leather boot-like arrangement. He placed the boot over the tip of the prop blade that was pointing straight up—it was a three-bladed prop—and attached the other end of the cord to the tail end of the truck.

While the two men held on to the blade closest to the fuselage, I was in the cockpit with my hand on the magneto switch. Then the truck started to move slowly away from the engine in the same plane in which the prop would rotate, and the shock cord started to stretch. This was by then exerting a strong pulling action on the propeller, which was being restrained by the two men. When the truck had moved perhaps sixty feet, and the shock cord had stretched to more than twice its original length, the chief yelled at the two men to let go of the prop blade. When they did, the contracting cord imparted a high velocity spin to the prop. As it did, I turned on the mag switch, and the engine caught immediately. I got out of the airplane to thank the chief who looked me in the eye and replied with impressive sincerity, "Always glad to help the air corps, Lootenant."

Now you may think that the good thing that happened here was that we found a handy way to start an engine in an emergency. That was nice enough, to be sure, but that wasn't the good thing. The good thing was the way that old Marine looked at me when he said, "Always glad to help the air corps, Lootenant."

Other good things happened. About once a month, I would fly to Miami for various important reasons. Regulations required that we make a position report to the navy at Guantanamo when we got abeam of it. This was a safety measure designed to protect us, but we didn't particularly appreciate it. I think it is fair to say that flying safety didn't receive as much emphasis in those days as it did later on.

We carried a radio operator, and he would make the position reports in Morse code. The sending key he used was a GI type—an old fashioned kind like the one seen in the telegraph office on "Gunsmoke." The navy operator on the other hand, was using a "bug," or high-speed key.

Now radio operators are a breed unto themselves. They are great technicians and proud of their ability. They like to talk only to each other, preferably in code. They are also highly competitive within their own league. What would happen is that our operator, using his slow key, would contact the navy operator and transmit the position report. The navy operator then would reply using his "bug" at a speed our operator could not read. This forced our operator to send "IMI," shorthand for "please repeat." Naturally, it is very humiliating for an experienced operator to be forced to confess publicly that the transmission of the other operator is too fast for him to read. And with his slow key, our man had no way to retaliate. It was soon apparent to the rest of us on the crew that our operator was suffering real agony.

Finally, after three such experiences, the operator asked permission to install his own "bug" for our next trip to Miami. Now, for some reason in those days, the use of a "bug" in an air corps aircraft was prohibited by regulation. But this seemed to me to be an extraordinary case, the implications of which far transcended anything that the author of the regulation could have visualized. I could see no reason why our operator should be publicly embarrassed just because the author of the regulation had been short-sighted.

"Higgins," I said in a Jovian sort of way, "install the bug."

We left the next Friday for Miami. As we approached the area where contact with Guantanamo was to be made, I turned around to take a look at Higgins. His eyes were unnaturally bright, and a fine film of moisture had formed on his upper lip. As I watched, he made the initial contact with the navy operator. He started to transmit slowly and then began to accelerate. In thirty seconds he had the bug singing. It was all over in another minute or two. He came forward.

"Did you make contact with Guantanamo?" I asked.

"Yes, sir," he replied.

"What did he say?" I asked like a good end man.

A marvelous grin appeared on his face, and he replied, "He said, sir, IMI!"

We did a lot of flying in our B-18s. My Form 5 shows that I averaged fifty-four hours a month for the year from November 1940 to November 1941. Our training program consisted mainly of practice bombing missions using 100-pound practice bombs called "Blue Blazers," navigation missions, and weekend cross-country flights. On these weekend trips, we could fly to almost any of the Caribbean islands, such as the Bahamas, Haiti, Cuba, Jamaica, Martinique, Barbados, and Trinidad. These missions were very valuable to us. We navigated into strange areas with little or no navigation aids, and landed in strange little grass airstrips where no maintenance facilities existed. It taught us to be self-reliant, to improvise, and somehow to scramble out of the difficult situations into which our ignorance and inexperience would betray us.

In these adventures, the B-18 was our steadfast ally. It patiently tolerated our youthful exuberance, our mistakes, and our occasional recklessness. It even understood about hangovers. It forgave us all but our most grievous errors. We, in turn, treated the airplane kindly. We tried to land gently and to brake smoothly. But more importantly, we understood its limitations and would not embarrass it by forcing it to exceed them. It was a highly satisfactory relationship.

You may not remember the story of the B-18s and the French aircraft carrier, the *Jean d'Arc*. In early December 1941, the *Jean d'Arc*, with a deck load of American P-36s for the French air force, left the United States bound for France. Very shortly after the carrier had left port, France capitulated to Germany. The *Jean d'Arc* ended up in the harbor of the Fort de France in Martinique. It was imperative that the carrier and its cargo not continue to France, and to the Twenty-Fifth Bomb Group fell at least a partial responsibility for preventing its escape.

To that end, a task force of six B-18s were dispatched from Borinquen to Antigua, a distance of 180 miles from Fort de France. Our instructions were to conduct surveillance over the harbor and to report any attempt by the carrier to put to sea. If the carrier did attempt to leave, we were to stand by for orders to sink her. Our system was to have one aircraft on surveillance patrol outside the harbor while the others remained on strip alert back at Antigua. This operation continued for about two weeks and stopped when the government of Martinique agreed to impound the *Jean d'Arc* for the duration.

For better or worse, this precluded what might have been an historic confrontation between the B-18s and an aircraft carrier. Who knows what might have happened had such a confrontation taken place? Supposing the B-18s had sunk the carrier. On the strength of such a performance, the B-18s might have been sent to Europe to the Eighth Air Force to ravage Germany, or sent west to become the scourge of the Pacific. But it was not to be, and I think we were happy with that outcome for several reasons—not the least of which was that we had a secret feeling that it didn't seem right or fair that this amiable old airplane with whom we had enjoyed such a companionable relationship should be used as an instrument of violence.

Once the United States had entered the war, the B-18s were used mainly for anti-submarine patrol, and in this department they did yeoman duty. Loaded with depth charges and working out of bases around the Caribbean, they patrolled millions of square miles. They performed this dull, enervating duty with distinction. In all kinds of weather they flew, doggedly, persistently, faithfully, and—you guessed it—at 135 miles per hour.

Well, the era of the B-18s is long past now. I suppose that they are all gone, but I like to think that there is at least one left, someplace. I like to visualize it, an old abandoned airplane, weather-beaten and beyond repair, but still sturdy and squatty, sitting on the edge of an old airstrip on a Caribbean island, slyly contemplating the distance to the trees at the far end of the field.

Winton R. Close spent his entire military career, with a few exceptions, in heavy bombardment. His flying career began in B-18s, ended with B-52s, and included almost every bomber in between, particularly the B-29, which he flew in World War II.

C-54 Skymaster

John F. Ohlinger

My first encounter with the Douglas C-54 was at the Douglas Plant at Orchard Field (later O' Hare International Airport) near Chicago late in 1943. Since, as the saying goes, "everything is relative," I found myself subconsciously making numerous comparisons of the C-54 with the C-47 "Gooney Bird" on which I had amassed considerable flying time. Instead of a cramped cockpit, the C-54 cockpit seemed almost of conference-room size. One could slide into the pilot's seat without fear of getting his cranium bumped on protruding switches and other gadgetry—a noted occupational hazard for "Gooney" crews. The steerable nosewheel, a remarkable invention of those days, eliminated the vexing problems of cross-wind taxiing. Internally operated control locks did away with externally affixed battens with their attendant complexities. Four fans rounded out this delectable package—foretelling many safe and comfortable flying hours with less apprehension of the dangers of engine failure than in the case of the two-engine variety. I noted with some satisfaction that a new crew station had been added—the flight engineer—situated on a jump seat directly between pilot and copilot. For some reason, I formed the opinion that this was a definite status symbol that moved the pilot from the working class to the executive category. This opinion was reinforced later when I learned that Air Transport Command had authorized navigators, radio operators, and flight attendants as regular crew members. The "Gooney" crews of this time never had it so good.

We usually entered the C-54 through the rear cargo door, climbing either a ladder that was part of the airplane equipment or an externally provided loading ramp. There was also a small crew door just behind the crew compartment, but this was seldom used.

Opposite page: The C-54 Skymaster in flight.

These were the days prior to air crew standardization and the vigorous adherence to checklists. Hence, for starting engines the crew loosely collaborated in assuring that fuel valves were open, cowl flaps open, wing flaps up, master ignition on, engines properly primed, mixture and ignition applied at the proper time as each engine was turned over by the starter. Mixture controls were located almost out of sight of the flight engineer, who eventually took to selecting the correct one by feel. Failure of an engine to start could frequently be traced to the flight engineer's having fingered the wrong control.

Although the steerable nosewheel greatly facilitated ground handling, there were other problems. Recommended speed for taxiing was 800–1,000 revolutions per minute. However, at this low engine speed, particularly on hot days, the plugs had a tendency to foul; if they were not cleared the result could be an aborted mission. One alternative was to taxi at higher revolutions—say 1,200—but this brought on another problem: at this power an excessive use of brakes was required to keep the taxi speed down to safe and manageable limits. Brakes on the early C-54s were very likely to overheat, leading to brake lockage—or at the worst, brake fire—so this alternative to the fouling problem had to be used with caution. Another option was to taxi out on only two engines, No. 2 and No. 3, and then start up 1 and 4 in the run-up position. When only two engines were used for taxi, 1,200 or 1,400 revolutions per minute could be safely used without fear of either engine fouling or brake overheating. However, this required two engine starts away from the flight line and hence without the protection of a fire guard; it was widely condemned by supervisory personnel.

Engine run-up and preflight check differed little from that of other prop-driven aircraft of the day: oil pressure, fuel pressure, hydraulic pressure, oil temperature, cylinder head temperature, mag check, etc., all within limits. One notable addition was the check of the two-stage supercharger. Just before commencing takeoff roll, the internal control lock had to be released and control surfaces checked. To preclude takeoff with the control locks engaged, Douglas had thoughtfully provided a pin suspended from the ceiling of the cockpit on a ribbon which could be reeled up when not in use. The locking mechanism was on the cockpit floor and was spring-loaded in the disengaged position. The pin was inserted in the device to hold the locks in place. Thus, when the locks were engaged, a broad red ribbon extended downward from the ceiling as warning that all was not as it should be. Despite this obvious indication there were more than a few aborted takeoffs due to locked control surfaces.

Takeoff was greatly facilitated with the use of nosewheel steering up to about 60 miles per hour, when rudder control became effective. At ninety or so, depending upon gross weight, the aircraft eased effortlessly into the air. Climb-out was accomplished at 120 miles per hour, thirty-five inches of manifold pressure, and 2,350 revolutions per minute. Engine failure on takeoff, the ever-present danger in the C-47, was of little concern to C-54 drivers. Loss of either inboard engine was hardly noticeable. Control problems encountered with the failure of either outboard engine could readily be overcome with minor adjustment of trim tab, even with a full load. Maximum gross takeoff weight was 64,000 pounds; maximum gross landing weight was 56,000 pounds. For military emergency missions, gross weight as high as 72,000 pounds was authorized for takeoff.

Since the aircraft was not pressurized, normal cruising altitude was usually between 8,000 and 14,000 feet. With supplemental oxygen, cruising as high as 20,000 feet was possible through engagement of the supercharger. As to cruise power settings, the fine art of cruise control had not been perfected in the early days of C-54 operations, hence each pilot developed his own rule of thumb. Some insisted on straight 30/20 at all times—thirty inches of manifold pressure and 2,000 revolutions per minute. Others insisted on constant airspeed—usually 180 miles per hour. At high gross this required excessive power at the early stages of long-range flight with gradual power reductions as gross weight was reduced, as fuel was burned off, and airspeed tended to increase. METO power (maximum except takeoff) was 40 inches and 2,550 revolutions per minute, and there were a few intrepid and impatient aviators who took this literally and insisted on cruising just below this setting. (I am here again speaking of the time prior to standardization boards. Late in 1944 things began to improve as the idea of standardized flight procedures began to take hold.) The C-54 carburetor was the automatic type; it could be set to the auto-lean position that would automatically adjust the fuel flow to the proper fuel-air ratio depending on altitude. However, there was a manual range between auto-rich and auto-lean which some pilots used in lieu of the fixed positions. One pilot of my acquaintance claimed he could identify an improperly adjusted carburetor by the color of the metal tarnish just outside the exhaust stacks. He was an ardent advocate of manual adjustment and did his best to convert others to this theory, with little success.

Compared to other aircraft of similar size at that time, the C-54 was extremely light on the controls, very maneuverable; and this was prior to the invention of hydraulically boosted control surfaces. The airplane could be flown manually for long periods without excessive fatigue to the pilot, but it had a fairly reliable autopilot which we usually used for long-range operations.

The prime feature of the C-54 that brought out the high admiration of the flying fraternity in those days was its great range and cargo-carrying capacity. Although early versions had to rely on fuselage tanks for extended range, cutting down on cabin cubage, later versions carried all fuel in the wings—a total of 3,600 gallons. At conservative power settings, fuel consumption on a long flight could be reduced to 200 gallons per hour (fifty gallons per hour per engine); an endurance of eighteen hours could be expected from full tanks. As a consequence the C-54 was able to outstrip all other contenders as the vehicle for global air support for U.S. forces in World War II. A distant contender at this time was the cargo version of the Consolidated B-24 known as the C-87. As rapidly as additional C-54s came off the assembly line and crews were trained, the airplane became the workhorse of the Crescent Caravan, a military airline of the Air Transport Command operating from New Castle Army Air Base, Wilmington, Delaware. Crescent's scheduled runs eventually spread through Europe, Africa, and India as far east as Calcutta.

For instrument operations the C-54 was remarkably stable. Precision approaches using ILS or GCA (new inventions at this time and by no means universally trusted) were no problem whatever. Even in severe turbulence the aircraft seemed to have an innate affinity for the straight and level and could be brought back to an even keel quite readily despite the most severe gust. However, the airplane did have one dangerous potential known as "split flaps," which was of great concern to pilots on instrument approaches. Accepted procedure called for the lowering of quarter flaps to reduce speed prior to crossing high station (then known as high cone). In the early versions of the C-54, the left and right wing flap segments operated independently; variations in hydraulic pressure and other factors could result in asymmetrical flap configuration and even, at the worst, no flaps on one side and quarter flaps on the other side. When this condition was encountered unexpectedly—especially at night on solid instruments—the results could be disastrous. A number of fatal crashes were later attributed to this cause. A modification that interconnected the left and right flaps solved the problem once and for all.

The best landing technique in the C-54 was the power-on landing (about fifteen inches manifold pressure) until touchdown. This was especially useful in gusty or crosswind conditions or at high or uncertain gross weights. (The latter was all too common an occurrence in World War II; if you knew your weight plus or minus 1,000 pounds, you were doing well.) The tricycle gear configuration permitted "grease jobs" of a quality previously unheard of. However, the airplane was not immune to the bounce; I have ridden through crow-hop landings that would do credit to the old "Goon." This usually resulted from too low airspeed, too high level-off, and excessive nose-up attitude, followed by a controlled crash. Although the airplane was most forgiving of goofs of this nature, the operation of Murphy's law was clearly evident; that is, if it's possible to do something wrong, someone will find a way to do it.

For short-field landings the technique was to bring the airplane up into an extremely nose-high attitude, full flaps and power on, holding this attitude as long as possible after touchdown. When the nosewheel touched down, flaps were raised immediately and full braking applied. Under certain loading conditions the tail skid might scrape the runway, but this caused no structural damage since the skid was equipped with a hydraulic strut to dampen the impact. It has been reported that Royal Dutch Airlines KLM made tail skid landings routinely in their short-field operations in Southeast Asia.

Although the C-54 was admirably built for operations in all climes, it exhibited some strange characteristics in extremely cold weather, like Thule Bay and Sondrestrom, Greenland. For one thing, the seals on the landing gear oleo struts would shrink, allowing leakage of hydraulic fluid from the struts, thus effectively destroying their shock-absorbing action. Taxiing on a rough surface in this condition was somewhat akin to operating an automobile with no springs. A landing perforce had to be smooth to avoid fracturing the gear. If the condition was known to the crew, due precautions could be taken on landing. Unfortunately it could and frequently did happen in flight unbeknown to the crew. On extension the landing gear would appear normal, and the crew, unwarned of the condition, would allow the oleo to immediately hit bottom on a normal landing. (It was not possible to make a visual check of the landing gear from the cockpit of the C-54; however, it could be observed through the navigator's drift meter, and this instrument was frequently pressed into service for this purpose when some doubt existed that the gear was down and locked. Some pilots distrusted the visual and audial gear warning signals—horn and lights—and made this a standard practice for all landings.)

An important item in the preflight check was to see that the struts extended the proper amount. Proper extension for the main gear was about $2\frac{3}{4}$ inches and for the nose gear, slightly more than three inches. These dimensions equaled roughly the height of a standard cigarette package and a king-size cigarette package, so it was not uncommon to see flight engineers using these objects as a gauge for strut extensions. Nonsmoking flight engineers could only eyeball the situation.

Another cold-weather hazard concerned the fuel tank selector valves. To change tanks, say from main to auxiliary, one simply actuated a set of switches on the control pedestal between the pilot and copilot. By a pulley and cable linkage the tank selector valves were changed, causing fuel to flow from the tank thus selected. At extremely low temperatures some part of this complex linkage could become stuck, rendering it impossible to change tanks. This was a matter of grave concern if the flight at hand depended on the use of auxiliary fuel to get to destination. Fortunately this condition was not permanent; persistent manipulation by the flight engineer could get the obstinate valves unstuck, but not without some nervousness on the part of the flight crew. Associated with the fuel tank selector switches was the cross-feed system which permitted interchange of engine operations among the various tanks. This was particularly useful in making available the fuel supply behind a failed engine to the remaining good engines. The cross-feed could also be used to transfer fuel from one tank to another, but this practice was not recommended; the need for fuel transfer practically never arose.

I never had occasion to bail out of a C-54, nor do I have any knowledge of anyone who did. However, the rear main door provided excellent egress for potential bailors, but caution would be necessary to avoid being impaled on the horizontal stabilizer. A deliberate, precipitous, headlong jump rather than a slow, lingering departure would insure against this contingency. Likewise, I am not aware of anyone having ditched a C-54, but experts generally conceded that the airplane had good ditching characteristics. It was believed that a lightly loaded airplane would probably stay afloat for some time. It was recommended that the rear cargo door not be jettisoned before ditching for fear of admitting a large amount of sea water on contact. Two over-the-wing removable panels could be used to evacuate passengers quickly. For the crew up front the sliding glass panels beside the pilot and copilot positions could be used if these persons were not unduly obese. (There was no weight-reduction program in effect in the services at this time, and consequently our outfit had a few renegade blimps who would never have made it through this exit.)

The early C-54s carried a significant amount of special equipment, but most of it was common to that being installed in production line versions of contemporary combat airplanes such as the B-17 and B-24. LORAN (long-range aid to navigation) was a new development that greatly eased the work of the bubble-chasers and bolstered the confidence of the pilots in their work. VHF radio was a fine substitute for the old "coffee grinders," but it did not immediately replace them since some ground stations were very tardy in updating their transmitters. ILS receivers (then known as SCS-51 in U.S. Army jargon) were installed in most C-54s, but this equipment likewise was not immediately useful because of the lack of ground transmitters. Radio altimeter and a crude airborne radar set for severe weather avoidance and instrument navigation rounded out the special gear on the C-54s of this period. As primitive as it may appear in this day of advanced aerospace technology, the C-54 appeared to be almost a gift from heaven to war-weary "Goon" pilots like myself.

De-icing equipment in the C-54 was similar to that in other current large aircraft. (The heated wing was still some years away.) Inflatable leading edge de-icer boots, carburetor heat, and prop de-icer fluid were the sum total of the airplane's equipment for combatting this formidable hazard. But the profile of the flight surfaces was such as to cause the airplane to accumulate less ice than others, and what ice was gathered could be disposed of by the boots. We dropped a number of B-17s and B-24s into the North Atlantic because of wing ice, but no C-54s disappeared for this reason, although they were operated along the same routes in the same seasons of the year.

Late in 1945 the Crescent Caravan received orders from the Pentagon to begin operation of the world's first scheduled around-the-world flight. Starting and ending point was Washington National Airport, and relief crews were posted in advance at strategic refueling points. I had the honor of piloting the initial leg of the inaugural operation from Washington to Bermuda. The passenger list included many prominent journalists of the day such as Fred Othman and Inez Robb. The flight took off on schedule amid much fanfare and publicity, and we reached Bermuda without incident. En route a fine steak dinner was whipped up by specially selected flight attendants. We changed crews at Bermuda, and I returned to Wilmington aboard another C-54. I learned later that the original airplane didn't make it all the way and another was substituted. This was unfortunate, since the initial airplane I took to Bermuda had a special paint job to suitably advertise the nature of the flight, and its interior was fitted in a decor appropriate to the status of our distinguished passenger list. (Standard models of the C-54 were not designed for passenger comfort.) Despite its problems, the flight was a historical milestone of sorts and certainly demonstrated the global airlift capabilities of the C-54 and the Air Transport Command. Although far overshadowed since by high-flying jet transports, the whole idea of a world-encircling air operation was astounding at the time. It might be noted here that the same operation—but with different airplane types—has continued without interruption to this day. It was originally called the Globemaster; later it was renamed the Diplomat and is today known as the Embassy run. From time to time it has had to bypass India due to denial of overflight rights by this nation.

Some weeks later while on leave in my home town of Toledo, Ohio, I was amazed to discover the amount of publicity that had been given the flight in the local press. Although the newspaper accounts correctly stated my rather minor role in the whole affair, I found that my adoring public generally had the misconception that I had flown the entire around-the-world operation single-handedly. Being a swinging bachelor at the time, I did little to efface this hero image except when pressed with ridiculous questions such as "How did it feel to fly across the Himalaya Mountains?" I had to admit then rather sheepishly that I had flown only from Washington to Bermuda—a mere five-hour flight.

John F. Ohlinger was engaged primarily in air transport operations in C-47s and C-54s in all major theaters of combat during World War II.

P-51 Mustang

John A. De Vries

There were one-cushion pilots and two-cushion pilots, and, if you didn't use a dinghy buckled to the D-rings of your back parachute, there were three-cushion pilots. Early in 1944, the air corps decided that a man five feet eight inches or shorter was a hot fighter pilot. If he was taller, he was destined for multiengine flying. Thus, if a fighter pilot was fortunate enough to be selected to fly the P-51 Mustang, the multiplicity of cushions was necessary to boost him high enough to see out of the massive bubble canopy.

In 1946 the monsoon rains came early. Japan, and more specifically, Johnson Army Air Base, was socked-in for the last half of September. Assigned to the 40th Fighter Squadron, 35th Fighter Group, I had plenty of time to study the lean and wiry Mustang before I flew it the first time. The Squadron owned twenty-five of the bubble-canopied beauties, but only fourteen pilots were assigned, and there were plenty of "ponies" to choose from. My choice was number 56—a K-model. The P-51K differed from the D only in the particular that it had an Aero Products propeller instead of a Hamilton Standard.

While the relentless rains fell, I studied the one and only P-51 flight manual available in the Squadron. Not the usual "Dash One," the manual was a how-to-fly-it book, filled with cartoons and simple illustrations that emphasized the important factors for achieving maximum performance from the Mustang. Because the first flight would be solo, every word was important!

The rains continued well into October, providing opportunity for three activities prior to checkout. Many, many hours were spent just sitting in the snug cockpit of No. 56 while the monsoon beat against the hangar roof. Gear handle, flap handle, throttle, mixture control, and

Opposite page: Two P-51s supporting a B-25 raid in Burma.

propeller knob all fell closely at hand. The instrument panel was memorized as well as the armament control panel (which held switches for the six .50 caliber Brownings, the gunsight aiming point 16-millimeter camera, the arming controls for the twin bomb or long-range tank wing pylons, and the rheostat that adjusted the intensity of the light in the reflector gunsight). The "triggers" for all of the armament were clustered on the control stick hand grip. Soon I was able to pass the required "blindfold cockpit check"—touch any instrument or control instantly, without any visual reference.

The Squadron was only at half-strength as far as pilots were concerned. The crew-chief situation was even more desperate. There weren't any! Two master sergeants made up the entire maintenance section. They, together with the North American Technical Representative for the Group, established a crew-chief school for pilots. For eight weeks, we new Mustang drivers attended classes every morning and worked on our own planes every afternoon. Changing the twenty-four spark plugs of the 1,400-horsepower, twelve-cylinder V-1650-7 Packard Merlin engine is a darn good way of finding out what goes on inside the Mustang! When I was ready to make my first P-51 flight, I really knew its innards.

The weather began to clear enough for flying in the pattern. But before we new pilots were turned loose in our superbly maintained fighters (after all, we were our own maintenance crews), we had to go through the ordeal of rear-seat landings in the AT-6. The idea was that if you could land the skittery trainer from the back seat, you would do well "when it came time" in the Mustang. However, the "Powers-That-Be" failed to realize two important facts: the almost 1,000-horsepower difference in the engines of the two planes and that unless one were a giant the overturn structure of the AT-6 effectively blanked out any forward vision.

With six controlled crashes in the AT-6, I was really ready for my first Mustang ride. The walk-around inspection wasn't really necessary. I knew every rivet and Dzus-fastener on No. 56. To please the check pilot, I approached my mount from the left. No bird's nests in the left wheel well; the sole landing light was firmly bolted inside. No oil dripping from the underside of the Merlin, and all of the cowl sections were firmly attached. The big, four-bladed Aero Products propeller was nick-free, and the carburetor intake under the nose was clear. No drips or loose Dzus-fasteners on the right side of the nose, and the right tire (like the left) was brand-new and properly inflated. The oleo strut spaced out to the proper hand-span, and the leading edge of the right wing was smooth. Aileron and the dropped flap looked "right," and the fuselage-mounted alternate static air source was clear of any foreign substances. The tail assembly looked OK—the fabric-covered movable surfaces were taut (later, the elevators would be replaced with metal-sheathed surfaces). A quick glance at the left aileron and flap, and then it was time!

The hangar hours had proven to me that I was two-cushion pilot. Two cushions and a dinghy (the CO_2 cylinder of which my gluteus maximus would soon learn to hate) propped me to the proper eye level—the center of my vision coincided with the pipper in the center of the gunsight ring, when it was projected on the sight-glass of the N-9 100-mil gunsight (the P-51 Ds in the Squadron had gyro-stabilized K-14 sights). With a casual familiarity born of many hours of cockpit time, I buckled myself in and began the round-the-cockpit check: ignition off, mixture-in-idle cutoff. Capt. Bill Hook, the check pilot, pulled the prop through four blades to clear oil from the cylinders. The fuselage fuel tank (over the left shoulder) was filled to eighty-five gallons (each gallon was good for one minute's flight). Flap handle up, carburetor air in the "ram" position, trim set—5° of right rudder, ailerons at zero, and elevator at 2° nose down. The gear handle was checked down, and the propeller control was to be "full forward" (full increase rpms). The throttle was opened to the "start" position (about three-quarters of an inch forward). The altimeter was set to field elevation, and gyro instruments were uncaged. Control locks were released (a pin was pulled from the bracket that held the stick and rudder pedals, the bracket springing flat against the cockpit floorboards) and the rudder pedals adjusted (full back for us shorter pilots). With parking brakes set, both wing fuel tank levels were checked through their indicators in the floor (ninety-two gallons each), the supercharger switch was put in "auto," and the fuel selector handle was set to "fuselage" and I was ready to start.

With booster pumps on (to provide fuel pressure), magneto switch to "both," and battery and generator switches on, I had to pause for a moment and run the coolant doors open. Liquid-cooled, the Mustang had to have its radiator uncovered for starting. Although the doors in the rear belly of the P-51 were thermostatically controlled and operated automatically depending on the temperature of the thirty-percent-glycol-seventy-percent-water coolant mixture, their functioning had to be checked manually on the ground before starting.

A couple of tweaks of the primer switch and I raised the cover of the starter switch. Held in the "start" position, the lean Mustang shuddered

violently as the big prop turned over. After a few rumbles, the Merlin caught. I advanced the mixture to "run" and the oil pressure rose to the proper 50 pounds per square inch almost at once. The manual said to idle the engine at 1,200–1,300 revolutions per minute. All gauges "in the green" or coming up, the suction at 4.75 pounds per square inch, and I was ready to taxi. Captain Hook, who had been kibitzing over my left shoulder during the starting sequence, gave me a pat on the back and leaped to the ground. Thumbs-up—and he pulled the wheel chocks.

Suddenly, I was alone in a rip-snorting bucking bronco. Easing the Mustang's throttle open slightly, stick forward to unlock the tail wheel, I was on my own. Out of the parking area, I eased the stick back to lock the tail wheel in its 12° taxi arc (6° right and left). Lordy, that nose was l-o-n-g! Unless I S'd the bird, I couldn't see anything in front of me. The positive action of the disc brakes helped me taxi.

By the time I reached the run-up pad at the end of the runway, Hook had climbed the control tower and it was he who "talked" me through the engine checks. Revolutions to 2,300, check each magneto for not more than a 100-revolutions-per-minute drop (but no longer than fifteen seconds operation on a single magneto). Advance the throttle to thirty inches of mercury for one minute and exercise the propeller pitch-changing mechanism. A rapid glance around the cockpit—prop forward, supercharger auto, coolant auto, fuel booster on, hydraulic and suction pressures, oil pressure and temperature in the green, and I was ready to take the runway. Hook checked the pattern from his tower vantage point and gave the go-ahead.

Gently, ever so gently, I advanced the big spade-grip throttle ("liberated" from a K-14-equipped D-model Mustang—a "sexy" touch in my N-9-equipped K). The Merlin wound up. At thirty inches, the bird was as docile as an AT-6; at forty inches it was like riding a tornado; at the full sixty-one inches of takeoff manifold pressure I was caught up in a hurricane! The tail came up voluntarily as I pumped rudders to keep up with the enormous torque of the mighty engine. I could see over the nose, and the far end of the runway was approaching at an alarming rate. Somewhere along the route I'd attained flying speed, so a tug on the stick and No. 56 was blasting heavenward. Behind my left hip was the gear handle and I clutched at it before I exceeded the 225 miles per hour gear-door critical speed. The Mustang did an involuntary dip as I raised the handle. Before I knew it, I had reached 500 feet where the manual said I should throttle back to forty-six inches and pull the propeller control to 2,700 revolutions per minute for the climb.

Opposite page: The P-51 Mustang.

For the next hour and a half, I attempted to get ahead of my mount. The Mustang was a thinking pilot's airplane: think about it, and the airplane did it. There was enough pressure in thought alone to make 30° banked turns; rolls took only a wee bit of fingertip pressure. There was no combination of throttle, propeller, and trim tabs that would permit the Mustang to fly straight and level by itself. Oh, maybe its altitude would hold for five seconds before a bump would disturb its equilibrium, but hands-off, and the fighter would establish a climbing or diving spiral. You had to fly the P-51 every second you sat in the cockpit!

A series of stalls—power on and power off, flaps and gear up and down—were part of the first ride. At 10,000 feet the book said, throttle back, dump gear and flaps, and slow the P-51 down to 125 miles per hour. Simulate a final landing approach, and at the "landing point," jam on full throttle. It made me a believer: with a full sixty-one inches, old No. 56 turned every way but loose! I think I definitely did an inverted snap roll. I know the sturdy wings flapped! The point of the self-demonstration was to convince the neophyte pilot that the go-handle on the left side of the cockpit was to be moved deliberately but, oh so gently, particularly when the bird was near the ground.

Over Atsugi-Wan (Bay), over Mount Fujiyama, with rolls and loops, my first two Mustang hours were over. Landing time was fast approaching, so I headed east, toward Johnson. I dove down into the Tokyo Plain at an easy-to-obtain 450 miles per hour. With all of that Plexiglas around my head, the visibility from the cockpit was superb. No worry about running into another airplane.

I saw a field and let down to 400 feet—tactical traffic pattern altitude. The Mustang was difficult to slow, but by pulling back on the big spade-grip throttle we got down to the 240 miles per hour indicated as required for pattern entry. Turning north, I stabilized speed and altitude and lined up with the strip. As the end of the runway passed under the Mustang's nose, I pushed the propeller control to 2,700 revolutions per minute and honked the throttle back to idle. A sharp rightward and rearward tug on the stick, a boot of right rudder, and I was in a hairy chandelle. At its apex, I dumped gear and flaps (at about 180 miles per hour) and continued around my 360-overhead pattern. Depressing the throttle-mounted microphone button, I called, "Base leg!"

"Don't see you," said Captain Hook, calmly.

I continued in my fighter pilot's pattern. "Turning final," I announced into the VHF radio.

"Still don't see ya'," Hook replied.

It was then that I looked up. I was perfectly lined-up and at the proper approach speed of 120 miles per hour. But I was landing at Yokota—three miles south of Johnson! Coolly, I yanked the gear and flaps up and slowly fed the 100-octane to the Merlin.

"De Vries, where the hell are you?" Captain Hook blasted into the airwaves.

"I'm on one heck of a long final," I replied, trying to inject a note of confidence into my oxygen-mask microphone.

The abortive approach to Yokota had been good practice. The traffic pattern and landing at Johnson were good—for a beginner. I didn't notice, until I'd parked No. 56, the big prop grinding to a halt, that my flying suit was drenched and that there was a pool of sweat in my oxygen mask. The Mustang was a hot airplane in more ways than one! With only a couple of thin sheets of Dural between you and the Merlin, there was little protection from the engine's heat. But the heat was a small price to pay for the spectacular performance of the P-51—and it was very welcome on missions above 20,000 feet.

The engine stopped; I dumped the flaps to relieve the pressure on the hydraulic system and proceeded, round-the-cockpit, to turn every switch off.

After twenty hours in No. 56, with the basics mastered, flying the P-51 became sheer joy. The 40th was a tactical fighter squadron so we were called on to perform every conceivable fighter mission. Today, it may be firing the six 50s at a towed sleeve over the Mito gunnery range or dive-bombing and strafing ground targets. When the machine guns let loose, the Mustang shuddered and bucked like its namesake and the flying speed dropped ten miles an hour. With the 100-mil fixed gunsight, I qualified for aerial gunnery—put forty bullets out of 200 into a banner target. Dive-bombing was easy: each diverging slash mark painted on the upper surface of the wings was associated with a specific bombing-run entry altitude. As the target disappeared under the appropriate slash mark, you'd begin a diving turn onto the bomb run. The "crack" on top of the forward fuselage, where the two removable cowling panels met, was the "sighting line." Point the crack at the target, roll to keep it lined up and kill the effect of the wind, and, at the proper release altitude, push the bomb-release button atop the stick. The 100-pound practice bombs would "pickle" right on the bull's-eye!

Another day we'd escort a Russian PBY or IL-12 from over Sado Shima Island to Haneda airport, outside of Tokyo. With gear down and flaps half-extended (the flap-angle indicators were painted on the flap

Four P-51s on a practice run over the Alps.

hinge line as black and white alternating strips, 5° per strip) we'd "for-mate" with the Russkys to keep them from wandering around the Japan-ese islands, photographing every military installation in sight.

On Thursday, we might be scheduled for a "surveillance mission." With only a few radar sites to protect Japan, Mustangs were sent on low-level sweeps up and down both coasts and through the inland valleys, for visual reconnaissance. We were charged with recording the numbers from the sides of any aircraft, sailboat, or railroad locomotive we'd run across. It was a sporty course, holding No. 56 steady while flying up a mountain valley, chasing an errant Japanese locomotive to get its number! Wartime cable barricades were still in place, from mountaintop to mountaintop, adding spice to the proceedings. Coastal surveillance missions were the most fun. There have been instances when exuberant young fighter pilots have been known to fly low over Japanese coastal waters with the intent of blowing over the sailboats manned by suffering fishermen.

Friday would see the Mustangers of the 40th practicing close-support with ground controllers and the infantry at Camp Crawford, or simulat-ing interceptor missions with Hot Point Control, the Tokyo-area radar at Shiroi. On "special" days we'd sling 75- or 110-gallon drop tanks to our Mustang's wing shackles and fly seven- to ten-hour long-range missions. Often, our flights would be planned northward to the island of Hokkaido where dwelt the 4th Fighter Group. Arrival would be timed for about 5 A.M. so that our Merlins would act as alarm clocks for the sleepy pilots of Chitose Air Base. On one of these "alarm-clock raids" we dropped leaflets on the unsuspecting northerners. Shoved out the Very-pistol holes in the left flank of our Mustangs, they read, "Sleep soundly, 4th Fighter Group. The 35th is guarding your rest!"

Two and a half years saw 500 Mustang D and K hours in the log book. It was time to give up being a wingman and flight leader and move on. Later, much later, there would be 300 more P-51 hours, but this time it was in the H-model and the two-place TF-51D. The H was a lightened D with a towering rudder and a more potent engine. It cruised at 270-Indicated (compared to 240 miles per hour in the D), and was even more responsive to the controls than its older brother, but the pilot was just a bit more mature, a bit more cautious (with a wife and three kids), and the missions were much less exciting. Flying as an interceptor and target while new radar controllers learned their business wasn't really fighter flying!

I loved the hairy Mustang. With a single exception, every pilot I know who flew the P-51 loved it. The one "sourpuss" was a B-24 driver who experienced two dead-stick landings and one bailout in his first three Mustang rides! But, this one individual notwithstanding, the pilots of the 15,000-odd 51s that rolled from the North American production lines at Inglewood and Tulsa thoroughly enjoyed the calm—and the panic—of their hours in the $50,000 "Pony."

Col. John A. De Vries completed nearly 5,000 flying hours, spread over more than 100 types and models of military aircraft, including 800 hours in the Mustang. He also served as an instrument instructor for French cadets.

P-47 Thunderbolt

Mark E. Bradley with Helen Porter

It was big for its time—16,000 pounds and up—6,000 to 7,000 pounds heavier than World War II's other single-engine fighters, the P-51, Me-109, Spitfire, and FW-190. Officially, it was known as the P-47 Thunderbolt, but that's not what the pilots called it. With the large 2,000-horsepower Pratt & Whitney engine up forward, in the air it looked like a milk bottle with wings. The men who flew it affectionately called it "The Jug."

An all-metal airplane, sturdy and durable, the Jug could stand up to sixteen Gs in pull-outs. Its air-cooled engine could take unbelievable punishment and still get the plane home. Capable of well over 400 miles per hour at 30,000 feet, the Jug also had superlative fire power, including eight free-firing .50 caliber machine guns in the wings. It would carry a bomb load of up to two 2,000-pounders. But its size and weight prevented maneuverability equal to that of the lighter and smaller fighters. For this reason pilots took advantage of the speed and diving capability and generally avoided close-in-turning combat. The Jug was only a fair high-altitude fighter. Its specialty was ground attack. At this it was superb.

The first American production fighter (then called a pursuit airplane) with a completely cantilevered wing structure was the Seversky P-35. Its predecessor, the Boeing P-26, had been a monoplane with metal wings supported by external brace wires to absorb landing and flying loads. Close behind the P-35 came the Curtiss P-36, the Air Corps' second fully cantilever-winged fighter.

The P-35 had good range and top speed of something under 300 miles per hour, probably about 280. The P-36 had less range but was a bit faster and, according to Col. Charles Lindbergh, was superior in flight stability. (Lindy had flown both planes as an air corps colonel just before the start of World War II in 1939.) I had to agree with the Lone Eagle that

---

Opposite page: The P-47 in flight.

the P-35 would snap into a ground loop during the landing roll if not watched carefully, but in the air, with a properly balanced load, I thought its stability was pretty good. True, a mechanic or a deer in the large rear baggage compartment could create a condition of imbalance. Sasha Seversky used to carry his mechanic around in this fashion but was well aware of the hazard. I personally found out the effect of a deer on my way back to Wright Field from a hunt near Williamsburg, Pennsylvania.

The Seversky AP-4 was a new design similar to the P-35 but bigger and modernized with flush rivets and a turbosupercharger to boost its 900-horsepower Pratt & Whitney engine to achieve more power at altitude—a critical need. The supercharger was placed below the fuselage at the rear of the pilot, the same positioning to be utilized later in the P-47 design.

The Curtiss YP-37 had the same wing, engine, and empennage as the P-36, with the addition of a turbosupercharger like that in the AP-4. To balance the heavy engine and supercharger up forward, the pilot was moved far back in the tail, just in front of the vertical fin. I can vouch for the fact that this *can* be done and the airplane *can* be flown, as I flew the YP-37 from Buffalo to Wright Field in a snowstorm one February night so that it could participate in the upcoming flight evaluation. But it was definitely doing things the hard way. Putting the supercharger and not the pilot back there in the tail was a lot better way to go. Later I flew the YP-37 several times trying to measure its performance but was never able to get satisfactory operation out of the supercharger.

In January 1939 a competition was held for the first big (over 500) production order for U.S. Army Air Corps fighters. Competing were the Seversky AP-4, the Curtiss YP-37, and the Curtiss XP-40. The XP-40 had a P-36 airframe with an Allison 1,000-horsepower engine substituted for the previous air-cooled Pratt & Whitney engine of somewhat less power. The Allison was a conventional twelve-cylinder, liquid-cooled V; the Pratt & Whitney, an air-cooled radial. The XP-40 won the competition almost by default. The AP-37 engine-supercharger combination was never made to function properly and, because the extra altitude performance obtained from the supercharger was its main advantage, the airplane really never had a chance. Over 10,000 P-40s were produced before the end of the line in 1944. In spite of its shortfall in speed and performance at altitude, it put up one hell of a good fight.

Later in 1940, George Price and I took part in some trials of the XP-40 vs. Spitfire III at Ottawa, Canada, competing with RAF and RCAF pilots. The XP-40 held its own very well in all of the main fighter characteristics—speed, climb, and maneuverability. But that was before the addition of about 1,000 pounds of combat essentials. Small wonder that the P-40 declined in performance. Everything was added except horsepower. We were stuck with not over 1,000 horsepower in the P-40 for all its long life.

The reason the early P-40 did not keep up with the Spitfire in performance is not hard to find. First, the horsepower of the Rolls-Royce engine in the Spitfire was progressively increased whereas the Allison stood still. Second, the British were able to hold the weight of the Spitfire down, whereas we had to encumber the P-40 with six .50 caliber guns in addition to armor protection and bullet-sealing tanks to make it combat-worthy.

In 1939, as a gesture of appreciation to a talented and loyal contractor, thirteen YP-43s had been ordered from Seversky (to become Republic after a reorganization). The YP-43 was very like the AP-4 that crashed. Because it had only two .50 caliber machine guns and no armor or bullet-sealing tanks, it was not a really combat-worthy design. Nevertheless, the lessons learned while producing and testing the YP-43 were to prove invaluable.

Being aware of the old P-35's ground-loop problem, we insisted that the Republic engineers provide the thirteen P-43s with a good, strong tail-wheel lock—a device that prevented the tail-wheel strut from rotating. It was locked during takeoff and landing, but set free for turning and taxiing. No one seemed to know what caused certain aircraft to ground loop, but it seemed logical to me that the tail-wheel lock was our best chance to prevent it. How wrong I was!

Republic followed orders: the first YP-43 had a fine, strong tail-wheel lock. Nevertheless, on an early landing by an expert test pilot, the airplane ground looped so violently that it dug in a wing tip at high speed and flipped completely over, breaking the fuselage in two behind the cockpit. The pilot, luckily, was unhurt. But after this near tragedy, a concerned and embarrassed project officer set about grimly to find the cause and the cure of this violent maneuver once and for all.

The next P-43 was ready in a few weeks, and I went to Farmingdale on Long Island to begin my search. It was midwinter, so we moved over to the Floyd Bennett runways where there was better snow clearance. I began by landing damned carefully. I soon found the tendency to "snap the nose" to the right, at the same time dropping the right wing, to be definitely there at a point during most landing rolls. I found, as I had previously on the P-35 and at times on the P-40, that quick application of the toe brakes away from the turn at the instant it started would correct the snap and prevent disaster—all of which called for an extremely alert pilot with his foot ready on the brake pedal. A small delay or a push of the rudder instead of the brake, and Katie bar the door!

At this point the weather forced us to move to Langley Field in Virginia, and it was there that we were to find the answer we were seeking. I had had some previous dealings with NACA, the predecessor organization to the present NASA, so I asked them to help us find out what cooked with landing a P-43. Bob Gilruth, a young engineer who much later became the man behind the people in the Apollo project, was assigned as the scientific side of the house. In a try for "no wind" conditions, I had been getting up well before daylight to be ready for takeoff as soon as light came. Working alone, I'd found that the ground loop was worse at no wind and that at more than 10-to-20-mile-per-hour wind the tendency disappeared altogether. Then along came Gilruth. From there on, I bow to the scientific side, a procedure I have not always made a practice of following over the years.

In the meantime, Republic had placed tufts all over the vertical tail and wing for photographing during landing and the start of the ground loop. The pictures showed the tufts waving in all directions. But why? In addition, the company had built a new vertical tail of considerably more surface. This we put on and flew; but with no wind there was no improvement, just the same violent snap to the right.

Then one day after a period of considerable frustration Bob casually said, "I think if we raise the tail higher off the runway, it will help." So we took the tail-wheel strut off, took it to the NACA shop, put in a ten-inch extension, and put the lengthened strut back on the airplane. The next morning there was no wind and no ground loop. From then on, observant people probably wondered why all the P-43 and P-40 tail wheels remained hanging out in the breeze, even after retraction of the main gear. Because the P-40 had also had ground-loop problems, we fixed both planes at once. We lengthened all the tail-wheel struts, but since there was no time to redesign and change the fuselage and doors, we let it all hang out!

About the time it chose the P-40 for production by Curtiss-Wright, the Air Force, facing the need for capacity production by all our capable fighter producers, appointed a board of officers to decide what fighter Republic would produce for the war. I've been unable to get the names of the board members, but I have a strong hunch that Lindbergh was an adviser. When the board met sometime during the summer of 1939, the XP-47 was born. It was decided to start with Pratt & Whitney's latest highest-powered engine, the 2,000-horsepower R2800, equipped with a turbosupercharger similar to the P-43 installation, then to make the airplane large enough to accommodate the big engine, plenty of fuel, armor protection, bullet-sealing tanks, and, most important, four .50 caliber machine guns in each wing. Republic quickly came up with the design and the XP-47 was ordered.

By the fall of 1940, the XP-47 was in its early flight testing. It looked great, handled well, and had good altitude performance. It was the heaviest and most powerful single-engine fighter ever built, and the test pilots at Republic were creeping carefully up on the performance envelope. We did not want to lose our single prototype. I say we. Col. Mish Roth was Project Officer on the XP-47. I was assigned to the production program. However, because production was released long before the XP-47 flew, we were both in effect the project officers.

One day we had British visitors. They were outstanding RAF officers who had weathered the Battle of Britain and had come over to work with and advise their inexperienced counterparts in the USA. A few names come to mind: Boothman, Broadhurst, Malan, Tuck. These gentlemen flew all our newer fighters and bombers. Boothman and Broadhurst later became air marshals. Wing Commander Tuck, a fearless fighting and flying character, took the XP-47 up while visiting the Long Island factory. He ignored the untried areas of XP-47 performance. He took the one and only at full power to 40,000 feet, turned it over, and dived it to terminal velocity to 15,000, pulled it out successfully, and landed, full of enthusiasm for the future of the aircraft. When he told us of his treatment of our war baby, we were in a state of shock. We could have lost them both right there. The speed and gravity forces Tuck had put the plane through were much greater than its previous pilots had yet attempted. Later we too had pilots like Tuck, but they did not begin to appear until we were at war. I'd say Dave Shilling, Buzz Wagner, Dick Bong, Tom McGuire, Bob Hoover, and a lot more took over in the United States where Tuck and his friends left off in the RAF.

After our struggle with the P-35, P-43, and the P-40, we were well prepared for any ground-looping problems we might find in the XP-47, but to our great relief there were none. The Jug's landing roll was as stable as the landing roll of nosewheel aircraft in which all ground-looping tendencies are completely eliminated. Why? Because it had a low ground angle. The plane was longer and had relatively short main landing-gear struts so that when sitting on three points, its wing to runway angle was considerably less than that of the P-43 and P-40, even with their tails raised ten inches. The fact that the P-47's main gear was spread quite far apart undoubtedly helped, too. But the ground angle was the primary reason for the stability. Had we understood this sooner, we could have retrofitted the P-35s as well as the P-43s and P-40s.

Testing the XP-47 proceeded and we were finally ready to start production. Tail troubles developed in some of the early production models, and a few planes were lost. No such problem had been encountered in the XP-47, which we must assume had a stronger tail. Unfortunately, adding a stronger tail and making other necessary changes had increased the weight of the rear part of the airplane, resulting in a shift of the center of gravity to the rear and a consequent deterioration in stability. It goes without saying that with the loss of stability, an aircraft becomes dangerous. In a high-speed dive when a pullout is attempted, the airplane may tend to tighten up the pullout to the point of failing the wings or tail because of over G and resulting overstress. This, then, was the problem facing the P-47 in late 1941.

We had nothing we could remove. Every item of equipment in the P-47 was essential. (I can personally vouch for that.) Relocation of the battery was studied but was deemed to be of insufficient effect. We tried a "bob weight" installation, a lever with a heavy weight on its end, fastened to the control stick in such a way that gravity acts on the weight to push the stick forward; at the same time, during a pullout from a dive, because the center of gravity is at the rear of the plane, gravity is trying to pull the stick back. Today's bob weights are electronic, but ours then was strictly mechanical. I did not want to start production with such a weak reed in my bow.

As so often happened in those days, the Republic engineers came through practically overnight. They built a little five-inch bridge or trestle structure (or engine mount) to fasten the engine to the front of the airframe, moving the heavy engine forward five or six inches. We had it made. We had a solid, stable airplane with no tricks and no gimmicks. Production went full speed ahead.

Now, a bit of philosophizing. I want you to know that while I am not an inventor, during this period I did, with some help from Republic, outdo the developmental capabilities of the General Electric Company. Most of our fighters had only three handles on the throttle; the power lever, the mixture control, and the propeller control. However, the P-47 had an additional lever for control of the turbosupercharger. In general, it could be said that all of these levers move from the rear to the front as they go forward. It was obvious to me that we needed an engine control

---

Opposite page: The P-47D—the first of the Republic Thunderbolts to incorporate a water injection system for increased emergency power.

mechanism that would give us proper performance of all four functions by moving one handle. I gave the powerful and talented General Electric Company a contract to produce such a control. Unhappily, General Electric worked on the problem until all the money was spent but failed to produce a workable control.

In the meantime, I had talked the problem over with the Republic and asked them to try the idea of a mechanical link between the control levers. As an interim measure, we came up with a way of interconnecting the levers mechanically so that with the proper rigging at least the change from idle to full power and back could be done by pushing only one lever. This we did by adding some retractable ears to the throttle-control arm so that, when down, the ears moved all controls forward and backward. When the ears were pushed upward out of the way, the control levers worked separately. As far as I know, all P-47s delivered, except an early few, had this throttle control. The pilots used it and General Electric missed a bet for some added business. The air force had a simple, inexpensive control that never failed, and the pilot could use it or not at his own discretion.

From what I have seen of the wildly escalating complexities and costs of today's aircraft and weapons, we need more inexpensive and simple solutions like this.

At about this time we got into the conflict by way of the Japanese war lords' audacity. The P-47 production line was gaining momentum and a few production prototypes were almost completed. One of these contained the first production-designed armament installation: eight .50 caliber machine guns with 500 rounds per gun, with nicely designed, quickly detachable mounts—the heaviest fire power ever before placed in a production fighter aircraft. The Japs hit us on the 7th of December, and by the end of the month I had the armament airplane at Patterson Field for the first firing.

The reason for taking the P-47 to Wright-Patterson Field was twofold. First, the armament experts, a Mr. Ferguson and Earl Hatcher, were there. They knew the .50 caliber machine gun better than anyone in the world. Second, there was an old World War I firing butt down on the eastern edge of Patterson Field where we could do the shooting.

I won't forget New Year's morning 1942. The two of us—my head and I—rose long before daylight and went down to the P-47 parking spot in a pouring rain. I climbed into the Jug and prepared to start the engine for taxiing to the butt. On my first attempt to start the engine, all 2,000 horsepower of it backfired—an explosion so violent that it shattered an experimental plywood duct that ran from the rear-positioned supercharger through the cockpit floor. In spite of the size of my head, I had been able to don helmet and goggles, but my hands and face looked as though I had gone sliding down a cellar door upside down.

In case you're wondering about the plywood duct aluminum was very scarce at the time. The War Production Board was pressuring everyone to substitute wood for aluminum wherever possible. Wright Field had several lousy all-plywood airplanes built; for, as you know, when the pressure gets high enough people sometimes try to comply whether or not it is possible or makes any sense. That is what happened here. Needless to say, the victim of the explosion was the right man, the project officer. There was no more plywood tested or utilized in P-47s or in any supercharger duct in any planes that he had anything to do with.

Because no flight was required, after taking stock I again started the engine, this time successfully, and proceeded to the butt. The stage was set. The P-47, our cherished hope to defend us from the thousands of Zeros and Messerschmitts, was about ready to show its deadly fire power. We put the tail up on a rack and aimed at the bottom of the old pile of dirt, loaded all guns and fastened the gun covers. I climbed in and pressed the trigger. What happened was one of the greatest disappointments of my life. Instead of eight guns firing 600 rounds per minute, each with a deafening roar, we got a scattered firing of one to ten rounds from each gun, then deep silence. I finally released the trigger. First I was stunned, then depressed. Some gun mounts were broken, several guns had jumped off their mounts, and the remainder were jammed. I sat there for some time visualizing a lost war, somehow holding myself personally responsible.

It took a few days to find that the guns had been freshly delivered to the air force by Frigidaire. Because they were just starting production, their first products did not have interchangeable parts. The guns had been fired successfully after assembly, but during final teardown and reassembly, parts were scrambled, as required by the Ordnance Department. Naturally, the guns would not shoot. I should add here that Frigidaire did a great job later on.

It was probably just as well that the guns jammed that day. Of the hundred or so rounds fired, a sizable number apparently went through the old butt and scattered over Wright View Heights a mile away. Had we fired the 4,000 rounds, I'd probably be doing time!

By the end of 1942 production was such that the first two Jug wings were in England preparing to enter combat. In January 1943 I was sent over to help get them ready. I took the Clipper to Lisbon just one week before the next Clipper crashed there in landing. I was lucky; mine made it OK. In England I reported to Brig. Gen. O. D. (Monk) Hunter, head of the 8th Fighter Command at Bushey Hall outside London. A World War I fighter ace, Monk was one of our famous fighter generals. He made clear immediately what I was to do: get the P-47 radios to function properly and get more range in both the P-47 and P-51. After a later meeting with Lt. Gen. Ira Eaker, I had no doubt as to the critical nature of my mission.

We first attacked the problem of the radio. It seemed the R2800 engine ignition system and the VHF radio were completely incompatible. When the engine was running, the radio signal was drowned out by the ignition noise. I went to Debden at once and visited the 4th Fighter Group which had previously been equipped with Spitfires and manned by Americans serving in the RAF. It had formerly been called the Eagle Squadron and had an outstanding war record. Col. Ed (Andy) Anderson, an old friend from our Chanute Field days, was wing commander, and Chesley (Pete) Peterson was the group leader. They were eager to get the P-47s going but were frustrated by the radio performance. Another P-47 wing nearby, commanded by Armand (Pete) Peterson, had the same problem. Both of these Petes were exceptional leaders. Chesley, though downed at least twice in the Channel in Spits, had a notable war record and is now well and happy in retirement in Utah. Armand was lost soon after his wing went into action, and he died leading it to what became a tremendous record of success against the Luftwaffe.

It took several months, but the radio problem was eventually solved by making certain changes in the electrical system of the plane's engine. During this time at Debden I got a chance to do some flying with both the 4th and 56th, but about the time I was considered fairly well ready for a trip across the Channel, I was ordered back to Wright Field.

So I returned to Ohio in June 1943 with the radio mission accomplished with two new goals: immediate installation of bubble canopies on the P-47 and P-51, and extension of the range on both airplanes. In England I had seen what the bubble had done for the pilot's rear vision in the Spitfire. Republic installed a canopy on a P-47 in record time, and I flew the first airplane so equipped to the West Coast to show it to Dutch Kindleberger at North American Aviation Company. It wasn't long before Dutch had one going on the P-51s as well.

In a 1974 article for *Aerospace Historian*, "The P-51 over Berlin," I described at length how we managed to extend the flight range of the Mustang to make that feat possible. It is enough to say here that though the P-51 was already equipped with wing tanks, we were able to bring about a further increase in its droppable fuel capacity and resultant range by placing an additional ninety-gallon tank behind the pilot's seat. We had no such luck with the P-47.

There was no place to put more fuel in the P-47 except in droppable wing tanks. Earlier, Republic had developed what was called a "slipper tank," usable for ferrying only. Because it made the airplane unstable, it was not suitable for combat. In the end we used the same pylon and tank arrangement utilized on the P-38. The first such installation was made, not at the factory and not at Wright Field, but in Africa by Col. Claire Bunch, an enterprising officer working for Jim Doolittle.

Along toward the middle of 1943, our government allocated 100 P-47s to the Russians. They were to get the airplanes in January 1944, and in making arrangements for their delivery, I experienced the kind of Soviet negotiating we have seen many times since. In mid-1943 General Arnold decided we had the war won. It turned out he was correct, but at the time I certainly wasn't sure. Anyway, to show the enemy and the world our confidence, the General ordered all camouflage removed from new production air force aircraft. His order became effective in the fall of 1943. With a production rate of 600 a month, it was not possible to make any sort of special arrangement to leave the paint on the ones for Uncle Joe. So I went to the Russian colonel at Wright Field and presented him with the following proposition: they could have their 100 aircraft in January without camouflage, or, if they demanded the paint, we would have to have it done after delivery at the factory and they would get them in February. "Which do you want?"

The colonel was very polite. He said he would wire home for the answer. In about a week, he came back, "We want them in January with camouflage on." And such was their power in Washington—that's what they got!

By the summer of 1943 I had taken the P-47 and P-51 as far as they were to go when I was transferred from the fighter business and made Chief of the Flight Test Section. There I flew all the foreign fighters we had come by (FW-190, Me-109) as well as the new experimental planes being worked on by our development people, including the XP-59, our first jet, and the B-29 bomber.

All during the war our development people were up against a tough problem. Until the late 1930s aircraft development consisted of three main features: cleaning up drag through sleeker design, adding power (bigger engines with more power at altitude), and increasing size and carrying power for either loads or armament. Improvement in some of these areas tended to level out in the late 1930s. The piston engine was a definite limitation. For example, the Pratt & Whitney 4360 was about as big as a fighter airplane could accept. It had more power; but with its outsized propeller, size, and weight it was unable to provide much more speed than the previous smaller, lighter engines. We were fast approaching a point of diminishing returns in the development of bigger, more powerful, piston engines. Cleanliness of design had gone far, but again the propeller contributed to drag. Faced with doing the job with what we had, the piston engine, our designers began to experiment with rearrangement of the components or the elimination of parts. Toward the end of the war, we saw the XP-55, the Curtiss Ascender (we called it the Assender). It was a tail-first airplane, having the same general power setup but with a pusher propeller and the horizontal tail out front. I had a flight in it. It had about the same performance as comparably powered fighters, but its lack of stability and handling difficulties gave me the feeling of sitting astride a powder keg. I was glad to get it on the ground.

Another innovation was the tailless design. We had a fighter and a bomber. I flew an early model, a small tailless test vehicle, and had an even greater feeling of the powder keg. Once more landing was a pleasure. With apologies to my friend Jack Northrop, it seems to me that a tail is a very fine thing to have on an airplane. It balances the wing and, if of proper size and location, gives the plane needed stability. In addition, the intervening fuselage, which must connect it to the wing, is an ideal place to put things—from people to bombs.

A perfect example of trying to do the job better by rearrangement was the P-39. Larry Bell and Bob Wood came up with the idea of putting the engine behind the pilot and driving the propeller and forward-mounted gear box by means of a drive shaft that ran forward between the pilot's legs. I recall Larry's saying that one reason the P-39 would be an outstanding fighter was the location of the engine, the biggest weight in the airplane, on the center of gravity. But we young pursuit pilots viewed the design with grave apprehension. We did not like the idea of the flex shaft travelling forward between the pilot's knees. What if it broke? Well, to this day I've never heard of one that did.

Although the flex drive shaft always performed well, that is not to say we had no trouble with the rest of the aircraft. Though at first glance Larry's proposition seemed to make sense, a little bit of analysis and experience proved the opposite. At the center of gravity it is far better to have the disposable load—the fuel, oil, and ammunition—not the engine or the pilot. In the case of the P-39, there was gasoline in front of the center of gravity, and all of the cannon ammunition was stored somewhat forward. This meant that firing of the cannon or using certain tanks of gas would lighten the forward load and make the airplane more and more tail heavy. The P-39 was famous for what pilots called "tumbling," a series of violent snap rolls or stalls, no doubt caused by depletion of ammunition up forward and too much fuel in the rear.

As Chief of Flight Test, I inherited the B-29 engines that overheated and sometimes caught fire. My coworkers were Col. Ozzie Ritland, Bob Ruegg, and Harney Estes. (Harney was later lost in the Far East while I was in Okinawa just after the war.) One of our tasks was to put time at high power on a B-29, testing the improved engine-cooling equipment being incorporated in the field. We flew the tail off that airplane at high power (highest authorized continuous) and never had a failure. We flew it all day long for several months with no more problems.

When there was a slack hour or so, just for relaxation we flew the old XB-19, then recently equipped with four 2,400-horsepower, 24-cylinder Allison engines. It was relatively slow and had a built-in delay in the elevators. That is, when one moved the wheel back in order to climb, nothing would happen for perhaps five to six seconds, then the nose would start up. Test pilot Maj. Stanley Umstead discovered this peculiarity the hard way when he took the plane up for its first flight several years earlier at Santa Monica. It was natural to keep pulling farther and farther back to get some reaction. When he finally got it, the nose went up—way, way up, and rapidly. He damned near lost the airplane. But Stanley was a great pilot and managed to get it under control. Later he was able to tell the rest of us about the lag so that we could act accordingly. But enough of these bomber stories. I'm really a fighter man at heart.

In late 1944 I received orders to France to join the 1st Tactical Air Force (Provisional). I never found out why it was provisional; it certainly didn't sound very permanent. But permanent or not, it put out a tremendous war effort. The war in Europe was rapidly folding as the Germans retreated on all fronts. The Battle of the Bulge was just winding down as I got to Vittel, headquarters for the 1st TAC at the time. That fine fighting unit had come all the way from North Africa via Marseilles, supporting General Patch's 7th Army. Gen. Ralph Royce was commanding when I arrived. Here I was—a fighter pilot, a test pilot, a project engineer—arriving very late in a war where the things I had been producing, testing, and flying were being used in battle. The crews and pilots were old hands; I was a newcomer. It wasn't easy!

My first assignment was to help the French Air Force Service Command, then at Besancon, with the support of their aircraft. While there, I was able to go over to Dijon where Brig. Gen. John Doyle had a B-26 bomber wing. I got out on a couple of B-26 missions, including a big one in February on which the entire enemy front was saturated with Allied airplanes. No German fighters were seen, only scattered antiaircraft. Victory was close.

One day while working with the French air force, I had reason to fly into Nancy where an American P-47 wing was operating. Soon after I arrived in early January, I landed a C-45 on the snow-covered Nancy runway, and while taxiing down toward the far end between the walls of piled-up snow at the runway edges, we saw a P-47 coming in on his downwind leg for an emergency landing, engine on fire, smoke and flames engulfing the entire plane. He was deadstick and had only one place to land—right where we were. No more taxiing to the runway end, we had to clear! So we headed at full speed for a wall of snow. Just as our tail cleared the right half of the runway, the Jug slid past down safely. It was my first contact with my old friend P-47 for some time.

As the war continued to wind down, I was called back to Vittel and assigned to set up support for the 358th Fighter Wing at a sand strip on an old GAF base called Sandhofen, near Mannheim on the Rhine. The 358th Group, equipped with P-47Ds, was commanded by Col. Jim Tipton, an outstanding fighter commander. After working for a few days at getting bombs and ammunition stores in proper shape, I managed a couple of P-47 missions with the wing, Tipton leading. The strafing mission was interesting. We had about fourteen or sixteen aircraft, and we swept the countryside for about 150 miles toward Berlin. I had known that the technique, particularly when flying at low altitude, was to weave and turn continually. Well, that we did, and violently, too. There was little movement on the ground. No enemy aircraft, some ground antiaircraft, but mostly weak, no losses. We shot up a bunch of railroad cars and locomotives, mostly stopped before we arrived. We saw one soldier on a motorcycle scooting down a narrow street through a small village. A couple of P-47s went after him, but I felt relieved when I saw bullets hitting all around him and not getting him. When we passed, he was still riding like all hell. I was glad he got away. He was no challenge, and he could do no harm to us or our armies. My P-47 flew like a dream. When we landed at Sandhofen, the Crew Chief found what looked like a .45 caliber slug sticking in my tailpipe. I don't know when or where I got it.

Opposite page: Another P-47D.

The second mission was a bombing and escort trip to Friederich-shaven on the Baden Sea. When we got there an overcast had moved over the target, and for some reason, we not only did not drop our 500-pound bombs but we took them back to Sandhofen. I am sure Jim Tipton felt it foolish to drop them indiscriminately as had often been done in the past when the target was denied. It was easy to see this war was won. Once more I had been able to see my P-47s in action, escorting the bombers, but there was little or no drama.

Recently I wrote to Jim, who is enjoying a leisurely retirement in Alabama, asking him to comment on the Jug. His answer: "It was the greatest ground attack aircraft in the war, without a doubt. It took punishment like no other and delivered firepower, guns, and bombs with authority and versatile attack techniques unlimited. Indeed, it is doubtful if we ever achieved its full potential in that respect. With most of our effort devoted to dogfighting ground units, we sighted our eight guns to converge at 1,000 yards, for example, and psychologically sledge-hammered army units and equipment."

In 1945 we moved to Okinawa, and after a short time the war ended. We moved into Japan right after General McArthur and set up headquarters at Johnson Field, then the Irrumigawa Air Base, an old primary flying school for the Japanese. I flew our headquarters P-51 up from Oki and was glad to get on the ground. There were no radio aids, and I had to do the last 200 miles over the clouds. I'm probably not the first pilot who was tickled pink to see Fuji rising above the clouds and to find a hole just beyond it over Tokyo Bay.

About this time General Ennis C. Whitehead was appointed Far East Air Force Commander, and I became 5th Air Force Chief of Staff, but not for long. I was just getting used to some fairly plush living in Tokyo when General Whitehead told me I was to go back to Okinawa (February 1, 1946) to take over the 301st Fighter Wing under the overall command in Oki of Brig. Gen. Pat Timberlake. And guess what—the fighter wing was equipped with P-47Ns. The N was a P-47 which had been put into production after I left the production business. It had more fuel and more wing, and hence was a lot heavier than the predecessors. It was so heavy it could hardly be called a fighter, but it was all we had to protect Okinawa. It had about the same rate of climb as an empty C-47 Gooney Bird. If you're asking, "Who needed to protect Okinawa with the war won?" the answer is that you obviously never worked for General Whitehead!

Along with the P-47Ns, I took on a wing that had no experienced airmen for mechanics. To a man, the mechanics who had been there all the way from Australia had been sent home. I had several hundred willing but inexperienced ex-machine-gunners released to the Air Force from Army ground units. In addition, I had about seventy young pilots who had just finished flying training. Most had never flown a P-47N prior to arrival in Okinawa. I did have some good senior lieutenant colonels and a couple of colonels, among them Stetson, Coleman, McCombre, Keeling, and Cory. Instead of fighting, they had spent the war in the training command. They were in Okinawa hoping at last to get into the war when it all ended. We had to improvise everything. There were no skilled mechanics, so we had the pilots crew their own airplanes. They did pretty well, except for two or three bad accidents, which I always felt might have been averted had we had more experienced maintenance.

I was happy to have command of a fighter wing, and a wing of P-47s at that; but living and working conditions there at that time were pretty rugged. What little had been built during the short period after Okinawa had been captured was wiped out by the September 1945 typhoon. My whole wing was in tents. We were based at Yontan Airstrip, which had no hangars and no buildings of any kind, just a coral strip 6,000 feet long. We started to build. First, we needed a water system with filtration. A team of lieutenants built one: welded sheet steel tanks, midnight-requisitioned from the navy, pumps and all. It took water right out of the Bishagawa Creek and made it potable. The mess where we ate was ghastly. I fired the so-called mess officer and put a fighter pilot named Green in his place. The mess improved.

Later, the only ice the airmen's and officers' clubs could get was from two lieutenant fighter pilots who had managed to come by an ice machine, had set it up in an old bashed-in Okinawa house, and had gone into business. These two entrepreneurs I found to be furnishing a regular supply of ice to at least two clubs and receiving a regular payment of so many bottles of booze a week in return. This sort of operation is not routine in the air force. So when I heard about it, I called these two icemaker pilots into my headquarters and said, "I understand you gentlemen have an ice machine with which you are supplying ice to the wing. Is this correct?"

"Yes, sir."

"Well, great! I think you deserve commendation for your diligence, and further I'm going to appoint you Wing Ice Officers. Henceforth it will be your duty to furnish ice to the wing, in addition to your flying duties." It worked beautifully, but the profit from their enterprise fell off dramatically.

During the next eight or nine months, we put up Quonset huts for mess halls, headquarters, clubs, living quarters, and latrines. And we set up a retractable flag pole that could be laid on the ground when typhoon danger approached. To accomplish all this, we used for some time about 100 Japanese POWs who were more than happy to be alive and put in a full day for a full belly. Obviously we had some time off, especially during the rather frequent passage of typhoons. During one of these I remember a day-and-night long-endurance game of bridge held in my shack. About midnight, the wind still screaming and the rain coming down by bucketfuls, we decided to call the game because of dealer incompetence. The long cocktail hour had resulted in one player's receiving seventeen cards on the deal.

Although we worked hard, I am afraid we were not very combat ready. We tried though. Finally, after a year of effort, we managed to "intercept" a B-29 coming in at 30,000 feet over the island. The boys had been trying for a long time but couldn't get up there fast enough. Their technique had been to climb at maximum power toward the reported position of the incoming bomber, but it would always go over them before they reached 30,000 feet. I didn't tell my staff, but I figured if I climbed directly over the target instead of toward the incoming bomber, I'd have more time to get to 30,000 feet. Well, it worked. But with the B-29 speed at that height, it was still almost impossible. General Whitehead, who had been less than understanding about our inability to intercept, was pleased, and I made a little hay in the eyes of my 301st wing pilots, too. I think that was the very last time I flew a P-47.

I was ordered home in November 1946, and so ended my association with the Jug. I respected it and I loved it!

Gen. Mark E. Bradley retired from active duty in 1965 after more than thirty-five years of service.

CG-4A Glider

Arthur J. Thomas

Soar to Victory on the Silent Wings of a Glider: Become a Glider Pilot in the U.S. Army Air Corps. Thus read the USAAF recruiting pamphlet released in the spring of 1942. That we played a part in the victory has been established. Our capability for "soaring to victory," however, left much to be desired.

Generally, if in the spring of 1942 you were between the ages of eighteen and thirty-five, could walk and talk, and were warm, you qualified as a glider pilot candidate. But not in my case! Having initially been rejected for being six pounds underweight, I ate thirty cents worth of bananas and drank lots of water before my next examination. When told that I was still underweight, I could no longer hold the load and proceeded to dirty up the gymnasium floor where the physicals were being held. The kindly old physician smiled and said, "Sonny, if you want it that badly, you're in!"

The CG-4A—designated Glider, Heavy Transport—was strictly a utility glider with little or none of the soaring capabilities attributed to its little sister, the high-performance sailplane. With an aspect ratio of 8.2 and a sink rate approaching 950 feet per minute at 100 miles per hour, there was only one way for the CG-4A to go after tow release—down!

When first introduced to the CG-4A at South Plains Army Air Field, Lubbock, Texas, in mid-1943, I was immediately impressed in two ways. First, it was the largest aircraft most of us had ever seen; second, if not the largest, it had to be the ugliest!

The CG-4A, designed to be used for troop and cargo transport, was a strut-braced high-wing cabin monoplane. It had a wing span of eighty-three feet, eight inches and a wing area of approximately 852 square feet. The overall length was forty-eight feet, three inches. Empty weight was

Opposite page: Attaching a towline to a glider.

3,089 pounds; with a useful load of 3,711 pounds total gross weight was 6,800 pounds. The nose could be opened upward; when the glider was equipped with tactical landing gear, a jeep could be driven inside and securely fastened for transport in a very few minutes. Pilot and copilot were seated side by side. The seating arrangement along the sides of the aisle accommodated thirty fully equipped soldiers. Entrance doors on the right and left of the fuselage aft of the wing were sufficiently wide for a fully armed man to walk through with ease. Emergency exits on each side of the fuselage were located under the wings. Visibility was generally good for the pilot and copilot, and there were six round observation windows along each side of the fuselage. The tech manual stated: "These windows are to help minimize airsickness on the part of the airborne troops. . . . men aft of the center of gravity tend to become airsick very easily." There were two racks of sanitary containers in the ship for this possibility.

Wing construction was conventional for that time—two-spar wood construction, fabric covered, and built in four sections for quick disassembly. The wing planform was straight with elliptical tips and little or no dihedral. Fuselage construction, square in cross section, was of welded steel tubing with a plywood honeycomb floor and fabric cover. One peculiarity was in the landing gear: the takeoff gear was to be jettisoned after leaving the ground and the landing was to be made on wooden skids under each side of the belly. On gliders used for training purposes, a more permanent landing gear was added, with brakes and shock absorbers; but in the original design of the glider the added strain of the training gear was not included in the fuselage structure, so it was quite easy to pull the landing gear loose on rough landings. The tech manual noted that "this weakness should be kept in mind and rough landings should be prevented as much as possible."

The aircraft had dual-control wheels arranged side by side, and it could be trimmed in respect to all three axes with three separate trim tab controls above and between the pilot and copilot seats. Instruments consisted of an airspeed indicator, a sensitive altimeter, bank and turn indicator, and rate of climb indicator; a few had a two-way radio, which was generally not in operating condition.

Another unique feature of the CG-4A was the spoilers. With this device the pilot was able to kill off a large percentage of the lift created by the modified Clark-Y airfoil. A lever was located on the outboard side of each seat in the cockpit, so either the pilot or the copilot could activate the spoilers. Use of the spoilers could increase the rate of descent from a normal 950 feet per minute at 100 miles per hour to as much as 1,600 feet per minute. Thus the glider pilot soon learned to plan all approaches on the long or high side so that in the final moments before touchdown the spoilers could be utilized to put the glider on the intended spot.

The CG-4A was to be flown not more than 25° up, 20° down, or 20° to the right or left of the extended longitudinal axis of the tow ship. Maximum indicated airspeed was placarded at 120 miles per hour. Minimum load was a pilot, copilot, and 600 pounds of ballast—300 pounds located immediately behind each pilot seat.

As was standard in nearly all training programs of the day, before the student pilot began his transition flying, he was required to spend at least one hour of familiarization in the cockpit of the CG-4A. We used gliders grounded for repairs to learn the location of the trim tabs, and their action when turned to the right or left was memorized. Blindfolded, we had to demonstrate to the instructor that we could locate the airspeed indicator and altimeter.

During this period we were impressed with the necessity for promptness in checking out parachutes and being in the assigned gliders as soon as possible after receiving our assignments for the day. In spite of the fact that we had spent thirteen months to complete ten weeks of training up to this point, we were informed that time was not expendable and every minute of delay was holding up the training program.

At last the big day arrived! We were terribly excited at the prospect of finally flying the glider that was to be our combat airplane. Comfortable seating in the CG-4A for the pilot depended to a great extent on how large he was and how many pillows were available. The seat itself was not adjustable, either up and down or fore and aft. After finding a reasonably comfortable position, probably the first thing we noted was the extreme cockpit roominess. Never before had we flown in an airplane where two pilots sat side by side with room between for another pilot, and off our outside elbows it was at least twelve or fourteen inches to the outside wall of the cockpit.

Although our span was almost as large as the Lockheed Lodestar tow plane, our pre-takeoff checklist was extremely simple: "Control checks off and securely fastened, pitot tube uncovered, controls checked for full movement, read the form 1-A status of the aircraft, safety belt fastened, 300-pound ballast in place and properly fastened, trim tabs set to neutral, meter pin flush in the towrope release mechanism, altimeter set, brakes off, ailerons in neutral position." When this had been accomplished, the pilot gave the signal to the ground crewman, who in turn relayed it to the tow plane, and the Lodestar started to take up the slack in the rope.

Initially, the control wheel was held in the full back position to apply up elevator, so if the tow plane took up the rope slack too quickly there would be some assistance in keeping the glider from nosing over and riding on the skids. The towline fastening on the glider was mounted high on the nose, and there was quite a tendency for the glider to nose over on the initial pull of the tow plane. As the glider began to move, the wheel was moved gently forward until the glider was in level position, rolling on the landing gear. Enough rudder was used to keep the glider directly behind the tow ship; when a sixty-mile-per-hour airspeed was reached, the wheel was gently eased back until the glider was approximately twenty feet above the runway. At this point it was necessary to ease the wheel forward so that the glider was in a slight diving attitude to put a slack in the towline, thus allowing the tow plane to leave the runway. After the tow plane was airborne the glider was flown level until the tow plane came up to its proper position, which was just below that of the glider. If the glider was flown too high immediately after takeoff, the tow ship was unable to leave the runway. Takeoff commenced with the elevator trim tabs in a moderately nose-down position. As the glider gained airspeed there was an appreciable nose trim effect. The glider student was cautioned, however, to devote his undivided attention to keeping proper tow position and to signal the copilot or instructor to trim the nose or wings immediately after takeoff if that were desirable. A more experienced glider pilot was able to make the takeoff with one hand and trim the aircraft with the other.

Techniques for takeoff were slightly different when the glider was fully loaded. The glider pilot had to bear in mind that the tow ship was dragging $3\frac{1}{2}$ tons of weight, in addition to the full load of the tow ship itself, and needed every assistance. We were cautioned not to increase drag by climbing too fast during the early stages but to wait until the tow ship had accelerated to its approximate liftoff speed; then by increasing the angle of attack we slowly transferred the weight from the landing gear to the wing so that the glider left the ground at approximately the same time as the tow plane.

In anticipation of problems due to our lack of experience in flying aircraft with side-by-side seating, the tech manual cautioned pilots that they were sitting approximately eighteen inches to the left of the longitudinal axis of the glider and hence the same distance to the left of the point where the towrope connected. "By leaning to the right and sighting along the towrope the glider student can easily see if he is lined up with the center of the tow ship fuselage; if not, he can correct his posi-

---

Opposite page: A towed glider leaving the ground.

tion accordingly." We found that this maneuver of leaning over toward the center of the glider in an attempt to line up the towrope with the tow aircraft increased the chances of vertigo, particularly during night flying.

Danger of taking off in a low tow position was emphasized. "Added drag of the prop wash could on occasion cause a towrope failure. On the takeoff the [glider] pilot should always be ready to release the towrope in the event one of the tow ship's motors failed or if the tow ship encountered difficulty leaving the runway." If the towrope were to break, the procedure was immediate release, to prevent the dragging rope from catching on obstructions on the ground. The only path left for the glider pilot in such an emergency was to make the best possible landing. If a glider was flown low enough to get into the prop wash during takeoff, it was difficult to control and much additional strain was placed on the towrope. Flown too high, the towrope became taut and exerted an upper pull on the tow ship's tail. The best position to fly was that which maintained constant sag in the towrope and constant airspeed.

The bank and turn indicator needle was the only cockpit indication of a good towing position. The needle was centered with rudder, the ball centered with aileron, and any pressures relieved by proper trimming. Occasionally a wing became so heavy that slight pressure would be required on the opposite aileron to maintain proper attitude even with full trim corrections. In smooth air light pressure on the controls was all that was required; the prime difficulty of beginning students was overcontrolling. The cargo glider tended to oscillate while on tow; this characteristic was not experienced in the sailplanes and other light gliders we had previously flown. We soon learned that the tendency to overcorrect would result in an increasing oscillation, and we learned to pick up the low wing with the opposite rudder and use as little aileron as possible. To stop the oscillation after it had started, slight cross-controlling was necessary. This was almost identical to the corrective action taken today to stop the "Dutch roll" of the Boeing 707. In moderate turbulence the tow plane and glider bounced around considerably, and heavy pressure and large control movements were required to make the glider respond when the air was gusty. Keeping the glider in proper tow position required undivided attention on the part of the glider pilot, and on tows of longer than half an hour it was recommended that the copilot take over for a few minutes to give the pilot a chance to rest his eyes and look around.

Turns presented no particular problem as long as the pilot could clearly see the tow plane. As the tow plane started a bank for a turn, the glider pilot did likewise, matching the angle of bank observed. Very little control pressure was required to bank the glider; when the desired bank had been accomplished, a slight pressure in the opposite direction was required to prevent overbanking. In climbs a glider pilot maintained his position slightly above the tow plane, and during descent moderate use of the spoilers dissipated altitude without excessive diving.

The most crucial thing a glider pilot had to learn—and learn well—was the determination of the tow release point. The critical factors involved in this decision were altitude, surface winds, and the path of the tow plane during the final moments.

The CG-4A had a gliding ratio of 9.25 in calm air at 100 miles per hour, but it covered well over 12 feet forward for every foot lost at our normal 70 miles per hour glide. Indication of surface winds can be quite misleading. As is well known, a wind velocity of twenty to thirty miles an hour on the ground can be considerably higher at altitude. In stronger winds glide speed was increased from the normal 70 miles per hour to 100 in order to cover any appreciable distance over the ground. At 100 miles per hour the rate of descent approached 950 feet per minute. In these conditions the glide ratio was reduced to as little as four to five feet of forward distance to every foot of loss of altitude. A pilot cutting loose downwind from the field in winds of high velocity had very little opportunity to plan an approach and land in the designated area. If the tow plane failed to put the glider in the proper position on the upwind side at the prearranged altitude for release, the glider pilot could elect to stay on tow until a position was attained from which he could make a safe landing in the designated area. Except in an emergency, the glider pilot always made the tow release decision.

Prior to release, the glider was pulled up gently to slightly above the normal tow position and all slack taken out of the towrope. The glider was then put into a moderate dive to create slack for releasing. Excessive speed was used to gain additional altitude if required. As the airspeed settled down to approximately 70, trim tabs were adjusted so that the glider would fly "hands off."

Training maneuvers consisted of coordination exercises (rolling the aircraft about its axis with the nose on the horizon). The practice of stalls involved a very gentle entry with the ailerons in a neutral position. After the nose dropped below the horizon, it was necessary to pull the wheel gently back again to establish a normal glide speed. Much time was devoted to the practice of needle-width 360° turns at a constant speed of 70 miles per hour. However, it should be pointed out that a large radius was necessary to make a needle-width turn and that the loss of altitude was considerable. If this type of turn was used in a landing pattern, it was extremely difficult to plan a rectangular approach from a key altitude.

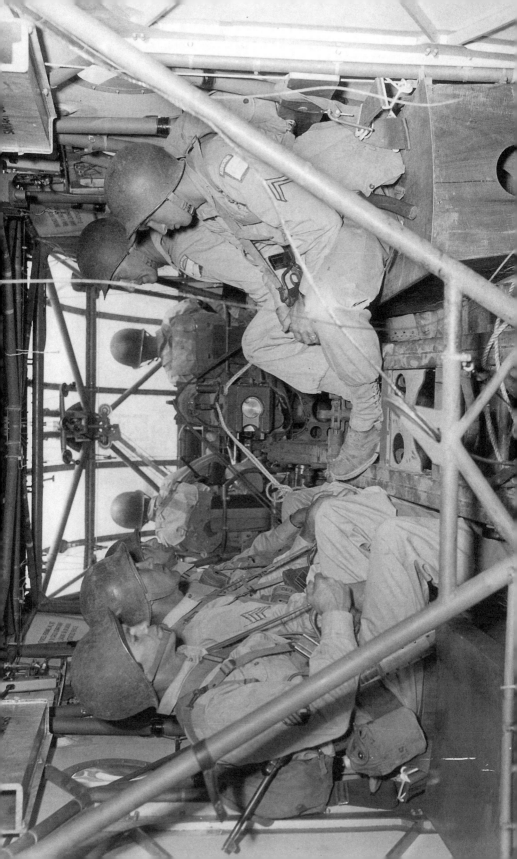

This was compounded by the fact that there was not time to observe the traffic and judge the velocity of the wind while on the base leg. Three-needle-width turns were far more practical. In a three-needle-width turn at seventy miles per hour altitude loss approximated 400 feet in 360° of turn or 100 feet in a 90° turn. Therefore, in traffic patterns steep coordinated turns were used. The lazy-8 maneuver in a glider was not too different from the lazy-8 in most other airplanes. At 90–100 miles per hour, the glider was put into a 20° bank toward the checkpoint, and the nose lifted in a coordinated climbing turn. As a near-stall condition was reached at the top of the 8, the nose was eased through the checkpoint; during the downward swing almost full aileron travel was required to maintain the proper altitude, and this pressure gradually eased off as the glider gained the speed necessary for the second half of the 8. This was the only maneuver the glider was stressed for other than steep turns and gentle stalls.

Under no condition was a cargo glider to be allowed to spin or get the nose high enough for it to "whip stall." We did find later in the overseas limited-supervision environment that the CG-4A would perform a beautiful loop. If executed immediately after a tow release, two loops could be performed with practically no loss of altitude. During a contest among unemployed glider pilots at Guidonia Airfield in Italy a record of fifteen loops was accomplished off a high-speed tow from a release point some 3,500 feet above the runway. The holder of this dubious honor did contact the ground on the final pullout, tore off the landing gear, and caused one wing to collapse. In addition his landing roll was somewhat shortened.

The normal landing pattern was a rectangular side approach; the glider entered downwind at 1,200 feet, passed abeam of the landing spot at 1,000 feet, turned onto the base leg at 800 feet, and completed the final approach turn at 400 feet. This was entirely theoretical; the size of the field, velocity of the wind, and the load carried were the ultimate deciding factors. On days with a wind velocity of more than twenty miles per hour, the base leg was made just outside the landing area, the approach purposely high, with spoilers used during final approach. Student pilots were taught forward slips, but this was considered an emergency maneuver; spoilers were preferred on both the base and final approach. Final approach speed (well over stalling speed) ran 70–90 miles per hour, depending on the load. Touchdown was approximately sixty. The CG-4A fully loaded was never glided at less than eighty, and a speed around ninety was preferred.

Opposite page: Inside a CG-4A.

Landings from a 200-foot-altitude tow release both straight ahead and with a 90° turn into final approach were practiced, but only after the student pilot had at least three hours of experience in the airplane.

A third type of approach, known as the "dive approach," was taught as a result of experience in the British heavy glider training program. It was designated as a measure to avoid fire from enemy ground defenses. In this approach the glider peeled off from an altitude of 1,000–2,000 feet and dived at a predetermined spot on the ground, as much as a mile from the intended landing point. Before diving the pilot made a mental picture of the intended flight path. After pulling out of the dive as close to the ground as possible, the pilot hedgehopped over and around obstructions until he arrived "unexpectedly" at the landing zone. This approach—though considered very effective—allowed very little margin for pilot error in estimating wind strength, flight path, and excessive speed necessary.

No discussion of the approaches of the CG-4A would be complete without some mention of the "Curry glide" (named after Colonel Curry who was its greatest exponent). Actually it should have been called the "Curry mush." Colonel Curry's objective was to land the glider with the shortest possible landing roll after touchdown; thus the Curry glide was a minimum airspeed approach. Because of the positioning of the pitot tube on the CG-4A, the airspeed indicator was of little value on this approach; when it was properly accomplished, the airspeed indications fluctuated quite widely. The best point of reference the pilot had was the bottom surface of the wing out near the wing tip. When this surface indicated a positive angle of attack as related to the horizon beyond, he was approaching the proper attitude. This actually produced a flight condition of riding just on the burble of the approaching stall. The burble felt in the ailerons was probably the best indication of the proper glide speed. The maneuver was quite successful in reducing the amount of ground run. The CG-4A in this configuration could be landed over a fifty foot obstacle and stopped with less than 300 feet of ground roll without use of wheel brakes. Unfortunately, since the rate of sink was around 1,500 feet per minute, quite often the gear collapsed on touchdown. In this case, landing roll was considerably shortened.

Perhaps the most interesting and exciting stage of training for the glider pilot was the "night blitz landings." These were made under blackout conditions with a low-altitude release at 200 feet on a base leg followed by a 90° turn to final. The only reference point out in that big black void of a field was a smudge pot sitting on the ground. This

---

Opposite page: The cockpit of a glider.

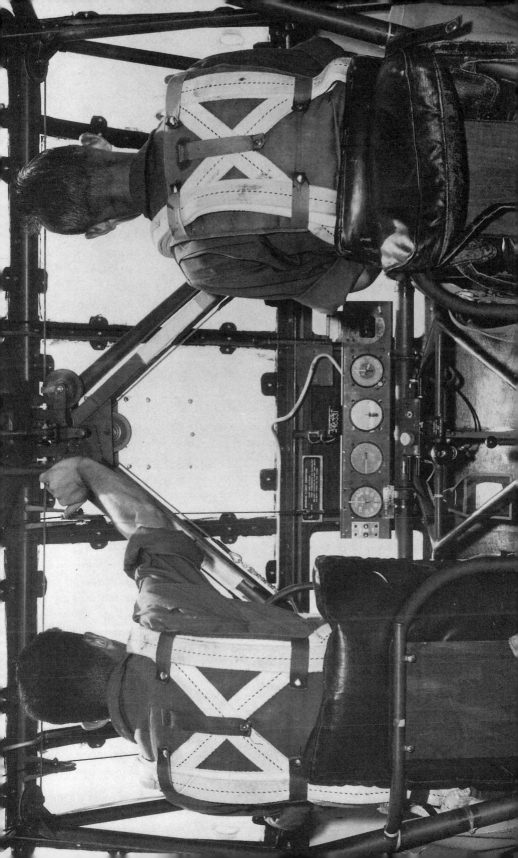

maneuver was performed with as many as twenty to twenty-five gliders which arrived at the tow release point at intervals of approximately thirty seconds. The idea was to make your turn, line up with the light on the ground, and park the aircraft so that your left wing tip was over the smudge pot. The copilot immediately jumped out of his seat, ran out the left rear door, picked up the pot, ran behind the glider, and placed the pot fifteen feet outboard of the right wing tip. Thus the next aircraft in line would have a designated parking position. It was not unusual for the pilot turning final and lining up on the smudge pot to see the light all of a sudden jump up and follow an erratic course approximately 110 feet to the right. Taking this element of surprise into his mental calculations he readjusted his estimate of his final destination and realigned the glider on final approach so that he could wind up with the light under his left wing tip. Shortly after touchdown, during the landing roll, he might again see the light picked up and moved to the right. Not infrequently after an evening of this maneuver, the glider program shut down for a day or two so that maintenance could catch up on their repair work.

The only emergency procedure discussed at any length in regard to glider flying concerned an error in judgment on the part of the pilot. From the Cessna-produced tech manual dated December 17, 1942:

> If the pilot sees that he made an error in judgment, the first consideration is to save the equipment and thereby prevent injury to himself and his passengers. In a strong headwind the speed of the glider must be increased to 100 to 120 miles per hour to make any headway over the ground. If it is evident that the glider will hit a fence or other obstruction at the normal gliding speed, the speed should be increased by pointing the nose down at the top of the obstruction and a few seconds before reaching it pulling the wheel back gently and zooming over. It is possible to lift the glider from 50 to 100 feet in this manner with an airspeed of 100 miles an hour. Do not fly along at sixty miles and guess whether or not the glider will clear the obstruction. Put the nose on the object and make certain that it will clear by lifting over it at the proper time.

Surely the Cessna writers had good intentions, but I have yet to see or hear of a case where this emergency procedure actually succeeded. An error in judgment invariably resulted in a horizontal fence, a demolished outhouse, or a bashed-in chicken coop as well as a very sick glider. [I used to do this with the Cessna Crane in 1944; it was a new maneuver to the RCAF!—Editor]

A typical cargo glider combat mission took place on August 15, 1944, when some seventy-five tow planes and their gliders left Rosignano Air Field just west of Rome at 3:30 in the afternoon for the invasion of southern France. A low altitude was flown en route to preclude detection by enemy radar, which had recently been installed in the Genoa area. Flight time from Rosignano to the landing area in southern France was some three hours and fifteen minutes. Arrival time over the southern coast of France was planned to allow one hour of daylight in order to make our landing, discharge our load, and set up a perimeter defense in enemy-held territory for the night.

Of the seventy-five gliders that departed on this mission, all but two made it to the area of the designated landing zones. One turned back because somebody had failed to remove the down lock pins in the C-47 tow plane under carriage. The other was literally blown out of the sky shortly after we passed checkpoint Orbitello. It was later ascertained that this glider was carrying ten drums of gasoline destined to be used in jeeps which were carried in several of the gliders.

Upon our arrival in the landing area just north and east of Frejus, France, visibility was extremely poor because of smoke from fires created by "softening up" fighter and bomber attacks, which had taken place in the area during the day. The landing area (according to intelligence reports at our premission briefing) was large, perfectly clear, and almost level. The fields designated for our landings had, however, unbeknown to the briefers, been planted in vineyards and a peach orchard. Choosing the lesser of two evils, the first fifteen or twenty gliders landed in the vineyards, which offered the least hazard to a safe landing. Those of us who were farther back in line took the peach orchard. The last few gliders had little choice of a decent landing area but did the best they could, with some rather disastrous results. The intelligence information must have been somewhat outdated!

The glider pilots had been admonished with the threat that any pilot who did not make a successful landing and leave the glider in a recoverable condition would surely sign a statement of charges for the same. An estimated seventy-five percent of the gliders were completely demolished. We soon found that it would be to our advantage to burn the gliders, after unloading their contents, to deprive enemy snipers of their protective cover. This we did, but I have not yet paid the charges.

The glider payloads, for the most part delivered in good operable condition, included miniature bulldozers, gasoline, ammunition, airborne troopers, and—of all things—a chapel organ, hymnals, and a Red Cross doughnut-making machine. Not faring so well, however, were the pilots themselves. Multiple fractures of the lower extremities were most numerous. If only somebody had told us to place our feet up on the instrument panel prior to mowing down a row of young peach trees! The fabric-covered $^3/_8$-inch plywood beneath our feet offered little protection.

The glider pilot's job after he got on the ground was that of an infantryman. During our long, drawn-out training program we had been qualified in the use of most of the armament of the foot soldier; it was not at all unusual during the early hours of that invasion to see glider pilots firing bazookas, 75-millimeter pack howitzers, 60-mmillimeter mortars, and .50-caliber air-cooled machine guns.

The CG-4A glider was a big flying machine—an ugly flying machine; it was uncomfortable, and the missions were hazardous. If ever the statement, "I wouldn't swap the experience for a million dollars nor do it again for another million dollars," was appropriate, it certainly applies here.

Lt. Col. Arthur J. Thomas was a glider pilot in World War II.

The P-40

Bruce K. Holloway

There were slightly over 15,000 P-40s produced, and they were flown by more countries of the Allied nations of World War II than any other combat aircraft. Models ranged from the B to the N production series, plus an experimental model called the Q, of which there were only one or two built. All were powered by Allison V-1710 liquid-cooled engines except the F, which had a Rolls-Royce/Packard Merlin V-1650.

The P-40 was not a spectacular performer. It was, however, except for the very early models, a rugged, simple, reliable aircraft which would take more punishment and get home safely more often than any other fighter of its era except possibly the P-47. The first encounter I had with this venerable machine was the P-40 (blank) at Wright Field in the summer of 1941. It truly was a blank, and on a couple of rare occasions when it was in commission, I was allowed to fly it. From the firewall back it was essentially identical to the P-36. However, it had less power than the P-36, was about 2,500 pounds heavier, was aerodynamically less stable, had about half the rate of climb, had 7,000 or 8,000 feet less service ceiling, but slightly more range, and possibly had a few mph more speed under ideal conditions. I don't recall whether there was any armament in this first model, which I believe had an X designation, but the B had six guns. This was three times as many as the P-36, but they were not very reliable. There were two .30-caliber guns in each wing, and two .50s firing through the propeller. All of them had mechanical cable rechargers, which was fortunate because jamming varied between often and systematically. There was a small center-line bomb rack which would carry a few thirty-pound bombs or a fifty-gallon drop tank.

After this first experience, of which my general reaction was "why bother," it was nearly a year before the P-40 and I met again—in China.

Opposite page: P-40s in string formation.

The AVG (American Volunteer Group—more popularly known as the "Flying Tigers") was equipped originally with B models, but later—and very shortly before all assets were amalgamated into the 23rd Fighter Group—received some Es. As best I can recall, the C and D models were quite similar to the B, but the E was a big improvement. Most of this was in the armament, but it also had more power, better armor, and a little more fuel capacity. Bomb-rack size was increased, and eventually we could carry a 500-pound bomb on those racks. The basic armament, however, was what made the P-40 a combat aircraft worthy of the name. There were three .50-caliber guns in each wing, and they performed extremely well. The ammunition load was fairly respectable for those days, and the guns rarely jammed. The E model also incorporated an illuminated reticle gunsight which was, of course, a major improvement over the ring and bead iron sights of previous series. The only really disappointing thing about the E was that it had no improvement in service ceiling and only slightly more speed. Climb performance was infinitesimally better, but—like speed—was achieved only because its newer model engines could be operated at considerably higher power settings. To the end, except for the experimental Q, the most significant deficiencies of the P-40 were climb and altitude performance.

In my opinion the P-40K was the best of all series. Principally this was because it was the fastest. Horsepower ratings were then up to 1,350, but the old style streamlined propeller blades were still used. Subsequent series, the M and the N, had a slightly lower wing loading, an extended fuselage, and a paddle-blade prop—ostensibly to improve climb and altitude ratings. They were better in these regards, but not much, and certainly not enough to counterbalance a degradation in speed and cruising range at lower altitudes. They also had the annoying habit of nosing over rather easily on the ground.

I flew approximately 100 combat missions with something over 300 flying hours in P-40s, and most of this was in E and K models. Both of these series really would go straight down and hang together at speeds of over 450 miles per hour (with both feet on the left rudder pedal). Also, their speed would bleed off much less quickly at lower altitudes after leveling off than would that of later series. This was tremendously important in the tactics we used against the Japanese Zeros, Zekes, Tojos, and a few Heinkels that we engaged, because we were no match at all for these lightweights in the climb, at high altitude, or in a turn at any altitude.

In contrast, they were no match for us in armament, ruggedness, or diving speed. Their best fighter, the Tojo, was faster than a P-40 in level flight above approximately 10,000 feet, but slightly slower below that (very slightly, if any, in the case of our Ms and Ns). Accordingly, we emphasized our superiorities through various forms of working in pairs (doctrinally), seeking initial advantages in altitude and surprise positioning, and never, under any circumstances, attempting a turning or climbing fight. Many people have described CBI tactics with the Jap fighters as hit and run, but I consider this an inaccurate description. Certainly we always tried to hit, and hit first, but the running part consisted in getting away when cornered or tailed by diving out and hopefully losing the pursuer long enough to get back up and acquire a new position of advantage. This usually could be done even when substantially outnumbered, either by the element leader or the wingman always covering his alter ego. The cardinal rule of working in pairs—no matter what happened to the entire formation in an aerial mêlée—plus the unravelling dive speed of the Japanese of about 375 miles per hour, plus the inherently better eyesight of Americans made these air combat tactics most successful, with an over-all air-to-air kill ratio in the CBI theater of about twelve to one in our favor.

One time we captured a Zero. It was the latest model at the time—a Mark 4 I believe—and we called it the Zeke. It had been shot down and was more or less intact, so after a month or so of work by Gerhard Neumann ["Herman the German," who was later director of General Electric's jet engine division] and some of his local talent, he pronounced it fit to fly. Several of us took a turn at some local flying around Kumming before looking for a volunteer to drive it across the Hump for eventual shipment back to the States. It was a revelation. My general reaction was one of riding a motorized orange crate, and I was thankful as never before that we had the P-40s and they had the Zeros instead of the other way around. After a couple of familiarization rides, Maj. Grant Mahony and I decided to do some side-by-side testing.

We squared off first for level speed runs. As expected, the P-40 was faster below about 12,000 feet, but above that the Zeke had an advantage which became greater as the altitude increased. Because we had no oxygen equipment compatible with fittings in the Zeke, we did not try anything above 20,000, but at that level the Zeke was still climbing at about 1,000 feet per minute and the P-40 was essentially through. Grant said, "now let's try some dives," and I responded, "not on your life. I'm afraid to nose this thing over enough even to get back to the field."

One of the questionable factors in these very fragmentary tests was how close we were operating the Zeke to its specified engine and airframe

limitations. Because it was delivered without any tech data, we never did know for sure, and in fact did not even know what some of the gauge calibrations meant. However, the tests came out about as expected, and all of us who flew the Jap fighter went back into battle with renewed respect for and confidence in the P-40.

The primary mission of fighter forces in China was defense of the Kumming Aerial Port Complex. This was not surprising, as that was the reception and distribution center for all traffic and supplies coming into that part of the CBI (China-Burma-India) theater of operations. Everything was completely dependent on that 500-mile aerial supply route and terminus remaining secure. We nominally kept one squadron of the five-squadron 23rd Group there at all times, and occasionally more if increased enemy activity was expected. Most of the time, however, the rest of the force was deployed for duty farther east at Hunan and Kwangsi Province bases. The P-40s did a little of everything. Base defense was, of course, always a prime consideration, but most operations were of the offensive type. We escorted bombers (B-24s and B-25s), ran fighter sweeps against targets of opportunity like lake and river traffic during rice harvest season, attacked shipping in Hong Kong harbor with dive-bombing raids, worked over railroad traffic with both skip-bombing and AP and incendiary .50-caliber ammunition, and patrolled the lower Yangtze and Pearl Rivers for opportune boat and ship targets. The P-40 did rather well in this jack-of-all-trades type strike force. We operated from the hub of a wheel, and had a radius of action of 200 to 350 miles depending on the load and mission—and on the status and condition of the belly tanks. They were made of bamboo, and the quality varied greatly according to where they were made and how they were treated in transit from source to squadron supply points. Some of them were rejected outright; some were good for one mission; and a few lasted for three missions before they leaked so badly as to be dangerous (as well as being marginal range-extenders). A three-mission tank was a "ding-how" piece of merchandise.

One technique we used in dive-bombing was called the Rodeo, and it worked quite well—especially in situations where fighter opposition was light and anti-aircraft relatively heavy. One flight formed a rough circle, weaving back and forth and undulating up and down between the altitudes of about 4,000 to 6,000 feet above the target area. The pattern was made as irregular as possible, with the target approximately in its center, and engine/propeller noise was made as loud and as rasping as possible by constantly moving prop controls back and forth between about 2,500 and 3,000 revolutions per minute. Once this was well estab-

Opposite page: P-40s.

lished, the dive-bombing flight came right down through the middle of it to deliver the bombs. This confused the anti-aircraft considerably, as gun-laying was usually done with use of the old sound-focusing horns.

I have already mentioned that one of the big plus factors for the P-40 was ruggedness. It really was a tough bird. I have personally seen 450 indicated miles per hour on the gauge in dives, and have never heard of one coming apart. The P-40 terminal velocity was not quite high enough to encounter noticeable local compressibility phenomena, but it was great enough to run out of enough leg-power on the rudder to keep the ball in the middle. In view of this, it was surprising to me that the canopies did not come off at terminal speed. I guess it was because it was built ruggedly, like the rest of the airplane. The locking mechanism was not like that of the bubble canopies of later model Jugs and Mustangs, but just the plain old sliding type with crank and cable operation, with fresh air cracks along the track.

John Alison, a fighter pilot and leader whose skill and courage was second to none, came back from an encounter with several Japanese fighters in as shot-up a condition for still being airborne as I have ever seen. The airplane looked like a bunch of fire-sale spare parts going along in formation. The whole fuselage back of the cockpit was riddled, part of the engine cowling was gone, only a rag was left that was once a rudder, and one elevator was completely missing (with the other one looking pretty limp). As I recall he had no brakes or flaps, but the engine still ran, and he got her down well enough to walk away. It was a stirring sight, and the kind of thing that prevented anyone who flew P-40s in combat from ever damning this airplane in spite of its rather marked deficiencies of performance.

The engine, too, was essentially as rugged as the airframe. One of the things that got so many wounded P-40s back that would have helped many a doomed P-51 was coolant location. Both engine and oil radiators were up front, with commensurately short interconnecting lines. Almost all small arms ground fire had a tendency not to lead low-flying aircraft enough, so that the hit pattern was usually in the aft section of the air-craft. The P-51, with its aft radiators and long connecting lines, was thus more vulnerable to ground fire than the P-40 (but this was about its only significant weakness).

The P-40's Allison 1710 was just plain sturdy. Its power output never was raised to anywhere near the levels of the Merlin 1650 (which in the P-51H was rated 2,200 horsepower at three yards of mercury). Accord-ingly, bearings were conservatively stressed, and rarely ever gave trouble even under emergency or wounded conditions. Once, while strafing trucks, I received a hit in the scavenge oil pump and immediately lost all oil pressure. Power was reduced to a low setting, and the engine ran for nearly four minutes with no oil! This was enough to get me back over friendly territory, and sit her down (with a few convolutions through several rice paddy dikes) pretty much in one piece. A post-mortem, as best I could conduct it, showed that actually failure had occurred in the reduction gear box rather than the engine proper—a finding which tallies with the fact that an internal engine failure would probably have resulted in a fire.

In 300 hours of combat flying, the only problems I had with the 1710 other than enemy action were a broken throttle linkage (fortunately near the field) and a sheared distributor rotor. This was in spite of a fair amount of operation well over red-line limitations. The sheared rotor creates a rather frightening condition, with random firing of the cylinders as the rotor debris makes contact with the pins while sloshing around inside the distributor cap. The best description is that of a convulsive engine without appreciable power and with fire occasionally shooting out the intake scoop ahead of the prop. It scared me plenty, but again I managed to get into a field. Curiously, this same thing happened to me again in a P-51A much later, but that time I recognized the symptoms, switched to the good mag only, and proceeded to the nearest base with maintenance facilities.

A final word about the P-40 must include the Q. It was quite a bird, and I was privileged to participate in some comparative operational tests at Eglin in 1945 between the Q, an advanced experimental model of the P-63 which I believe was called the L, and the P-47J, which held the world speed record for propeller aircraft until another Republic product, the Rainbow, broke it by a few miles per hour.

The Q, like the other two contenders, was designed to capture a piece of the fighter market which by 1945 had gone almost exclusively to North American, Republic, and Grumman. It was a delight to fly, and had performance which made you forget that it was a P-40; but it was strictly a bread-board model that required several high-priced specialists to keep it in commission. Although the Q may have had a modified wing—I don't remember—the principal enabling ingredient for this new hot-rod was the engine. It had, among other things, a two-stage blower with an interstage carburetor. In other words, the carburetor was rammed by the first stage. Moreover, the second stage was driven through a liquid coupling with an aneroid control in order to maintain constant manifold pressure for any chosen throttle setting right on up to whatever altitude the air finally gave out. The P-63, incidentally, used

essentially the same engine, and thus the comparison between these two hopefuls was unusually meaningful.

I have often wondered why Curtiss and Allison did not do something like this sooner; or Allison independently; or Curtiss in conjunction with another engine manufacturer. The answer on the latter is probably that other suitable engine contractors were booked to capacity. Curtiss did put a Merlin in their F model, as mentioned, but it was an early version and provided essentially the same performance as the Allison-powered Es and Ks. In any event, the Q was too late and caused no ripples at all. As far as I know, it did not pick up a single zealot in uniform, which is highly unusual, but even if it had caught on there was a lot of work to do before it could be satisfactorily produced.

Thus ended the saga of the Curtiss Hawks, a long line of successful fighters that saw action all over the world. Although never in the prima ballerina role, they nevertheless performed well in a variety of mission applications, and, principally through their close identity with the shark-mouth of the Flying Tigers, have achieved the enshrinement of stardom in the hearts and minds of all who love to fly.

EDITOR'S NOTE
The following is an informal exchange of correspondence regarding the P-40 between the editor and Gen. Bruce Holloway which we thought would be of interest to our readers.

March 2, 1978

Dear General Holloway,

I like what you have written, for it tells us a lot of interesting information. The main thing I find missing is much about the feel of the aircraft—you once mention two feet on the left rudder pedal, but that is about it in that delicate area of feel. May I ask you for further comments and clarification on the following points . . .

Page 1.   By the way, you will be interested to know that we have a piece from General Mark Bradley on the P-40 at Wright-Patterson and that we have been able to get the Canadian report on the same aircraft on its visit to Ottawa. How did you happen to join the AVG?

Page 2.   How many 500 lb. bombs did the P-40 carry? Would you compare the E-model to the Zero here? You say that the old-style propeller blades were used on the

Opposite page: The P-40 in flight.

P-40K, but I think you also said that the paddle blades were no improvement. Can you clarify this? Some Jug pilots claim the paddle-blades made all the difference in the world.

Page 3.   The sentence on the cardinal rule of working in pairs does not read very clearly; could you please expand upon that? Am I right that "Herman the German" Neumann later went on to manage the GE jet-engine program?

Page 4.   Would you please make greater comments upon the Zero, especially as to why you were afraid to dive it? What you have to say seems to contradict what pilots in the SW Pacific said about the Zero.

Page 5.   Do you mean AP *and* incrediary 50 caliber ammunition?

Page 6.   Is it John Alison with one L?

Page 7.   I have not heard the expression "three yards of mercury," could you please clarify? Do you mean fire shot out of the intake scoop, located aft of the propeller, so hard that it went ahead of the spinner?

In general: Could you please supply a paragraph or two on the following:

What was the P-40 like to taxi and take off on various surfaces in the USA and China and what were the techniques used?

What did you do inside the cockpit in combat areas and situations?

How did the aircraft feel in the air and what were its idiosyncracies, including in stalls and tight combat maneuvers?

What were the combat limits apart from diving, which you have covered well?

What about bailing out? Easy or hard and the technique? Did people always try instead to get to base?

What were crash-landing techniques, especially in your own experience?

What was the P-40 like to land under ordinary circumstances and with a bombload or drop tanks?

Thank-you so much for your contribution and for your patience in answering these questions.

With best wishes,

Yours sincerely,

Robin Higham

March 16, 1978

Dear Mr. Higham,

Thanks for your letter of March 2 regarding my offering on flying the P-40. The answers to some of your questions follow, but from the outset I would like to ask that the story not be modified. . .

The following responses are keyed sequentially to your questions:

[Page 1.]—I did not join the AVG. Was sent to China as an observer to work with and fly with them preparatory to formation of the 23rd FG from all AVG assets on July 4, 1942. I was in such observer status for about six weeks prior to that date.

[Page 2.]—One 500 pound, bomb, and it did well to manage that. The airfoil prop was better for the P-40 in my opinion because it gave more speed at lower altitudes—which, as explained, was one of our few—and saving—advantages. The P-47 was a different story. It had plenty of power at altitude—especially the M and N models, and had to use paddles to absorb this power. It was more a matter of structural integrity than aerodynamics, and the choice was either paddles or counter-rotating airfoil props. In this case I could also cite the C and KC-97. The KCs were converted from airfoil to paddle props because of the high failure rate of the former. When this was done however, both climb and high speed performance were severely reduced.

[Page 3.]—You are right. Gerhard Neumann is one of the great success stories of my experience. I did not and do not call him "Herman the German," although we did call him Herman occasionally.

[Page 4.]—I was afraid to dive the Zero because of its relatively frail construction.

[Page 5.]—Yes.

[Page 6.]—Yes. One L in Alison, John.

[Page 7.]—One of the main readouts for piston engines is manifold pressure, and it is normally expressed in inches of mercury. I believe three yards of mercury expresses well the very high operating limits of that late model engine, and should be broadly understood. I said it that way for the impact of such a high BMEP, and believe parenthetical or other explanatory remarks would be counter-effective. As regards the random firing of the busted distributor rotor, yes—the flashes did extend ahead of the leading edge of the intake scoop.

—Misc. questions:

—The P-40 was quite conventional in taxing and take-off. Early models had a tendency to ground-loop after landing and when slowing through the 60 mph zone because of a slight change in lateral CP at that speed.

—Stall and spin recovery were good, and there was plenty of stall warning. There were no characteristics I would call vicious, and believe I mentioned all of the idiosyncrasies felt to be pertinent.

—Combat limits on the engine varied from about thirty-seven inches of mercury on the B model to fifty to fifty-five on later models as best I recall, and 2,700–2,800 rpm. I do not remember exactly, but these are technical data that I am sure could be supplied by the Air Force (AFSC). Airframe limits were—I think—about 8g maneuver and 400 mph IAS, but again I am a little fuzzy. The main point is that it was a rugged machine, and we habitually—when necessary—exceeded the red-lined diving speed limitation.

—Crash landing preference also varied. Flaps down was prescribed and universally accept as good. However pilots were split on wheels. The only time I crash landed was wheels-up, and I elected this because, like everything else on the P-40, the landing gear was rugged, and I believed that it was more likely to promote cart-wheeling than to reduce shock by breaking off. My spot was a series of rice paddies, and although the airplane was ruined, it was a good decision (no injuries).

—The P-40 had no landing tricks, and most preferred three-point types except in cross-winds or heavy load conditions, when a main wheels first condition was preferred.

Hope this helps—a little.

Sincerely,

Bruce Holloway

Gen. Bruce K. Holloway was Commander-in-Chief of Strategic Air Command at Offutt Air Force Base, Nebraska.

B-26 Marauder

Douglas C. Conley

The B-26 was a World War II medium bomber with twin Pratt & Whitney radial engines (R-2800) equipped with four-blade Curtiss electric propellers. It was designed for low-altitude bombing, but a high loss rate in low-altitude combat forced us to operate it at 12,000 feet. The craft carried a crew of seven and a normal load of four 1,000-pound bombs. It had a cigar-shaped fuselage and short stubby wings, and it was fast and "hot" for its time. At this time, in the more or less embryonic world of flight, an aircraft that landed at a high rate of speed was referred to as "hot." The principal difference between the B-26 and most other aircraft of its day was a landing speed about twenty miles per hour faster and a cruise speed comparable to the fastest fighter aircraft. This increased speed coupled with a higher wing loading represented an advancement from the design standpoint and confronted pilots with a whole new ball game in the art of flying. The first B-26s stalled at 130 miles per hour, came "unstuck" from the ground at 135, and cruised at 220 indicated; instantaneous engine failure precipitated a vicious control problem.

The stubby wings were responsible for her nickname of "Flying Prostitute"—she had no (or very little) visible means of support. The serious control problem upon engine failure earned her the name "the Martin Murderer," and the reputation of "a Marauder a day in Tampa Bay" was assigned to her at about the time I began flying her in the fall of 1942.

In spite of this, I loved her, as did nearly every pilot who flew her. In all honesty, however, there were a few pilots who had great difficulty checking out in a B-26 at McDill, probably because of her reputation. A performance average of one crash a day from unknown causes and with all hands killed is reason enough to make anyone jumpy, and I must admit to considerable apprehension on each takeoff.

Opposite page: B-26s in formation.

I reported to McDill Field at Tampa in September 1942, proud of my new silver wings and my recent promotion to SSgt Pilot. (We received many faltering uncertain salutes from old line chiefs because of the pilot's wings in spite of the staff sergeant insignia.) Upon graduation from flying school we had received our assignments, and although disappointed at not getting fighters we were resigned to flying the B-17 (reportedly at McDill). Imagine our chagrin to discover upon arrival that there were no B-17s in sight but B-26s everywhere. We were already aware of the B-26's reputation for being dangerous, a reputation undoubtedly embellished for shock effect during "hangar flying" bull sessions throughout the Air Corps. With the hope that the rumors might not be true, I began dual flight instruction to check out as first pilot.

Each transition flight carried an instructor and two student pilots, who took turns taking off and landing. Because of control problems accompanying engine failure, we were required to fly a rather peculiar flight pattern. On takeoff we made a long low run to assure earliest gaining of flight speed sufficient to provide maximum airflow over the control surfaces, so that the sharp control movement required to counter the effects of engine failure would not be so likely to result in a high-speed stall. Most aircraft flew a few miles out over the swamp before attempting to gain more than fifty feet of altitude. After the climb to pattern altitude, we reduced to the final approach airspeed of 140 miles per hour indicated and made what was called a one-shot approach and landing: at 140 miles per hour without using power to drag it in or to delay the stall after round-out, a pilot had only one chance to put the aircraft in proper position for landing before the stall occurred. When the far end of the runway disappeared below the nose, we cut all power, nosed over, and made our round-out and touchdown without the aid of power. Fortunately, old Glen L's people designed her with one of the sturdiest landing gears I have ever seen. There were no touch-and-gos; we taxied back to the takeoff area after every landing, and the crew chief got out to perform a walk-around inspection before the next takeoff.

After we had shot a few landings, the instructor pilot got out. The other student and I then took the aircraft up for a few stalls and practice landings, alternating in the pilot's seat. The other student pilot made me extremely nervous by the careless way he flew the aircraft—riding the burble of a stall, as it were, almost continuously in the pattern. I expressed my concern to him in no uncertain terms. We didn't crash.

The next day I was assigned a different student pilot to continue our familiarization program. We went out over Tampa Bay to practice stalls and single-engine procedures, and we found that the B-26 actually flew well on one engine, provided care was used in shutting the engine down and feathering the propeller. After completing this air work we headed back to McDill to shoot some landings. Upon approaching the field, we observed a large plume of black smoke rising from the middle of the field and suspected the worst. I discovered upon landing that the student pilot I had checked out with the day before had "spun in" to crash, and all on board had perished.

While I was at McDill, one of our older pilots, a captain in his mid-twenties, achieved the then unheard-of distinction of surviving a crash in a B-26: he had a runaway propeller and belly-landed in a swamp. The R-2800 engine was very reliable and seldom failed, but the electric propeller was another matter. It was responsible for most of the crashes. Carbon brushes on a slip ring transmitted the electric power to change the pitch on the prop. This mechanism was new and unfamiliar, and it was the maintenance man's nightmare. Dirty brushes and changing clearance due to wear resulted in the loss of many aircraft. The high-pitched screech caused by a runaway propeller could be heard for miles. A break in electrical contact caused the propeller to go immediately to flat pitch, and an extreme overspeed condition resulted. When this happened, there was suddenly no thrust from that engine—with the same effect as engine failure.

The design of the aircraft was responsible for the control problem resulting from engine failure. The cylindrical fuselage required engine placement well out on the wing to provide clearance for the large propellers. (A flat-sided fuselage like that on the B-25 would have provided the same functional space internally but would not have extended so far out toward the wing.) With the two engines so far from the centerline of the fuselage and so far from each other, we had to contend with extreme aerodynamic forces when one quit suddenly while the other was still churning. The wing on the failed side immediately "fell back" and stalled while the good engine torque and thrust worked the opposite effect with the other wing. The result was a snap roll. Admittedly, the above is "lay" reasoning, but to me it explains the probable cause of the tendency to flip when an engine failed.

We moved from McDill to Lakeland, Florida, for combat crew training. As pilots and maintenance personnel became more proficient, the accident rate declined dramatically. After forming our crews, we practiced skip bombing and .50-caliber target practice on dye markers dropped in the gulf. I was fortunate to be assigned the best crew in the air force.

While at Lakeland I had an experience with weight and balance of the B-26. One day when we were walking out to the aircraft for a practice bombing mission, an airman asked if he could go along for the ride. I told him he could hop up in back with the gunner. We almost finished that takeoff in the company of angels. There were twelve 100-pound practice bombs in the front bomb bay and ten in the back; with the addition of one extra man in the back, the plane was very tail heavy. The first inkling of this condition came at about ninety miles per hour when I lifted the nosewheel off. To my surprise, the nosewheel kept coming up and at such a rate that I had to shove forward quickly to keep the tail from dragging the runway. In retrospect I should have chopped power immediately, taxied back, and reconfigured my load; instinctively, more or less, I decided to try to fly her in that condition, so I let her roll and build up speed. (Looking back today from a position of maturity and experience, I am horrified at that decision.) At the time, the engines were developing full power; my sense of control was improving with each second as the speed increased, and I felt I could fly her off and reconfigure my load in the air. On the theory that any decision resulting in success is a good decision, I made a good decision. She overcame the stalled angle of attack at 160 miles per hour, just before we ran out of runway, and struggled into the air riding on the burble of a stall just above the pine trees. My knuckles were white on the control wheel, and I'm glad I didn't have a mirror to see the look of terror on my face; I made my sigh of relief as inaudible as possible so as not to alarm Junior (my copilot) unduly. When I moved my passenger from the rear to the front, the plane flew beautifully.

We moved from Lakeland to Lake Charles, Louisiana, to fly tactical missions in support of the mock war being staged by the "Red" and "Blue" forces of the U.S. Army. Having done one stint at maneuvers in the Louisiana swamps while a squad leader in the combat engineers, I thoroughly relished dive-bombing the "ground pounders" with small paper bags filled with flour. As we approached a marching column walking down a dirt road, we could see them dive for the ditches and cover as we flew over skimming the treetops. Our group commander, in keeping with the low-altitude design of the B-26, told us when we began the maneuvers that he didn't want to see a damn one of us above 500 feet unless we were in the traffic pattern. Since buzzing was and is illegal, this was all we needed to turn a chore into an exhilarating adventure. We cut grass in level pastures, made wakes on water with prop wash, and straddled lone pine trees with our props. Junior tried to get me to fly under

---

Opposite page: A B-26—the *Loretta Young*—on a raid over Europe in 1945.

the Port Arthur bridge; all the crew agreed except Starky, our navigator, so we never did it.

At Lake Charles I learned by mistake a peculiarity of the B-26 that was later to save my life. Too steep an approach and too sudden a round-out (at the right altitude, luckily) and she shuddered from a high-speed stall, sat down, and stuck. I later used this feature when belly-landing, after combat damage, in a vineyard that was too small to land in.

We checked out our copilots at Lake Charles. I drilled Junior repeatedly by telling him every move to make, and if he didn't do it at the right time, I did it for him. He rounded out high and stayed there until I let it down; he bounced it in, overshot, undershot, etc., until it looked hopeless. I finally realized my method of instruction was becoming counterproductive because he was waiting to be told to make every move. On the next landing I told him he was flying with an armless deaf-mute and he had to make a good landing or kill us all. He made a good one and had it "made" from that time on.

From Lake Charles we went to Savannah to pick up new B-26s to ferry overseas to combat. We hopped down to West Palm Beach for our leaping-off point, and while there we named our aircraft *Phoebe* and painted the name under the window by each crew station. She was a good bird; she got sixty-five missions in before being demolished in a belly-landing after combat damage.

Upon arrival at Oran in northeast Africa, our beloved *Phoebe* was assigned to another crew; our crew was split up, and the veteran combat copilots were given crews of their own. (It was a personal tragedy to lose a crew who had flown together through training and whose teamwork and demonstrated proficiency had convinced us they were the best crew, to a man, in the whole damned air corps.) The veteran combat copilots had an average of eight missions. They had crowded in a lot of experience in those eight missions. They had tried low altitude with six-ship formations; after losing all aircraft to deadly antiaircraft fire they were flying at 12,000 feet by the time I got there. The ex-copilot, J.C., who was now my first pilot, was a pretty darned good pilot. He had about ten hours of first-pilot time, and I had over 300.

We were returning from our second combat mission when I noticed the oil pressure falling off on the right engine. The oil temperature did not rise, nor did the cylinder head temperature, so I concluded that the oil pressure gauge was faulty. But we were losing oil, as we were to discover shortly. We were letting down in a six-ship formation to enter the pattern to land; we were the left wingman, lead element, in a left turn at a comfortable 200 miles per hour when the right engine froze with a sudden, final shudder. As quickly as we perceived what had happened, both the pilot and I stomped the left rudder to the floor; the plane did a half snap roll right through the middle of the formation, past the nose of the No. 4 aircraft, and ended up in a vertical right turn. I never saw our formation, during or after our recovery, because I was completely occupied with trying to regain control. (I can only imagine what would happen shortly after takeoff at low airspeed if an engine froze.) Now for one of those rare single-engine landings to get her down safely. J.C.'s face had an ashen pallor, and again I was glad there was no mirror to reflect my own color. Something about the look on his face and the way his knees were shaking struck me as funny, and I managed something less than a hearty laugh. I'm sure this helped to relieve the tension as we set about trimming her up and preparing to land.

I had long before worked out a single-engine procedure to use if necessary: no go-around, no dragging her in at low speed on one fan. We picked the nearest runway, approached high and fast, and set her down across traffic. The rest of the returning aircraft were landing on the runway perpendicular to ours at thirty-second intervals. We could not raise the tower to interrupt the flow of cross-traffic, and when a collision looked inevitable at the intersection, J.C. opened the throttle on the good engine to full power. This accelerated us enough to pass in front of the approaching aircraft, but it also caused us to jump up on one wing from the sudden torque. We made it.

While flying with this same pilot, I had another experience with weight and balance. We were approaching Pantelleria for a bombing run with a bomb load of four 1,000-pounders and an extra crewman, a photographer. As we crossed the IP inbound, the photographer quietly went to the rear compartment to record the bomb strikes from the camera hatch. Suddenly the airspeed fell toward a stall. Since there was no ready explanation for it, there was panic in the cockpit—at least for a moment. J.C. added full power to no avail, and the formation was passing us by as if we were standing still. I never felt a stall approaching, but because we were not gaining speed at full power J.C. salvoed the bombs, dived out of the area, and headed home. Then it occurred to us we had too much weight in the tail. We brought the cameraman up front, and that (or the now empty bomb bays) corrected the weight and balance problem. We chalked that one up to the cost of learning.

Later J.C. and I were given a crew to share. He would fly pilot on one mission, and I would fly the next one. One day J.C. was flying: the flak was intense, and we had numerous holes in our aircraft; our airspeed and hydraulic systems had been shot out; to cap it off, as we returned to base across the Mediterranean, bad weather caused us to lose sight of our formation. As wingmen, without a navigator, we were lost. As our fuel got low, we sighted the North African coast, but it was completely unfamiliar. We decided to belly her in before we ran out of fuel, while we could still choose the pasture where we wanted to land. I suggested to J.C. that we "drag" a farmer's field that looked level—near a town so we could get help if we were bleeding.

We decided to go in with wheels up (a brilliant decision, since we had no hydraulics to lower the gear), and I would cut off all electrical power on final. Also, just before touchdown I was to feather the props to keep a blade from shearing and coming through the fuselage.

J.C. buzzed the field from about 500 feet to his satisfaction; since I was expecting him to go across at about ten feet, I was surprised to hear him say, "I'm on final, cut the power!" I turned off the master switches, waited a moment, and hit the feathering buttons; the props didn't feather of course because they were electrically operated, but by this time I was too preoccupied with the approaching touchdown to correct the error. Perhaps terrified would be a better word: the "field" was a vineyard with short tree-sized stumps of old grapevines, and we were coming in cross-furrow. Worse yet, when we leveled at about three feet to play out our speed, the field suddenly seemed to shrink in length until collision with the sharply raised roadbed at the end appeared inevitable. Almost instinctively I yelled at J.C. to snap-stall her in. He apparently had not experienced what the B-26 would do under those circumstances, so he just sat there continuing to play her speed out, as it were. I waited a microsecond or two for him to move, but when he didn't, I grabbed the control column and snapped it back in my lap. She shuddered and sat down immediately. She skidded on her belly for perhaps a hundred yards, slewed around to point in the opposite direction, sheared off a prop blade which went through the fuselage behind my head, and stopped just short of the embankment. The engines were almost torn from their mounts, but the fuselage was intact. No one was hurt—a remarkable fact which attests to the B-26's structural integrity. People came to help almost immediately; so we posted a civilian policeman to guard the wreckage, borrowed a truck, and drove to our base (which turned out to be just over a small range of mountains). The miracle of adrenalin was demonstrated to me that evening. I was on an unbelievable "high"—keenly alert and filled with boundless energy—until all of a sudden, in fact in moments, my energy drained from me with such a rush I could hardly make it to my bunk before collapsing from exhaustion.

There are many stories of how well the B-26 did in combat—coming back with unbelievable damage, making two-wheel landings and subsequent cartwheels with no one killed, and so on. She was a sturdy craft that demanded skill in emergencies, but she was sweet to handle—the real seat-of-the-pants feel to flying was there. She did beautiful wingovers. My favorite "exuberance" maneuvers were a dive followed by a vertical climb and a negative G pushover describing a perfect half-circle to level flight at a speed across the top a fraction ahead of a stall; or a dive followed by a vertical climb to near stall as she did a slow wingover through the top of a brilliantly white cumulus cloud. As a pilot gained experience in the B-26, he could "strap her on his back," become integrated with her, fly formation within inches of the lead aircraft and never vary the distance, and "grease" her in on landing with a featherlike touchdown time after time.

Years later I visited the Air Force Museum to see the B-26 on display there. As I walked around her, memories came back of the people I flew with and the many successful flights she carried us through. My vision blurred as I gave free rein to thoughts of another day in time and space and I took a flight on the wings of nostalgia.

Lt. Col. Douglas C. Conley flew a B-26 from North Africa and Sardinia in operations over Italy and southern France during World War II. He received a battlefield commission as second lieutenant in 1943.

Lt. Gen. Jacob Devers and Maj. Gen. Ira C. Eaker wishing the crew of the B-17 *Memphis Belle* good luck on their trip back to the States after their twenty-fifth operational flight.

The Flying Fortress
and the Liberator

Ira C. Eaker

Often, in the last thirty-five years, I have been asked which bomber, the B-17 (Flying Fortress) or the B-24 (Liberator), contributed most to victory in World War II. I generally have expressed the view that it was most fortuitous that B-17 crews preferred their plane over the B-24, and vice versa. Neither were happy when asked to crew the other. It would have been a serious morale factor had it been otherwise. Combat airmen always wanted the best airplane. Naturally, that was the aircraft which they thought gave them the best chance of survival and mission accomplishment.

The reasons Fortress crews gave for preferring their bomber were that it was a better gun platform with better visibility in the upper hemisphere due to its low wing, it was sturdier, it could come home with more battle damage, and, when forced to ditch in the English Channel, they had more time, again because of the low wing, to abandon ship, get into their dinghies, and launch survival gear.

The reasons the B-24 crews gave for their preference for their Liberators generally included the fact that their plane was a little faster, had a higher service ceiling and therefore was better able to cope with flak and enemy fighters, their prime concerns. They also felt that its high wing gave them better visibility for navigation and on the bomb run into target.

Each of these arguments had validity, but the main reason combat crews preferred their respective types was because they had been trained on them in the flying schools at home, had flown them across the Atlantic safely, and had delivered them successfully into combat. They knew no other combat air vessel. As the cavalryman loved his horse, and the sailor his ship, so this new air gladiator, only lately come to warfare,

loved his airplane. Yes, combat crews do have a deep affection for their major weapons.

All the senior commanders had an understandable preference for the Flying Fortress. It was "the original." It had been the first long-range, four-engine bomber around which they had built their theories of strategic bombing in the GHQ Air Force and at the Air Tactical School. Its performance in the flight to Buenos Aires in 1938, and other dramatic demonstrations of its intercontinental capability, had won the recognition and regard of the planners who devised air strategies and doctrines for World War II. It was the combat weapon with which Arnold, Andrews, Spaatz, and others hoped to prove the validity of the visions of Trenchard, Douhet, and Mitchell. The Flying Fortress had a head start in demonstrating the concept of daylight bombing against Hitler's Europe and its anticipated significance against the Japanese warlords.

When in command of the Eighth Air Force, 1942 and 1943, operating out of England against German-occupied Europe, I expressed a preference for the B-17, as did Gen. Jimmy Doolittle when commanding the Eighth in 1944 and 1945. Gen. Carl Spaatz, the over-all commander of Strategic Air Forces in Europe, concurred and supported our recommendations. But none of us spurned the B-24 when it became available to augment our effort. It, too, was an adequate, four-engined daylight bomber, most welcome in our hard-pressed struggle.

Our preference for the Flying Fortress did ease General Arnold's problems at home. It enabled him to supply the Liberators to the antisubmarine "Battle of the Atlantic Lifeline" and to Gen. George Kenney, MacArthur's airman, in the Pacific Theater, where the Fortress's longer range was especially valued.

The history of World War II is interesting in this comparison of the two great bombers. It records that 12,677 B-17s were delivered to the war theaters, whereas 18,190 Liberators saw service in that war. There were thirty-three B-17 groups and forty-five B-24 groups committed to combat, worldwide. It also records that combat crew losses, as a percentage of sorties, were slightly less for the B-17 than for the B-24.

The B-17 was designed in 1935, and first procured in group strength in 1937. It represented the best that the state of the art could produce in long-range, four-engine bombers at that time. The B-24, designed in 1939, tested and produced in the remarkable time of less than two years, exhibited some technical advantages, such as increased altitude, speed, and range.

Opposite page: The B-24.

Both played effective, indispensable roles in proving the case for daylight bombing in World War II. And this was made possible by their equally gallant crews, who in my opinion will always deserve the primary credit.

Lt. Gen. Ira C. Eaker was Chief of the Air Staff of the USAAF from 1945–1947.

Opposite page: WASPs prepare for a B-17 flight in Florida.

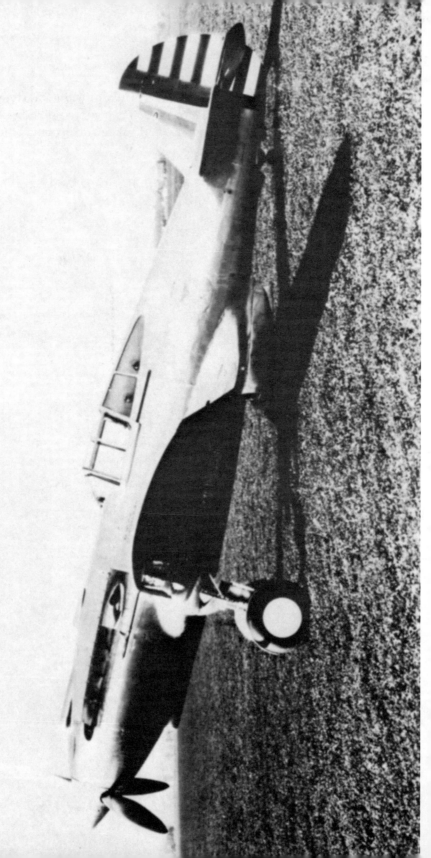

The XP-40

Mark E. Bradley

The United States entered World War II woefully unprepared. We were out-gunned and out-performed by our enemies on practically every side. Even with two years of war in Europe and the warning therefrom, we had a big catching-up job to do. Luckily, then we had time to do it. What I'm leading up to, of course, is that many of us old fliers can also look backward and forward at the same time. True, we look back with pride, with a sense of accomplishment, with excitement rekindled, and, let's face it, with nostalgia. But we also look back with horror at what happened, what almost happened, and what could have happened. And more and more we look forward with dread to what can happen long before the year 2000 if we refuse to learn from the past.

When the United States entered World War II in December 1941, just about the only fighters we had were a few groups of P-40s, with most still on order and yet to be delivered. The XP-40, not a new airplane, was what today's aircraft builders would call a "derivative." Actually, it was nothing more than the old Curtiss P-36 with a new engine. The P-36, a low-wing, all-metal fighter, was powered by a Pratt and Whitney air-cooled engine of about 900 horsepower. Two groups of these fighters had been operating since 1936 and were still in use into 1941 when the first P-40s became available. In late 1938 Curtiss removed the engine from a P-36 and installed the Allison V1710 liquid-cooled V-12, an engine rated at 1,000 horsepower at about 15,000 feet. Behold! The XP-40!

Armament in the XP-40 consisted of two .50-caliber machine guns, fuselage-mounted and fired by synchronization through the three-blade automatic electric propeller. Amazingly, this method of arming fighters in the USAAF had remained constant since World War I, the only difference being that in 1918 the guns were .30-caliber. The XP-40 had none of the

Opposite page: The XP-40.

213

defensive equipment already found to be so necessary in European combat. It had no leak-proof fuel cells and no armor plate. It had too few guns and too little ammunition, to say nothing of many lesser insufficiencies. It was not a combat aircraft.

At 15,000 feet, top speed of the XP-40 was 360+ miles per hour. As then equipped, or rather *unequipped*, the aircraft was fairly light in weight for its 1,000 horsepower and, therefore, had quite a good rate of climb and a good turning radius at high altitude/high speed. But these advantages were to be negated by the addition of a lot of weight, an obvious necessity. By the time the P-40E arrived several years later, it had six .50-caliber wing guns, leak-sealing fuel tanks, armor, bullet-proof windshield, and 1,200 rounds of ammunition. Unfortunately, no more power was forthcoming from the engines, and thus the later versions of the P-40 were less than adequate. Turning at hi-g was poor; climb was poor. About all that the planes had was toughness, a good dive speed, and a tremendously gutsy bunch of young Americans to fly them.

I first flew the XP-40 in early 1939. Right after that a competition fly-off was held at Wright Field to select the airplane for what turned out to be the first sizable buy of fighters for our air force for World War II— 541, I believe the number was. Competitors of the Curtiss XP-40 were the YP-37 and the Seversky AP-4. The YP-37, so designated because a total of thirteen of the model had been ordered for service test, was also a derivative of the P-36. (YP was used to designate a service test lot, usually thirteen, while XP designated the first experimental model). Again an Allison liquid-cooled engine had replaced the P&W, but in this case the engine was equipped with a turbine-driven supercharger, having a potential for superior altitude performance, instead of the more conventional gear-driven supercharger used in the XP-40 engine. However, I can't say that the XP-37 benefited from a second major change from the P-36 configuration. This was the movement of the pilot's cockpit about four feet aft in order to obtain a weight balance for the forward-mounted turbo-supercharger and its intercooler. It was not the best place for a pilot back there, just in front of the tail surfaces, but a sizable number of us flew from there. It could be done.

The AP-4 had typical Seversky lines and was similar in design to its predecessor, the Seversky P-35, except for its turbo-supercharger which was located under the fuselage just to the rear of the pilot's cockpit, a better positioning by far than that found in the YP-37, I assure you.

Because all three competing prototypes lacked defensive protection and adequate armament, in that respect they entered the fly-off as equals.

I should mention here that the specifications to which the production planes would be delivered did require the addition of essential combat equipment. With hindsight, I would suggest that at the time of ordering, additional specifications should have been issued to insure a 20 percent increase in engine power as well. Obviously, this was not done.

I remember well a cold night in January when I was assigned to fly the YP-37 from the Curtiss factory in Buffalo to Wright Field for participation in the competition. It was snowing, I had no radio, and the turbo-supercharger was not working. So I flew low and slow all the way, and managed to get into Wright Field an hour after dark. It was more than unfortunate that the engineers never did get the supercharger to function properly during the competition. Hence the YP-37 did not get a real test. This leaves us with some big "ifs." *If* the supercharger had worked well, which it could have if properly rigged, and *if* the improved altitude performance had been achieved (and appreciated by the testing board), it well could have been the P-37 that fought the war. Certainly its performance would have been greatly superior to that of the P-40 above 15,000 feet. Although it wasn't pleasant sitting back so far in the tail, it certainly was possible to do. We did it. Who knows how the war might have been affected had the YP-37 won the competition.

But all the "ifs" do not concern the YP-37. The AP-4 was lost during the fly-off. The company pilot, Frank Sinclair, was making some kind of check flight when there was a fire in the cockpit. Luckily, he was able to parachute safely; but the AP-4 was gone. Who knows? Had the AP-4 survived (its supercharger was functioning well), it might well have won the competition. Once more, no one will ever know how the war might have been affected.

It is not difficult to guess which airplane won the fly-off, if practically by default. With the competition over, the air force ordered the P-40s.

By May 1940, while the Battle of Britain was yet to be decided, both the RAF and RCAF had a considerable number of war-experienced young fighter pilots. The United States had none. The growing RCAF, having no fighters of its own at the time, arranged for the RAF to loan Canada a Spitfire III for familiarization and testing. Then they invited the U.S. Army Air Force to send whatever new fighters it had to Ottawa for combat trials against the Spit.

This was just about the time that the late Lt. Gen. K. B. Wolfe, then a colonel, had assumed his duties as the newly appointed chief of the aircraft production program. When it comes to K. B., I can hardly be called an objective reporter. The love and admiration I always shall hold for this man make it almost impossible for me to avoid hyperbole when speaking of him. I really believe that he was put here on earth at the right time and the right place to do just what he did. He energized the aircraft industry practically overnight, and within three short years saw it produce and deliver the 50,000 aircraft per year that President Roosevelt talked about and that the world considered impossible.

But this was the spring of 1940 and K. B. had not yet had time to perform his miracles. All we had to take to Canada was the XP-40. No P-40s had been delivered. P-39s and P-38s were not yet available, and the P-47 was two years away. Thus, it was arranged that K. B. would accompany the XP-40 to Ottawa. For participation in the trials, he chose Capt. George Price and a certain Lt. Mark Bradley. Only a few of our Air Force pilots had flown the XP-40 at the time and, pending the upcoming production program, it was our only bird. K. B., George, and a couple of mechanics flew to Canada in a DC-3. I took the XP-40 up and back.

The first night in Ottawa we were taken to the RCAF mess to take part in a *dining-in* in our honor. The dining-in is an old RAF custom, later adopted by our air force. Strange to the Americans was the rule against smoking until after dinner, at which time the ban was lifted by the lighting of a "smoking lamp." (I've never known our British cousins to pass up an opportunity for a ceremony!) Everyone was in dress uniform, and the atmosphere was quite formal. Then the toasts began. We started with the King, then the President. I don't think we stopped until we had toasted every captain and corporal in both air forces. At evening's end we were still in dress uniform but there had been a decided change in atmosphere. I can assure you that the group that started back to the hotel to prepare for the next day's trials consisted of some pretty mellow fellows.

The next morning we found the Spitfire there and ready. One of the two Spit pilots who were to participate was an RAF wing commander, Victor Beamish, an often decorated and highly respected veteran of the air war in Europe with many victories to his credit. The other was Archie McNab of the RCAF. I believe he was a squadron leader at the time. He, too, had been in the European air war and was quite familiar with the Spit in combat.

We spent the next several days becoming familiar with both aircraft and trading them off for mock combat against each other. You all know what I mean. We tried to get on to the other man's tail by any kind of maneuver: tight turn, fast climb, quick dive—anything we could execute. Because the object of the trials was to determine which airplane would have the advantage, we switched pilots continually in an effort to reduce pilot skill to some common denominator. I must say it was exciting. Our allies certainly gave a good account of themselves in both airplanes. Modesty prevents my describing the brilliant maneuvers of the American team. I'll just say that George and I held our own.

We had no serious problems, though bad weather added considerable risk to what should have been a routine mission. Neither airplane had a radio installed, and thus we had to stay in contact with the ground. For the three days or so we were flying, I do not think the ceiling raised to over 2,000 feet. Most of the time it was much lower. Up to that time the XP-40 had had probably fifty or so hours of flying, but the testing had been for handling qualities and general performance, not *combat* flying. Doing maximum performance turns at under 2,000 feet in a strange or untried new airplane is not necessarily conducive to a long career, but luckily we finished the mission without accident. Any real danger we encountered turned out to be mild in comparison to the near head-on collision we almost had with a truck as Squadron Leader McNab was weaving our way to the hotel after the "dining-in." If one of the front-seat passengers had not turned the wheel to one side at the very last minute, there might not have been flight trials for some time.

What turned out to be a minor problem occurred on the first day when we burned out the ignition harness on the XP-40. I'm sure we were taking more power from the engine than we were supposed to, but all that failed was the harness. The engine, fortunately, held together. K. B., the "getter-doner," took off for Buffalo and brought back another harness the next day. On his return, he failed to check in with Canadian customs, causing no small amount of excitement among customs officials. For a while it looked as though our leader might end up in the pokey. Things were worked out, however, and we were flying again the following day. George and I did get lost once during the trials while trying to make our way back to the airdrome after a flight. The weather was lousy. George had a map and no compass. I had a compass but no map. I shudder to think of it now, but we made it.

The Spit was a good, solid airplane, as we soon found out. It handled quite a bit like our fighters except it had a two-position propeller, whereas the XP-40 had an electric automatic. The Spit brakes, unlike our foot brakes, were actuated by pressure on the stick and kicking the proper rudder, but it flew like an airplane—a good airplane. The Spit had less trim change in a high-speed dive than the XP-40. In fact, it has been said that P-40 pilots have a much stronger left leg than any others due to the force required to hold her straight in a dive. Both aircraft as flown had good stability and good and effective ailerons for roll. The XP-40, having a controllable propeller, had slightly better takeoff and climb than the Spit but not enough for much advantage. I am sure that by that time in England the RAF was at least partially equipped with later Spitfires with automatic propellers. As I recall, the Spit had two .20-millimeter cannons installed, whereas the XP-40 had its two .50-caliber guns. The XP-40, as I have said, had no bullet-sealing tanks and no armor plate. Thus equipped, the two aircraft performed about evenly, any edge generally resulting from some stroke of luck or a bit better pilotage. We decided that the two airplanes were comparable. Unfortunately, as I have said earlier, the necessary weight added to our later production P-40s could only result in seriously reduced performance. For some reason, we seemed to be stuck with a maximum of about 1,000 horsepower and a 15,000-foot-best-altitude engine. The British, on the other hand, gave the later Spits more power and more altitude.

The late P-40 and the Spit IX could not be compared. They were not designed for the same kind of war. Why? Primarily because prior to 1940 our engine performance was dictated by the requirements of commercial aviation. At the time, high altitude was not one of the airline requirements. The money spent by our government on aircraft engine development prior to World War II was really a pittance. It was a crime and a disgrace. I only hope we are not headed the same way again, but each day I see indications to the contrary. I am highly suspicious of SALT. As far as I am concerned, salt is only good for seasoning, and the doctors say that isn't good for us either.

Should anyone be interested in what happened to the participants in the Canadian mission, I can say that, unfortunately, I never have seen either of our competitors since the trials. Victor Beamish went back to England and the war to distinguish himself further until he was lost on an operational mission. McNab, I understand, came through the war and by this time is probably retired some place in Canada. K. B. Wolfe, of course, soared on to clearer skies several years ago. That leaves George Price, retired and living in Santa Barbara, and myself, who at this writing am quite obviously alive. I guess that about accounts for us.

EDITOR'S NOTE

It is interesting that in this case we are also able to provide readers with the other side's view. Following is a duplication of the 1940 Canadian report, signed by Wing Commander Beamish, on the XP-40, kindly supplied to us by Dr. Brereton Greenhous, Senior Historian, Directorate of History, National Defense Headquarters, Canada.

U.S. Curtiss P.40 (XP.40) Production Model XP.41—Single Seater Fighter Engine

1. Allison 1090 H.P. at forty-two inches of mercury (twelve pounds boost and 2,950 R.P.M. at 13,200 feet on 100 octane fuel. No stop fitted on boost and engine can be over boosted on the wide opening of the throttle. The installation is not nearly as neat as that of the Merlin and it is estimated that twice the space is required by the Allison. Oil dilution system is fitted and the engine can be taken off after comparatively short run up (oil temperature about twenty degrees). Starting on XP.40 is from a twelve-volt battery, on the XP.41 there will be a twenty-four-volt system. Fifteen gallons of oil are carried. A Stromberg pressure carburettor is fitted, supposed to be unaffected by ice. A Curtis electrically operated constant speed propellor is fitted. During the tests the automatic governor failed twice and the manually operated had to be resorted to. Much minor engine trouble was also encountered (ignition leads, Prestone coolant leaks and plug trouble). The engine is lively and gives excellent acceloration but is not nearly as smooth as the Merlin.

AEROPLANE

2. The aircraft is a low wing monoplane with detachable wing tips but the wings are built integrally with center section and are not detachable. The all up weight with normal load is 6,828 lbs.

COCKPIT

3. The cockpit is very big and roomy with excellent visibility. A moulded safety glass wind screen is fitted which does not fog up in rain to the same extent as perspex. The lay out is good, with a very full complement of instruments. The controls are too far away from the pilot and adjustment is much too limited. A locker is situated behind the cockpit with the radio compartment again behind this locker.

PETROL

4. There are three tanks, two in the wings (centre) and one in the back of the fuselage. The wing tanks are filled when in service and the fuselage tank is kept for cross country purposes and

is not to be filled when combat work is undertaken—13 gals. of fuel being normally retained in it as tail ballast. The capacity is 103 American gallons (61 plus 42) in wing tanks. This gives two hours endurance at 75 per cent horse power and one and one-quarter hours at full power. An extra 77.5 gallons (American) can be carried in the fuselage tank giving an additional endurance of one hour at 75 percent power. Pressure feed is used and an emergency pump is fitted in the cockpit.

PERFORMANCE

5. The take-off and climb are excellent and the P.40 requires about the same operation space as the Spitfire—little longer landing run is required. Top speed at 15,000 ft. is 365 M.P.H. (corrected.). Top speed at ground level is 290 M.P.H. (Corrected). Cruising speed at 15,000 ft. at 75 percent power is 310 M.P.H. (Corrected). Cruising speed at 2,000 ft. at 75 percent power is 260 M.P.H. (Corrected). Best climbing speed 125 M.P.H. dropping off about 1 M.P.H. per 1,000 ft. The wing loading is 29. The stalling speed is 75 M.P.H. A gliding speed of 90-95 M.P.H. is required as the aeroplane is inclined to sink and also to drop a wing on landing if stalled a little high. The aeroplane will not spin easily unless held in. The recovery is normal but at least 2,000 ft. are required.

CONTROLS

6. The controls are positive but all, especially the rudder, are very heavy. The combination of rudder and aileron is very good. When flown hands off, marked hunting is noticed. As mentioned before the control column and rudder bar are too far from the pilot and little adjustment is allowed for the rudder. It is not an easy aeroplane to fly blind. There is little torque on taking off. Elevator and rudder tabs are similar to the Spitfire and the brakes (foot operated hydraulic) are very good. The undercarriage, flaps, and fully retracting tail wheel are worked by a hydraulic system electrically operated from a 12 volt engine charge battery. The wheels turn and fold backwards. Action is on the slow side. The flaps ore particularly smooth in operation. An emergency hand pump is fitted, but no emergency gear is fitted similar to the Spitfire.

GUNS

7. The guns fitted are:—(a) Two .50 above the engine, firing through the propellor (600 rounds per minute), loaded manually in the cockpit; (b) One .50 (perhaps) or one .303 gun in each wing. The empty links are retained. Five hundred rounds are carried for the wing guns and 200 rounds for the fuselage guns. A reflector sight, something similar to our own is fitted. The guns are electrically fired. At present no gun heating is installed.

GENERAL

8. In carrying out comparative air tests between the P.40 and the Spitfire, the performance of the two aeroplanes was practically the same. The Spitfire (L.1109—Merlin III Engine) was a new and good one but the old type and run on 87 octane fuel, with a V.P. two pitch propellor fitted. Unfortunately the tests could only be carried out up to 10,000 feet on account of thick clouds. The P.40 with its constant speed propellor could outclimb the Spitfire with its two pitch propellor. The speeds were practically identical. The American Pilots claimed that the P.40 was 8 m.p.h. foster.

The P.40 is a very big aeroplane (much similar in size and appearance to the Hawker Henly). It provides an excellent gun platform, but is very heavy to handle. In combat the Spitfire was much handier and more pleasant and far superior for any kind of aerobatics. The American pilots expressed much admiration for the Spitfire and its characteristics. In my opinion, from a fighter pilot's point of view, the P.40 does not reach the high standard set by our excellent Spitfire. Again the Allison engine is not nearly so compact or as smooth in operation as the Rolls Royce Merlin.

On 13-5-40 I carried out two flights of 35 minutes and 45 minutes in the P.40 and flew our Spitfire several times in comparative tests with it. Squadron Leader McNab, R.C.A.F., also flew the P.40 and is in full agreement with the opinions expressed in this report.

18-5-40   SGD: (F. V. Beamish)
                                 Wing Commander.

Gen. Mark Bradley reacts to Beamish's report in the correspondence that follows.

22 Feb. 1978

Dear Dr.—

I am amazed that you found the poop in the RCAF. 'Tis quite accurate too and seems to agree fairly well with Price's and my report on the two aircraft.

I'm sorry to see McNab has passed on—I knew Beamish failed to survive the war—Looks as if old George and me out lasted 'em.

It also appears that neither of us made much of an impression.

Obviously I do not object to your publishing the RCAF story along with mine. 'Tis quite a coincidence—

Sincerely,
Mark E. Bradley

23 Feb. 1978

My Dear Doctor,

I note in this report by Beamish a couple of questionable items. First the name of the team leader—Yeager. This must have come from a misreading of K. B. Wolfe's manuscript because he was in charge and the only two pilots flying the XP and Spit were Gen. and me.

He states that the XP-40 had either one .50 cal or one .303 or .30 cal mg. in each wing—I am quite sure this must be what he was told was to be in the production model—because we may be wrong. But both Gen. Price and I agree there were no wing guns in the XP-40—only two 50 synchronized. I would be inclined to agree with Beamish when he says "In my opinion, from a fighter pilot's point of view the P.40 does not reach the high standard set by our excellent Spitfire—"—**but it was all we had—**

Sincerely,
Mark

According to Ray Wagner's *American Combat Planes* (1960), 207–208, the XP-40 had one .30- and one .50-caliber gun in the nose mounted above the engine. The XP-40 was first flown in October 1938 after the order had been placed in July 1937. The first 200 production P-40s had twin .50s. Production was then delayed for French and British orders, and when the remaining 324 of the original order were produced they had a .30 in each wing in addition to the twin .50s in the nose. These Tomahawk IIAs of the RAF, or P-40Bs of the USAAC were not delivered until the first trickled off the line in February 1941, by which time, except in the Middle East, the British considered them training aircraft. The P-40C had twin .50s and four .30s in the wings.

Gen. Mark E. Bradley flew six combat missions during World War II for a total of thirty-two hours. He was Chief of Staff of the Fifth Air Force in Japan in October 1945 and assumed command of the 301st Fighter Wing in Okinawa in 1946.

The AT-6

Wayne S. Cole

We called it an AT-6 or a "6"; navy and marine pilots called it an "SNJ"; British and Canadian flyers called it the "Harvard"; youngsters and reservists who flew it long after World War II called it a "T-6"; and no one called it a "Texan" except journalists, promotional writers, book authors, and people who never flew it. Whatever the label, most who flew the airplane fell in love with it.

Just how much they loved it depended on what they compared it to—what they flew before and what they flew after. For me (and for many thousands of other army air force pilots) it came at the end of my aviation cadet training after sixty-five hours in an open cockpit 220 horsepower Boeing PT-17 Stearman biplane, and after seventy hours in a low-wing Vultee Valiant "Vibrator" BT-13. Compared to those planes, the 6 was supreme. The Stearman was more nimble, more fun, better suited for beginners—and more likely to ground loop. The BT would snap-roll (I never tried that in a 6 except when demonstrating cross-control stalls for students), and it was great for teaching cadets to correct for torque (and giving them enlarged right leg muscles in the process). It was pretty good for cross-country flying—if you had the patience and endurance to sit there all day. And it was all right for teaching basic instruments, formation, and night flying.

The BT had hand-cranked flaps and a two-speed propeller (that was incredibly noisy for those who listened from the ground). But it had too much wing and not enough power (450 horsepower). Its wide landing gear and tendency to float made it too easy to land and allowed one to get a bit casual about crosswind landings. It did not reward precision flying very much, and generally it did not punish sloppy flying very severely. Young men died in it (one of our classmates spun into the Mojave Desert

---

Opposite page: AT-6s in flight.

near Lancaster, California, one sunny day, and two classmates on a buddy ride spread themselves and their BT over the desert when they attempted an unauthorized "English bunt"). But the BT-13 generally was about as uninspiring as a Chevrolet station wagon. Coming after the Stearman and the BT-13, the AT-6 seemed like the closest thing to a fighter there was, short of the "real thing." And it was.

The North American AT-6 was an all-metal, full-cantilever, low-wing, tandem two-seater, single-engine, advance trainer. Despite its 5,300-pound weight, it did not seem underpowered with its nine-cylinder, 600- horse-power, direct-drive, Pratt & Whitney radial, air-cooled engine. Its forty-two-foot tapered wing was trimmer and racier than the larger, more cumbersome BT-13 wing. The plane had a cruising speed of 150 miles per hour (at twenty-six inches manifold pressure and 1,850 revolutions per minute). The book said it had a top speed of 205, but I never saw a 6 do that in sustained level flight. Normal climb speed was 110 miles per hour, with 2,000 revolutions per minute and 30 inches. It stalled at about 75, with wheels and flaps up, and at about 65 with them down. It was red-lined at 240. Its 110-gallon fuel capacity gave it about four hours flying time at normal cruise—less than the BT-13. Its constant speed, two-bladed Hamilton Standard propeller, its split-type flaps (maximum 45°), its con-ventional retractable landing gear, and its brakes all operated from highly reliable hydraulic systems. Altogether more than 15,000 of the various models of the AT-6 were built in the United States, and thousands more in Canada and other countries. When new during World War II, they cost the U.S. government, on an average, about $25,000 each. In the long (and continuing) life of the airplane, there were several models and countless modifications, with consequent variations in performance and procedures (most of my flying was in C and D models).

The early morning quiet at wartime flight-training fields was rou-tinely shattered by the roar of engines as ground crews preflighted the planes on the flight line (it came to be a familiar and even comfortable sound—unless one had been up late the night before). But that did not relieve the individual pilot from responsibility for his own careful pre-flight checks. When approaching an AT-6 parked on the ground, I thought it looked powerful, husky, and slightly stubby.

A standard walk-around ground inspection was a *must*—including visually checking the fuel supply in both wing tanks (fifty-five-gallon capacity on each side), checking landing gear struts (1 1/2 inches normal, one inch minimum), pulling the prop through ten blades if the engine had been idle an hour or more, making certain the cover was removed from the pitot tube that protruded spearlike at about eye level near the tip of the right wing, securing the baggage compartment and door, and checking that cowl fairings were fastened and that the control surfaces were clear and free. The walkway at the rear root of the wing on the port side and a small metal step protruding on the left side of the fuselage provided easy entry to the cockpit (though new cadets invariably managed to get their feet tangled on the first try). In the front cockpit the pilot checked the Form #1A on maintenance and servicing, unlocked the controls, zeroed the trim tabs, and made certain all switches were off. If it was to be a solo flight, certain chores had to be done in the unused rear cockpit (remove and stow the stick; secure the safety belt, shoulder straps, headset, and microphone; cage the gyros; and close the rear canopy).

In the cockpit, the bucket seat accommodated the seat-pack parachute the pilot wore (often supplemented by cushions to help him see out better). After adjusting rudder pedals and seat, fastening the safety belt and shoulder harness, and setting the parking brakes, the pilot went through a detailed checklist before starting the engine. The hydraulic, flap, gear, trim, and engine controls were on the left side of the cockpit; the radio was on the right side; and electrical switches were in front below the instrument panel. Starting procedure included setting mixture full rich and prop control for low rpm, cracking throttle $\frac{1}{2}$ inch, turning switches on (battery, generator, and ignition), priming (five strokes for a cold engine), energizing the starter for ten seconds, shouting "clear" (and *looking*), and engaging the starter. If oil pressure did not indicate within thirty seconds after starting, the engine was shut down promptly. Manually operated oil shutters were available for use during warm-up in cold weather (we did not use them much in Arizona and California). The pilot checked the operation of flaps, propeller, fuel lines, hand hydraulic pump, controls, engine gauges, and magnetos (maximum drop of 100 revolutions per minute on each mag at 1,900 revolutions).

On wartime models, the tail wheel was steerable by means of the rudder pedals but was disengaged to swivel freely beyond 15-30° on each side of neutral (depending on the model). Those I flew as a reservist at Offutt Field in 1947 after the war had been modified to full swivel, requiring use of toe brakes for steering while taxiing and locking for takeoffs and landings. As with most "tail draggers," the engine on the 6 blocked forward visibility on the ground so that it was necessary to "S" with small turns left and right to check that the path was clear of obstructions when taxiing. On an Arizona auxiliary field in 1943, I saw one Stearman whose tail and rear fuselage had been chewed to within inches of the rear cockpit by the propeller of a carelessly taxied AT-6.

We used a standard CIGFTPR check prior to takeoff (controls free, instruments okay, gas selector on proper tank, flaps up, trim tabs set, prop set for high rpm, and run-up). On takeoff, the pilot advanced the throttle smoothly to the sea-level stop, kept the plane aligned with the runway by increasing right rudder pressure to correct for torque, raised the tail slightly, and with light back pressure on the stick let the plane fly off the ground at about 80 miles per hour. When airborne, he toed the brakes to stop wheel rotation, pushed the hydraulic button, and pulled up the lever retracting the landing gear. Then he lowered the nose of the plane slightly to let the airspeed increase, throttled back to thirty inches of manifold pressure, set the prop control for 2,000 revolutions, and climbed out at 110 miles per hour.

To me the plane seemed brisk and responsive on the controls in flight, particularly on the ailerons. The AT-6 rewarded precision flying, and it revealed sloppy flying for what it was. But it had no unconventional quirks; it behaved itself properly and did what it was told to do. Its stalls were sharp but manageable. It spun furiously, but in literally hundreds of spins I never had one argue seriously with me about coming out of it if I commanded it firmly with brisk, almost violent, recovery procedures (in the spin the pilot reduced power, held full rudder with the spin, and kept the stick all the way back; for recovery, he jammed full opposite rudder and after another half turn he jammed the stick full forward briskly—that was no time to be gentle on the controls; as the plane stopped rotating, he neutralized the rudders, smoothly eased back on the stick to pull out of the dive, and reapplied power). In nearly 600 hours of flying in a 6 in all sorts of situations (as a cadet, a basic flight instructor, and a reservist), I never had an engine stop, a spin persist unduly, a gear fail to lower or retract properly, or a prop run away.

Chandelles and "lazy 8s" were precision maneuvers, but when properly flown in the 6 they were also real works of art and beauty—constantly changing bank, pitch, speed, and torque correction. The AT-6 was a fun airplane for aerobatics. My own personal favorite was the Immelmann (the secret, I thought, was proper entry speed—190 miles per hour—and crossing controls briefly at the beginning of the roll-out at the top of the maneuver). Entry speeds were 180 for loops and 160 for slow rolls.

Prior to landing, we entered the traffic pattern on a 45° angle to the downwind leg. We used a standard GUMP prelanding check (gas selector on the fuller tank, undercarriage down and checked, mixture full rich, and propeller set at 2,000 revolutions per minute). We flew the "45" and downwind legs at 120 miles per hour, the base leg at 110, made the turn onto the final approach at about 100, and flew the approach at 90. Flaps were lowered on base and on final as needed.

Personally, I enjoyed landing the plane. Its gear was narrow enough and its fuselage short enough to require the pilot's full attention and skill; it was not the sort of plane in which one could go to sleep on landings—either figuratively or literally. Pilots were known to find themselves in the midst of a ground loop on the landing roll-out, just after congratulating themselves on having made a nice landing. Proper correction for crosswinds was essential. Generally, I preferred the slipping or cross-control method of correcting for crosswinds. Using that method the pilot lowered the wing on the windward side to prevent the plane from blowing sideways across the approach path and runway, used opposite rudder to keep the plane lined up straight with the runway, and if necessary held the correction right down to touchdown. In unusually strong crosswinds it was necessary to use a combination of the slip and crab methods (but if the wind was that strong I probably should have stayed on the ground in the first place). With proper correction for crosswinds, with accurate airspeed control (normally ninety miles per hour on the final approach), and with gradual dissipation of airspeed in the flareout by smoothly coming back on the stick as the plane neared the ground, the AT-6 provided a neat, precise, three-point touchdown that gave a pilot a sense of pride in accomplishment. One learned to keep the stick back and to stay alert on the roll-out. The flight was not over until the plane was parked, the engine shut down, the controls locked, the aircraft forms filled out, and the wheels chocked.

During most of World War II, aviation cadets first experienced the AT-6 in advanced flying school (for me that was at Luke Field, Arizona), after already having successfully graduated from primary flight training in a Stearman and from basic in a BT-13. Near the end of 1944, however, that changed. I was then a flight instructor at Merced Army Air Field in California's San Joaquin Valley, a basic flying training field. But it was later rebuilt to serve Strategic Air Command planes and renamed Castle Air Force Base.

In November 1944, we began giving basic flight instruction in AT-6s rather than in BT-13s. That meant cadets went directly from the open cockpit Stearman biplane to the 6. The Canadians and British had been following that general procedure successfully all along, but it was quite a jump for the cadets (and for their instructors who had the responsibility for keeping them alive until they could master their mighty new mounts). At the time, I thought it was a bit like changing them from a kiddy car to a Buick. But most of them caught on more quickly than I had thought they might. It normally took a bit longer for them to solo in the 6 than in the BT, and the "wash out" rate may have been slightly higher, but the difference was not as great as one might have expected. And the clumsy BT-13 was bypassed completely, with few tears shed over its demise. I am told that for a time after the war, the air force used the 6 as a primary trainer—the first airplane the cadet flew in his pilot training; I'm glad the army didn't do that when I was a cadet and a military flight instructor.

The AT-6 was flown from the front cockpit solo (under a sliding glass canopy). For instrument training the student flew in the rear cockpit under a canvas "hood" to prevent him from seeing outside. The instructor flew in front when teaching instruments, and in the rear at other times. The forward visibility was reasonably good from the front but poor from the rear. Among the more challenging experiences in the plane was instructing cadets before solo when the main responsibility for assuring survival in landings lay with the instructor in the rear cockpit who got only tiny glimpses of the ground at each corner—with the instrument panel, front cockpit, cadet pilot, wing, flaps, and engine obstructing his view forward. But it was not at all impossible, and the difficulty enhanced the pride one felt in doing it well. Similarly, the forward visibility for the instructor in the rear cockpit when checking out cadets in night flying left much to be desired—particularly on a dark night when checking out someone else's students whose skills (or lack of same) were not familiar to the instructor. But the visibility from the rear seat of the 6 was sufficiently similar to that in single-engine, single-seater fighters of the era that it was excellent preparation for the transition to fighters later.

Back-seat landings in a 6 were a part of my preparation for flying P-40s in transition at Luke Field in 1945. The Curtiss P-40, of course, was more powerful, faster, and performed better than the AT-6. Its handling characteristics on takeoffs and landings, however, were enough like the 6 so that those of us with instructor time in the back seat of a 6 had advantages over other pilots in transition. But the P-40's temperamental electrical systems and liquid-cooled in-line engine never seemed so comfortably dependable to me as the AT-6's reliable hydraulic systems and its problem-free, air-cooled radial engine (though that may have been partly because I had more experience with the latter).

The AT-6 was used for every imaginable flying purpose: instruments, aerobatics, formation, cross-country, night flying, aerial photography, gunnery, and even combat. I flew it during gunnery training at Ajo Army Air Field in the deserts of southern Arizona, firing its .30 caliber gun at both aerial and ground targets. (When one of my bullets severed the aerial target tow cable, and the metal rod for the target knocked a six-inch hole in the leading edge of my right wing near the pitot tube, the plane continued to fly normally and permitted a beautiful wheel landing that did not need the services of the fire equipment and ambulance that alert tower people had arranged to have available when I touched down.)

One AT-6 was credited with sinking a German submarine in World War II, and others downed Japanese Zeros. As a "spotter" plane, it saw combat in the Korean war in the early 1950s. In the 1960s, some countries modified the 6 as a counterinsurgency light attack plane, with gun pods under the wings and assorted external weaponry. It served as a training plane in the air forces of more than forty countries, and as late as 1973 was still in service with more than thirty air forces. In 1974, Dr. Richard P. Hallion of the Smithsonian Institution saw 6s flying in the Netherlands Air Force and also saw the three Harvards still used by the RAF at its Empire Test Pilots' School in Wiltshire, England. They were in "magnificent condition"—more than a generation after the first AT-6s came off production lines.

One still sees weary looking AT-6s tied down at remote corners of airports all over the United States and the world. And many of those planes are still flying. They are still challenging the skills of dedicated airmen. They still inspire the love of those who flew—and fly—them. It was—and is—a great airplane!

Wayne S. Cole served in the U.S. Army Air Forces from February 1943 until October 1945 and received his commission and pilot wings at Luke Field in Arizona in February 1944. He served as a basic flight instructor at Merced and Minter Fields in California.

B-25 Mitchell

Arthur J. Thomas

Much has been written about the combat record of the B-25 Mitchell medium bomber, and its successes in World War II are well documented. Those who flew a B-25 in battle can still today make a keen showing in competition with "Jug" jockies, Lightning riders, and P-51 pushers when it comes to retelling hair-raising tales. The initial U.S. Army contract for 148 Mitchells was awarded to North American in September 1939, and the first B-25 was test flown in September 1940. (Compare that with today's lead time on new aircraft!) Subsequently many models evolved with changes and improvements dictated by combat experience. Among the long list of firsts accredited to the B-25 are: first to see action on all fronts; first to pack a 75-millimeter cannon; first army airplane to sink an enemy sub; first medium bomber to fly from a carrier deck; and first U.S. plane over Tokyo.

But let us look at her twilight years (1945 through the late 1950s) when the "Baker Two Bits," as she was affectionately known, served as the backbone of the Air Force's multiengine pilot training program.

In the pilot training program established in 1939, there was no provision for separate training of pilots for two-engine aircraft. Soon after World War II began in Europe, however, such a program was initiated; by Pearl Harbor, aviation cadets were receiving advanced training in B-18s at Barksdale Field, Louisiana. Seven multiengine bases operated eventually. To augment the supply of trainers, commercial types were accepted by the air corps—mainly the Beech AT-10 and the Cessna AT-17. Because the Curtiss AT-9 was an all-metal craft (thus difficult to procure), its use was limited, even though it was the best two-engine trainer at the time.

In late 1942 exhaustive tests were made using the B-25; they proved that students with limited knowledge and average skill could readily

---

Opposite page: A B-25 in flight.

learn to handle the plane. General use of the B-25 for training started in July 1943, and by May 1945 all multiengine training was accomplished in this airplane. Redesignated as the TB-25 and downgraded from "medium" to "light" bomber in descriptive phraseology, the trainer provided an excellent student learning tool.

By 1950 the TB-25 had to be considered an old aircraft, particularly when compared with the current combat types of the day. A popular comment at the time (paraphrasing a more dramatic speech) stated in effect, "Old airplanes never die, they just get turned over to the Training Command." True, heaters didn't always work; many windows were checked and crazed, limiting visibility; starters burned up; cylinders cracked; spark plugs glassed over and became glow plugs in the Texas dust; and instructors on the whole seemed to be determined to log as much single-engine time as multiengine time. However, techniques of multiengine flying acquired in this program were carried over and applied to the newer, heavier, and hotter aircraft flown even today in the USAF.

B-25 students and instructors of the 1950s remember the bases in Texas and Oklahoma with acres and acres of concrete ramp and anywhere from 85 to 135 airplanes staked out. Most were J models, with a few Ks and some L, M, and N model series. The latter models had such goodies as more nosewheel tread on the runway, larger escape hatches, Holley carburetors, relocated feathering buttons, cockpit lighting, and more advanced electrical panels and navigation equipment.

Each plane approximated 33,000 pounds for takeoff, was fifty-three feet, six inches long with a span of sixty-seven feet, seven inches, and stood sixteen feet, four inches high. It was a big machine for students previously familiar with such types as the Stearman PT-18, Taylorcraft TG-6, and perhaps the North American T-28A. It was powered by two Wright Cyclone engines rated at 1,700 horsepower each on 100/130 octane fuel, having two-speed centrifugal impeller blowers with ratios of approximately 7:1 and 10:1. With a 974-gallon fuel capacity, endurance approximated six and one-half hours—longer of course with long-range economy power settings.

Oddly enough, this was one airplane in which range could be slightly extended by lowering one-quarter flaps. At an economical cruise setting (160 miles per hour) the aircraft maintained altitude in a slightly nose-high attitude. Because the fuel tank outlet was located in the forward portion of the tank, this nose-high condition made about forty gallons of fuel unavailable. Lowering the flaps raised the tail of the aircraft, and the fuel could then be used, easing the fuel shortage tensions that sometimes permeated the cockpit toward the end of a westbound, headwind-plagued flight.

We soon learned not to rely too heavily on this extra reserve fuel. An instructor with two students on a weekend cross-country to Florida departed Reese Air Force Base one Friday night and made it to West Palm Beach Air Force Base nonstop with an adequate fuel reserve. Reluctant to leave the glorious beaches and the even more glorious girls thereon, they delayed the departure from West Palm until late Sunday afternoon. To cover up they decided to make a nonstop flight home. About forty minutes east of Lubbock Texas, the flaps were lowered; twenty minutes later No. 2 engine died of starvation; ten minutes later they were safely on the ground at Lubbock Municipal Airport—ten miles short of destination. A quick purchase of fifty gallons of gas for cash and a safe landing at Reese shortly thereafter would make a nice ending to a hairy story. But who just happened to be at the Municipal Airport that night? None other than Colonel C. P. West, base commander at Reese. His inquisitiveness about the fact that one of his B-25s landed at another airport with one engine feathered and that cash was being paid out of the crew's pockets for fifty gallons of fuel must be commended. The next morning we had a new maintenance officer at Reese—the flight instructor involved became the flight line fuel servicing officer.

In approaching the TB-25 for the first time, one could not resist the feeling of awe it inspired! It was more than a great big T-6 with two of everything. It had bomb bay doors, gun turret positions, a bombardier's position in a glass nose, engine nacelles that looked as big as the T-6 fuselage and emitted a mighty roar as the upperclassmen applied power for takeoff from the nearby runway. Perhaps even a little apprehension was mixed with the awe when we realized that during the next 110 hours of flying time we would have to become intimately familiar with this machine. At this point mastery of emergency procedures, formation flying, navigation, and instrument flying seemed a formidable task indeed.

Our instructor, Captain Billie D. Smith, was certainly one of the "old pros" at instructing. Like many of the Reese instructor pilots at the time, he was a recent returnee from the Korean conflict, a very capable B-25 pilot, and most adept at analyzing student errors and unspoken thoughts.

The initial "dollar" ride was truly a joy! Apparently sensing our misgivings, Captain Billie D. capitalized on them. His personal competence and confidence in the airplane were reassuring and his enthusiasm most contagious. One of his first "pearls of wisdom" was the fact that "North American engineers put propellers on the B-25 just to keep the pilots

cool." To prove his point he feathered No. 1, and sure enough the neophyte pilot in the left seat at the time began to sweat profusely. Nonsense, of course, but just what was needed to establish the desired rapport. (I have since used this gimmick with new students of my own many times and have found it always works; "student sweat" is a most effective ice breaker. No pun intended.) This sense of humor cropped up repeatedly during the next six months with Billie D., particularly when the situation was looking most grim from a student standpoint.

While that engine was feathered, each of us had the opportunity to crawl into the seat and make steep turns (60° bank) both left and right. This just had to be verboten—we had known for years that no pilot ever made steep turns with an engine out, and certainly turning into the dead engine was just plain asking for it. Imagine our surprise and chagrin when we found that it could be done, and all hands survived! Billie D. explained that the maneuver could be accomplished safely if done properly. This led into my being talked through a single-engine stall, and although we wallowed around the sky a good bit, the point was made that "the safe single-engine speed on the B-25 is 145." We were told in dead seriousness never to forget that fact, and I never have. At 140 miles per hour, directional control was tricky, to say the least. Between 130 and 135, it was well-nigh impossible. Below that, you just went where the airplane wanted to go until the airspeed was increased and/or power on the good engine was reduced.

Billie D. promised us that if ever he read less than 145 on the airspeed indicator (except on the short final of a landing approach or during an intentional stall series), he would guarantee us the loss of power on one engine or the other. He kept that promise several times.

I didn't get caught with a slow airspeed until several months later, during the instrument flying phase of training. When our group had about six or seven hours of basic instrument training, our instructor found the situation he had been looking for: visibility through the Texas Panhandle was reduced to three miles in dust and at Amarillo further reduced by moderate snow showers. While we didn't think we were quite ready for low-frequency range approaches, Captain Billie D. just couldn't pass up such a good opportunity.

En route to Amarillo I kept hoping we'd get there between showers and it wouldn't be too bad. As if reading my mind, Billie D., with a big grin on his face, hollered across the cockpit, "Buck up, things are going to get worse!" And they did. At Amarillo we encountered thunder and lightning, snow and dust, static on the radio, light turbulence (it seemed

---

Opposite page: Inside the cockpit of a B-25.

more like severe turbulence), brown slush on the windshield, and possibly more brown slush on the student pilot's seat.

While I was trying to decide whether to follow the close-in range procedure or turn outbound for a procedure turn, a quick glance at the airspeed indicator (showing 142) explained the sudden loss of power from the left engine. If ever a naive, overburdened student compounded his problems by his own ineptness, this was the time. The only help from the right seat came in the form of an admonition to "maintain control of the aircraft." By the time the "dead leg, dead throttle, simulate feather" emergency checklist was completed, I was completely lost. Flying was like wallowing around inside a great big bottle of chocolate milk—I couldn't see anything, I was not too sure which way was up, and I certainly had no idea where the range station might be.

Ground controllers at Amarillo in those days were apparently used to Reese students floundering around in their airspace and indicated no concern. A glance at our jolly instructor prompted the thought, "That idiot over there is actually enjoying this." Thirty minutes or so later, when the field finally came into sight, I too began to enjoy the flight. Captain Smith was so right when he said, "You'll never know if you can make an actual instrument approach until you make one."

This also was a turning point in the student-machine relationship. No longer was the TB-25 a formidable adversary that had to be conquered. Now it was to become a partner in developing skills and techniques that would lead to higher, faster flights over great distances.

The TB-25 was noisy, very noisy. Most instructor pilots suffered some permanent hearing loss during a two- to three-year tour of duty. Furthermore, temperature in the cockpit was uncomfortable—too cold in winter and very hot during Texas summers. On the plus side of the ledger, the cockpit was roomy enough for comfortable seating with adequate cushions. (Big instructors carried a personal seat cushion; little instructors carried two or more.) Head room and leg room were more than ample, and visibility was excellent. And the airplane was "honest" to the extent that an experienced instructor could predict to a very fine degree just how far he could let a student go before corrective action was required to preclude an uncontrollable situation.

Although the supply of parts dried up during the last couple of years the TB-25 was in service, maintenance was remarkably good. Utilization approximated eight hours per day, five days a week. Engines withstood the student abuse of rapid power changes, much time at the higher power settings due to frequent takeoffs and landings, and single-engine practice. Airframes were subjected to "bone rattling" hard landings and the severe buffeting of power-on full breaking stalls followed by secondary stalls when too abrupt a recovery was attempted. Occasionally single-engine stalls resulted in an inverted stall attitude when the student failed to reduce power on the good engine quickly enough. Weather avoidance radar was not yet available, so it was not unusual to plow through a Gulf Coast thunderstorm on a night cross-country. With all this, actual engine failures were rare; with the exception of occasional superficial hail damage or an antenna fused by lightning, structural failures were practically nonexistent.

The TB-25 was safe, simple, and forgiving. At the same time it was complex enough to require learning the effects of a power loss; aircraft configuration versus performance; emergency or alternate operation of landing gear, flaps, hydraulic system, and air brakes; and fuel management with a cross-fed system. These things, learned well, have made a significant contribution to USAF's operational success in more modern multiengine aircraft.

Lt. Col. Arthur J. Thomas was a glider pilot in World War II.

C-47 Dakota

Robin Higham

The first time I was really impressed by a Dakota was in 1945 when we were taxiing around Kemble, England, in an Oxford and passed a C-47 standing next to a Halifax. I was surprised to find that the Dakota appeared to be much bigger than one of RAF Bomber Command's heavy bombers. What made the Dakota so impressive was the round fuselage compared to the slim rectangular one on the Halifax; otherwise their dimensions were about the same, though the Halifax had four engines and the Dakota only two.

On the ground the Dakota had a tendency to look massive from the tail because of the great fin and rudder and elevators and the size of the fuselage; from the nose it looked like a dainty bird with a clean rounded beak, compared to the cluttered noses of most contemporary multi-engine military machines with their guns and the like. Like all pretricycle-gear aircraft the Dakota stood high off the ground so that the cockpit towered above a spectator. Today of course a DC-3 (the civilian C-47) looks like a puppy following a mother 707 around O'Hare.

The impression of size was further accentuated for the novice when he first climbed into the rear end of the cabin, walked a long distance up the cabin toward the cockpit, opened the door, went past the navigator's table and the outside cockpit door (both on the left side), and finally entered the cockpit. From here he looked down about twenty-five feet to the ground. Moreover, for one just out of an Oxford (as I was), the wingspan seemed enormous; there was as much wing on one side as the whole span of the Oxford. Neither pilot could see the wing on the opposite side of the aircraft, which made taxiing alone very dicey—in fact, in the RAF it was forbidden. The constant fear of getting a black mark for

Opposite page: A C-47 releases its payload—simulated bombs —in a training operation over the California desert.

an accident made us especially careful, for in 1945 no one wanted to be thrown off flying. Size was further accentuated in the air where—although the C-47 was a very docile aircraft—its stall, which was at first ponderous and hard to achieve, was an abrupt and sudden dropping of the nose with a sinking feeling. But recovery was quickly achieved with some power and use of the great tail surfaces. The other result of size was the poor rate of roll with the ailerons, since they were very long and narrow. Thus while pitching and skidding were easily achieved, turns were rather gentle if done smoothly with the needle and ball properly centered.

Before a flight the copilot circled the machine, inspecting the controls and seeing that the wooden wedges that locked the three movable surfaces were removed. If there was much of a wind, we sometimes instructed the ground crew to leave the locks in until after the engines were started, in order to prevent flapping and to ease the strain on the pilots until George (the automatic pilot) could be engaged. This practice was frowned on by authorities, and quite properly, since the CO of the Transport Command Conversion Unit was killed shortly before I joined the unit when trying to take off with the locks in. He had also failed to follow instructions to check the controls manually and visually before takeoff, to make sure they were free. Preflight inspection included the oleo legs, tires, and fuel drain cocks, which were to be wired shut. The copilot also instructed the ground crew to pull the pins from the undercarriage legs once the engines were running and the captain gave the signal. These pins were $\frac{1}{4}$-inch affairs dropped into a hole behind each undercarriage leg to prevent the undercarriage from collapsing while the aircraft was without hydraulic pressure. After the engines were started and pressure had reached 825–875 pounds, the captain would hold up his left hand with the thumb and forefinger making a circle and then withdraw the index finger of the right hand from it. In the RAF where P/O Prune was the captain who could never get his finger out and so get promoted to F/O (Flying-Officer), this was usually a ribald signal, generally answered by the ground crew with an earthy rendition of Churchill's V for Victory signal of two fingers waved upwards. Once removed, the pins were handed to the wireless operator at the back door, who brought them to the cockpit, reported, and stowed them away.

Before starting the engines the pilot and copilot would run through the cockpit drill: intercom on, generator on, brakes on (even though the aircraft was against chocks), master switch off, George off, and cross-feed off. The battery switch was then set to "on" and fuel placed on "main

Opposite page: Inside the C-47.

tanks" and checked for fullness, since we never flew without full tanks if we could help it, especially over Burma. Next the throttles were opened one inch; the mixture set to "idle-cut out," propeller pitch to "fine," carburetor heat to "cold" (or on the MKIV to "ram"); the gills opened; and the master and individual ignition switches turned on. If the copilot was starting the engines, he usually started the starboard one first. This meant setting the starboard booster pump switch to "on" (or pumping the wobble pump on earlier models) and then switching on the energizer. Immediately there was a high whine, and the propeller would slowly begin to turn over. If all went well, it would begin to accelerate after a number of loud bangs, splutters, and a cloud of smoke from the exhaust pipe. If it did not catch in thirty seconds, the energizer had to be rested and another attempt made. When both engines were running, the battery cart would be waved away and the aircraft allowed to start warming up at 800–1,000 revolutions per minute. While temperatures were climbing to 40° C for the oil and 120° C for cylinder heads, a cockpit check was made, flaps tested on both hydraulic systems, and the blind-flying panel set up. On the MKIV, which was fitted with supercharged engines, the blower controls were moved at 1,200 revolutions per minute from low to high and back to low while the momentary drop in oil pressure was observed to make sure they were functioning.

An experienced pilot anxious to get off the ground would now wave away the chocks, look around to see if any unwary friends were in a position to have their caps blown off as he left the area, open up the throttles, and trust that the journey around the taxi track would give the engines time enough to warm up. Eager or experienced crews would then start the takeoff check—running the engines up to twenty-five inches, exercising the pitch mechanism, moving the mixture control to lean until the revs dropped, even opening up to thirty inches on both engines against the brakes and then pulling back to 650–800 revolutions to check slow running. In Burma we rarely had troubles with cold engines after the first start in the morning. Nor was overheating a great problem, even though we were once held on the ground at Akyab for fifteen minutes by a nervous controller who had a Mosquito coming in.

The actual takeoff check was the RAF's standard mnemonic HTMPF-FGG: hydraulics (825–875 pounds); trim to neutral and tighten throttle damping nut; mixture to auto-rich, carburetor heat to cold, and adjust oil cooler shutters; pitch to fully fine; fuel on and check contents again of all four tanks; flaps up; gills to trail; set gyros. Then open engines once to clear the plugs of oil from idling, and lock tail wheel after the aircraft is lined up on the runway.

Takeoff itself was not difficult with the great rudder available. Throttles were advanced to between thirty-five and forty-seven inches of boost, depending on the load. The copilot now did strapped-in contortions, his right hand keeping the throttles forward and his left down beside his seat on the gear lever. Normally we got the tail up as soon as possible, let her gain speed, and then lifted off at about 80 miles per hour indicated. Our favorite ploy at this point was to climb about thirty feet and then put the nose down and aim for the end of the runway. This allowed a rapid buildup of airspeed and a satisfying whoom up into the air at the boundary fence before settling into a steady climb at 125 miles per hour. Takeoff boost and revolutions were then reduced in stages starting at 500 feet. Upon reaching altitude, boost was generally reduced to about twenty-seven inches and revolutions to 1,850, though we normally aimed for 165 miles per hour on the clock and adjusted boost and revolutions upwards to achieve this. Since we nearly always flew with a full 5,500 pounds in the cabin and occasionally—with erratic weighing machines—up to 8,000, it took more power than the manual specified on operations.

When heavily loaded, the Dakota had a tendency to wallow. This happened to us particularly after a heavily loaded takeoff from Don Maung, Bangkok, with only 1,000 yards of runway available. As we thundered down the open half of the runway, she just was not getting off. We eventually dumped full flap at 950 yards and barely cleared the Japanese working party relaying the other half of the runway. We knew we were way over the 26,500-pound landing weight so could not turn back; we gradually staggered up in the hot air until, as it grew cooler higher up, the controls got firmer. But for an hour or so she still felt mushy.

Landing after a couple of hours of flight even with a full load was not so bad. We slid down into the circuit and on the downwind leg reduced speed to 130, lowered the undercarriage, pushed the mixture to auto-rich, checked the gills on trail, increased pitch to 2,400, checked fuel, and lowered one-quarter flaps. After turning on final and reducing to 120 miles per hour, with full flaps and fine pitch (a maneuver that at night we usually managed to do right over the village in the middle of the approach path at Conversion Unit), we settled down to a normal engine-assisted approach at 95 or a glide at 105 or a single-engine approach at 110. Touchdown was on the main wheels if fully loaded; three-point landings were permissible and encouraged, though there was a tendency for the light aircraft to bounce unless handled carefully. We once landed back at base with several spare crews as passengers; when the unfortunate skipper bounced it, the cabin rang to "One!" "Two!" "Three!" The brakes are described in the manual as "fierce"; "good" would be a better word.

Unlike British brakes of the day, they were reliable toe-operated hydraulic ones and brought the aircraft to a quick, smooth stop. We landed once at Chittagong, India, in 220 yards.

Dakotas were used extensively with airborne forces. This meant special kinds of flying. For paratroop work we flew in a close formation stepped up one behind the other, so that men dropping out of the leading aircraft would not smash into those behind and below—a lesson, we always heard, that had been learned the hard way. Quick anticipatory use of the controls was required in flying close formation, since it was very easy with that big rudder and small nose as a reference for a Dakota to get into a pendulum action skidding from side to side of the aircraft in front. Once mastered, a tight formation was a lot of fun; one of the games was to see if you could bump the top of the rudder of the plane ahead with your nose. For the actual paratroop dropping, speed was reduced to 90 with partial flaps, altitude about 600 feet.

Glider towing was another matter. The gliders were marshaled alongside the runway in use. Towropes were laid out on the ground. The C-47 tug taxied onto the runway and moved slowly ahead until signaled to stop by the marshaler. Then the end of the towrope was shoved up an orifice in the tail until it snap-locked. The copilot hastily checked that he was in communication on the intercom with the glider, and the marshaler waved the aircraft slowly forward until the 200-foot towrope lifted off the ground, whereupon he signaled all clear for takeoff. The Dakota pilot then opened up his throttles smoothly and fully, while the poor copilot twisted in his seat with his right hand backing up the throttles and his left over his shoulder holding the towrope release handle. The tug advanced, with much groaning, trying to keep as straight as possible. Usually the glider became airborne first, and it was at this point that the copilot's left hand could get itchy. If the glider failed to skim the runway and rose instead into the air, it would pull the tail of the tug up so that the tug could get no lift. If this happened, the copilot was supposed to shout a warning and pull the towrope release handle. This was not a popular move, both because it meant a time-wasting abortive launching and more particularly because if the glider pilot did not pull the release at his end first, 200 feet of elasticized nylon rope with a substantial metal fitting on the end could come zinging back through the Perspex of the cockpit and decapitate the glider crew.

If all went well on takeoff, the glider rose slightly above the tug, being careful again not to stall him, and rode just above the slipstream. The tug pilots anxiously watched oil and cylinder head temperatures and

---

Opposite page: C-47s over Germany.

reduced power as soon as they could. Once past 1,000 feet, both ends of the towrope could relax. A slow further climb would continue, as pilots watched carefully for the other elements of the glider stream as well as for rival ones. Once at cruising altitude, a glider with an experienced crew was no problem for the tug, though the aircraft still had to be flown manually. Fuel consumption was higher and speed lower than normal.

Arriving in the vicinity of the landing zone, the Dakota crew gave the glider crew a fix and a countdown to cast off. Once the glider left, the tug accelerated and tended to climb. The trailing towrope was eventually jettisoned at a recovery point or simply abandoned to black marketeers. The rest of the trip was flying a light aircraft home.

One peculiar problem we encountered one day was that our aircraft had an inexplicable tendency suddenly to start sliding toward another Dakota we were trying to photograph. This meant a hasty abandonment of cameras, both pilots on the wheel, shoving the nose down, and diving under the other machine. Once down behind, the aircraft would return to normal. It was not until I went back to the toilet that I discovered what was happening. We were carrying a load of Sikhs who did not speak English and who had not flown before. Apparently, whenever the other aircraft became visible, they undid their seat belts and went across to the other side of the aircraft to watch it. Most upsetting, but luckily not disastrous.

The Dakota was a joy to fly because of its general reliability. We had a slow flight from England to Chittagong—losing the high-speed blower on one engine right after takeoff from Down Ampney, having to replace both engines at El Adem, and two other maintenance problems—resulting in twenty-eight days en route. But out of Chittagong we flew the two jinx aircraft of the squadron's twenty-eight; the only time we had trouble in the air was when a battery boiled over while climbing away from base, causing us to return and make a gingerly landing at maximum weight. Given a choice, I would fly the "Gooney Bird" again without qualms.

Dr. Robin Higham served in World War II with the RAF.

The Martin Bomber
B-10, B-12, B-10B

Edward W. Virgin

Even in late 1933 when in training on the advanced stage at Kelly Field (San Antonio), stories were coming through telling of the Martin bomber under development, soon to be delivered to the air corps. The reports were exciting—a modern twin-engine all metal airplane with a speed of approximately 225 miles per hour. We were flying B-3s, B-4s, and B-5As—(Keystone) bombers—so our interest in something new and modern is understandable.

On graduating from Kelly Field in February 1934, the bombardment pilots were ordered to March Field, Riverside, California. When we arrived, we found that all normal operations were at a standstill. Most of the pilots and airplanes were being used to fly the airmail. As recent graduates, we were used only to ferry planes to and from the overhaul and repair depot at Rickwell Field, San Diego—thank God.

We began getting deliveries of our Martin B-10s and B-12s in the summer. They were beautiful to behold, and we swarmed all over the first ones. They were mixed in with our Douglas B-7s, and we still had some Keystone B-4s (box kites) and, believe it or not, one Curtiss-Wright B-2 on the field. It is hard to find words to describe the order of magnitude advance in this modern airplane over even the B-7, which was far, far ahead of the Keystones.

I mention the Martin B-12 because a service test quantity of this model was delivered. This airplane had two Pratt & Whitney R1690-11 Hornet engines, whereas the B-l0B, which was the principal production model, had the Wright R-1820-33 Cyclone engines. I made my first solo

251

flight in a B-12 on July 5, 1934. I was just four months out of the flying school and was checking out in a B-12—man, I had arrived.

A short description of the airplane can start from the bombardier's station in the nose and work to the rear. The entrance to the compartment was a trapdoor in the floor. Forward was a flat shatter-proof inclined glass window just ahead of the Norden bombsight base for forward visibility. The head of the sight (secret) was brought on board for the mission. Above this was a rotatable Plexiglas turret that mounted a single .30 caliber Browning machine gun. The turret was manually operated to swing and aim the gun. The bombardier was provided with a detachable chest-mounted parachute which was normally stowed. This gave him freedom of action when kneeling over the bombsight or swinging the gun turret without a cumbersome seat-type chute hanging from his rear end. The chest chute could be snapped on quickly in an emergency. There was no way to get into or out of this compartment (like a meat can) except through the floor trapdoor, hence a nose over or a wheels up landing was memorable for the occupant.

The pilot's seat was reached by climbing up the left side of the fuselage with handholds and foot recesses, over the top rail, and into the cavity uncovered by sliding the canopy back. This was luxury—a cockpit that could be closed and protected from the wind and rain. In the event of rain, which reduced forward visibility through the windshield, the sliding glass windows could be opened or the canopy partially cracked to provide good visibility for a landing. The control wheel was on top of the stick post, which came up between the legs. The seat was adjustable vertically; with seat up visibility was excellent even when the plane was in the three-point position. The instrumentation was the latest 1935 vintage, but by today's standards it was primitive. The PDI (indicator) transmitting direction signals from the bombardier was prominently placed front and center. Besides the normal complement of oil pressure, electrical, and fuel gauges there was the flight group made up of the clock, altimeter, turn-and-bank indicator, rate-of-climb indicator, directional gyro, and artificial horizon. The artificial horizon could not be trusted, as it tumbled on occasion when in a steep bank. The low-frequency radio equipment was good for interplane communications but was a poor crutch when flying the airway beams. By lifting the lever (switch) adjacent to the seat on the right side, the landing gear retracted electrically. This was a real luxury, as the B-7 gear had to be pumped up hydraulically by the pilot.

The bomb bay, which had about a dozen stations or racks, was just behind and below the pilot. The bomb load was 2,260 pounds maximum. The one 2,000-pound bomb was carried externally on a rack located between the fuselage and the right engine nacelle. The bomb-bay doors were operated electrically from the bombardier's station or by a crank from the aft end of the bomb bay at the navigator's station. The pilot had a lever he could pull that would split the nut on the doors actuating the screw jack so that the doors would fly open for an emergency. The crew in the rear of the plane bailed out through this opening.

Just aft of the bomb bay was the navigator's station. This was used by the officer copilot when dead-reckoning or celestial navigation were required for over-water flights. A small table, drift meter, clock, speed indicator, and aperiodic compass were provided. A kit containing all the other necessary implements for navigation was brought aboard for the mission.

The copilot sat on a fold-away seat under the rear sliding canopy. The control wheel was attached to a yoke rising from the floor on the right side of the fuselage so that a clear passageway could be had beneath the wheel when the yoke was uncoupled from the elevator cables and stowed forward. Clearing the passageway in this manner made it possible to fire the .30 caliber Browning machine gun mounted on a T-ring behind the copilot's seat or to operate the floor-mounted camera that could be installed just below.

When in position and acting as copilot, the officer could spell the pilot on a long flight even in loose or extended formation. Landing the plane effectively from the rear cockpit was out of the question due to lack of forward visibility, although I am sure that it could be done in an extreme emergency. The copilot's instrumentation was minimal—altimeter, airspeed indicator, turn-and-bank indicator, rate-of-climb indicator, compass, directional gyro, and clock.

The B-10's specifications and performance were as follows: span 70.5 feet, length 44.73 feet; height 11.42 feet; wing area 678.2 square feet; wing loading 21.30 pounds per square foot; weight empty 9,205 pounds; useful load 5,264 pounds; gross weight 14,469 pounds; fuel 452 gallons; oil sixty-three gallons; maximum speed 214; cruising speed at 67% power 190; landing speed with flaps 65; service ceiling 22,800 feet; rate of climb 1,465 feet per minute; cruising range 1,110 miles at 190 miles per hour and 10,000 feet (with 2,260-pound bomb load—600 miles).

In the fall of 1934, Hamilton Field, located just outside of San Rafael, California (Marin County), was completed, and the 7th Bombardment group was ordered to man the new station. The 9th, 11th, and 31st bombardment plus the 88th Observation Squadrons comprised the

7th Group. We were gradually provided with B-12, B-10, and finally a full complement of B-10B airplanes; the B-10B was the principal production model. The differences between the B-10 and the B-10B were minor. The first B-10s came out equipped with fixed-pitch Hamilton standard propellers and no landing flaps. The B-10Bs had manually operated (hand pump) landing flaps and controllable-pitch propellers. The engine exhaust outlets were relocated to reduce strain on the pilot's eyes when accompanying others in night formation flying.

The B-10s were real dreamboats. The ground handling characteristics were excellent—good brakes and small differences in throttle settings coupled with excellent forward visibility and no tendency for ground loops made for fast, straight-ahead taxiing and formation takeoffs as well as fast clearing of the runway after landing. The in-flight visibility was even better. The controls were effective and the forces reasonable (you could say well harmonized), making it an excellent close-formation airplane day and night. The plane was an excellent bombing platform because of its stability around all three axes. Directional changes, as requested on the PDI from the bombardier, could be made quickly. The airplane was very forgiving in every respect, not having any vicious characteristics even in a power-off stall. It would stall straight ahead with adequate warning (buffet). This resulted in a good, safe airplane during landings.

One point that is not absolutely clear is the airplane's capability with an engine failure. It was customary to practice single-engine flight by closing the throttle on one engine, putting the propeller in full-course pitch, advancing the power on the other side, and maintaining flight. This could be accomplished. Though I never had one, I know of two flights when engine failure occurred, which had different results. On one, the pilot was cruising along above 5,000 feet when the engine threw a piston, knocking off a cylinder head and damaging the engine cowling (causing increased drag); the pilot spiraled down for a landing in a field below. He believed that under the circumstances there was no alternative, although he was only thirty-five or forty miles from home base with no difficult terrain between. On the other flight, the left engine threw a piston, knocking off a cylinder head during takeoff. The pilot accomplished the takeoff, gained altitude to about 100 feet, circled around, and came in for a successful landing with the prop in a stopped (frozen) position. In both cases the airplanes were at light gross weights. One must conclude that without feathering propellers, the single-engine flying ability of the airplane was marginal; in the second case, the pilot was lucky and did everything right.

Opposite page: The B-10.

Looking back with a critical eye, I would say that the airplane had drawbacks in configuration and in systems. Perhaps the weakest feature was the tandem arrangement and the small fuselage that made it impossible for crew members to go from one station to another in flight. The second officer (copilot, bombardier, navigator) could not be completely utilized. If the mission involved bombing, he took off in the nose compartment and stayed there. So much more flexibility would have been possible if a tunnel had been provided from the nose to the rear section. But we have to evaluate the airplane as it was and not as it could have been.

Two systems deficiencies plagued B-10 crews. The lack of a heating system forced us to wear heavy leather winter flying suits and boots because at 10,000 or 12,000 feet for extended periods the cold was penetrating. The lack of a good oxygen system also adversely affected pilot and crew efficiency. Prior to flight liquid oxygen (—360° F) was poured by hand from a receptacle into an inaccessibly located generator—a dangerous operation. Once in the generator, the liquid oxygen could not be contained because it boiled off continuously with the result that when reaching Mount Whitney (14,401 feet) 1 ½ hours after takeoff, the supply was exhausted. All of our routine bombing runs for training and for record at 15,000 feet were done without the benefit of oxygen. Oxygen was provided for our runs at 18,000 feet, but the supply was generally exhausted before the mission was completed.

What did this great airplane accomplish to be remembered by? It participated in two pioneer flights and one exercise: the Alaska Flight, the Miami Flight, and the bombing of the battleship *Utah*. I had the privilege of being one of those involved in the deployment of a whole group of bombers from the West to the East Coast in less than twenty-four hours. Twenty-eight airplanes led by General Tinker left March Field, Riverside, California, around noon on December 1, 1935, landing at dusk at Biggs Field, El Paso, to complete the first leg of the trip. After fueling with hand wobble pumps out of barrels and providing necessary maintenance (engines had to be recowled and the rocker boxes lubricated with Zerk guns), we took off individually late that evening down the runway marked with kerosene flares. We landed at Barksdale Field, Shreveport, Louisiana, around dawn. We refueled (this time out of fuel trucks), provided necessary maintenance, and took off for our destination—Vero Beach, Florida. We arrived around 10:30 in the morning EST, which made the flight about 19 ½ hours elapsed time coast to coast with twenty-seven planes completing the flight together. The bombing of USS *Utah* (a remote-controlled target battleship) off San Francisco in August 1937 was a joint exercise with a reluctant Navy. Each of the above, however, is a story in itself.

I understand that the B-10 saw some service in combat with Allied governments in the early part of World War II in the Pacific, but I am not familiar with the record of effectiveness.

Looking back, I feel that the air corps and the Martin Company should be given high marks for the conception and development of this wonderful airplane that advanced the state of the art so greatly.

Edward W. Virgin received his Wings and Military Pilot's rating in 1934 and was sent to active duty as a Flying Cadet. He terminated active duty in 1938 and became an air corps inspector at North American Aviation, where he was later an engineering test pilot.

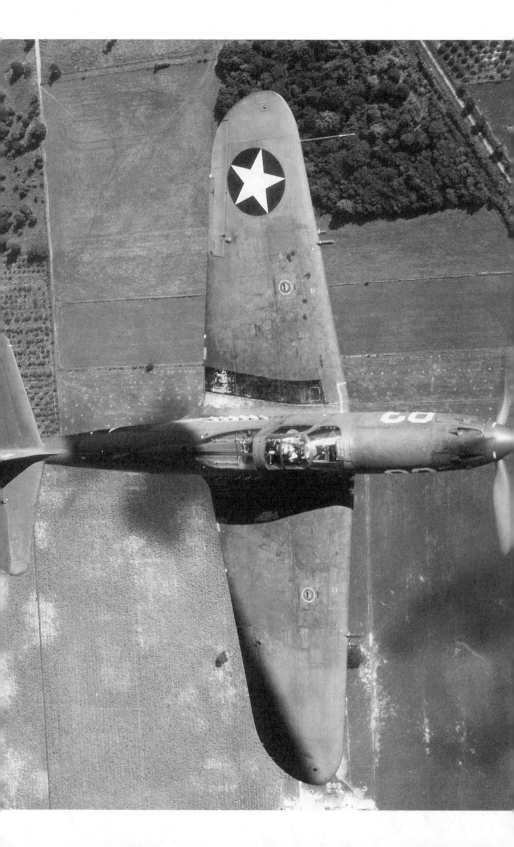

P-39 Airacobra

Richard D. Kent

It was in September 1942 at Napier Field in Alabama, while I was still a cadet flying T-6s, that I first saw the P-39. My desire was to be a fighter pilot (or pursuit pilot, as it was then termed), and watching this P-39 land and taxi up convinced me I'd made the right decision. It was beautiful— sleek, well armed, small—and the tricycle landing gear fascinated me since it was the first such gear I'd seen. In fact this was the first actual fighter I'd seen other than in pictures. The final reinforcement of my inclinations came when the P-39 took off, buzzed the field, and slow-rolled on the deck several times. Fortunately that deadly inhibitor now called "flying safety"—a fighter pilot really knowing his true flying abilities as well as his plane's idiosyncrasies—hadn't been permitted to dampen this P-39 pilot's spirit; the demands of the war took first priority.

My understanding is that the P-39 was designed and built prior to World War II to British specifications requiring a fast-climbing interceptor to destroy low-flying enemy bombers raiding England. The Airacobra was never used for that purpose for several reasons: the Germans attacked England with a different tactical approach, and the P-39 had a major flaw—extremely low fuel capacity—that severely limited its usefulness.

This aircraft was different in many ways from other contemporary fighters. Besides the revolutionary tricycle gear its in-line, air-cooled engine was located behind the cockpit. This feature permitted the use of a 37-millimeter cannon firing through the nose plus two .30 caliber machine guns firing through the prop and two .50 caliber machine guns in each wing. The pilot entered the aircraft from either of two doors similar to the two front doors of the modern automobile. To eject he could release either door, roll out of the seat, graze the wing, and fall under the

Opposite page: A P-39 in flight.

tail. In a panic he could release both doors and literally be sucked out of the cockpit. A major disadvantage was that, if wounded or for some reason unable to use the emergency release on the doors, he couldn't roll the plane over and fall out as was possible in other fighters.

The P-39 handled well in the air: it was stable, an excellent gun platform, and very sensitive to the controls, as was the P-51. Quick and very minute corrections when in combat with an enemy aircraft, particularly the outstandingly maneuverable Japanese Zero, were definitely an advantage. The P-40 and P-47 were deficient in this aspect, since sheer strength was required to execute a high-speed turn or to recover from a high-angle, high-speed dive; a skillful but less strong pilot was at a definite disadvantage in these aircraft in these instances. Other advantages of the P-39 were its exceptionally high rate of climb from the ground to 12,000 feet (better than any other American fighter used in World War II) and its rapid acceleration and high rate of diving speed at any altitude.

However, its disadvantages outweighed the advantages by far. Upon climbing through 12,000 feet, you felt as if you had hit a brick wall. In combat, and given the chance, the climb from 12,000 feet to 25,000 or 35,000 was at a snail's pace. Because of the stubby wings, maneuverability above 12,000–15,000 feet was nil and not very good below that altitude. Your only hope was to lure the Zeros to a lower altitude or make one run at the enemy at altitude and dive for your life. Many times I approached the speed of sound in the P-39 with no trouble. If you had altitude, you could easily leave the Zero far behind, because the Zero's wings had a tendency to separate from its fuselage around 350 knots. However, by this time your fuel was critical and/or the enemy did overheads on you from their height advantage.

To briefly summarize, the P-39 was virtually worthless above 15,000 feet, and this was at a time when the enemy flew routinely at 35,000–45,000 feet. Fuel was a critical problem: air time in combat was at best twenty-five to thirty minutes, and we flew routinely over the ocean at Guadalcanal. Additionally, other than the standby compass we had no navigational equipment whatsoever. Fighting over water, out of sight of land, against better and more enemy aircraft in almost every instance, tended to make the P-39 pilot a restless individual to say the least. Many such pilots died because of lack of fuel to make it back to that tiny island or because they couldn't find the island. Returning at night with runway flare pots out because of enemy ground action or bombing from the air or sea further thinned our ranks. "Somebody up there liked us," however, for most of us from our original group of thirteen pilots sent to Guadalcanal lived to tell war stories.

Certain taxiing, takeoff, and landing characteristics of the P-39 were excellent because of the tricycle gear. Runway width permitting, four-ship takeoffs and landings were routine. Taxi time and idle time on the ground, however, were critical, because the engines rapidly overheated. When flying with other aircraft (for example, P-40s, F-4Fs, P-38s), careful coordination with the other units was necessary; the short taxi time of the P-39s required that they take off either first or last. Because of the fuel limitations of the P-39, we generally took off last, to conserve fuel by eliminating the "form up" time lost when performing a coordinated mission or escorting bombers.

By far the most dangerous time was during the landing phase. Because of the short, stubby wings the stall symptoms normally encountered in other fighters rarely appeared in the P-39; many pilots were killed as a result of allowing their airspeed to become too low in the landing pattern. The very little, if any, advance warning of a stall provided too little time for the pilot to recover airspeed at the low level of the traffic pattern.

Another deadly factor was also due to the short wings and resultant airflow. When performing aerobatics at altitude or in ship-to-ship combat that resulted in an uncoordinated turn or too tight a turn, the plane was said to stall without warning and tumble end over end. Several pilots have told me this happened to them and it took 15,000 feet to recover. This tumbling characteristic was debatable—it never happened to me and, intentionally and unintentionally, I stalled the plane in almost every conceivable situation at high enough altitude to recover. Perhaps I was just lucky to stall it in such a way as to avoid the tumble. These stalling factors, however, caused many pilots to avoid flying the P-39 whenever possible and contributed to its reputation as a dangerous plane to fly.

The short taxi time of the P-39 due to overheating resulted in the death of one of the finest pilots I ever knew. He had just shot down his fifth Zero a few days before. On a predawn takeoff the P-39s were lined up at one end of the field waiting for four P-38 flights to take off. The P-38s were taking off from the opposite end of the runway, but wind was not a factor to any great degree in the tropics, and the P-39s were planning to avoid the long taxi to the other end. Because of the heat, the P-39 pilots were sitting on their planes' wings watching the P-38s take off. The thirteenth P-38 either lost an engine or became spatially disoriented on the instrument takeoff, rolled over in the air shortly after liftoff, and crashed into the waiting P-39s.

Our combat formation was conventional—four aircraft in widespread, finger-tip formation with the two elements far apart to permit each element to turn inside the other in case of a rear attack on either element. This was adapted from the advice given us from such great pilots as Joe Foss, flying there before our arrival, who incidentally had a much better fighter in the F-4F (Wildcat) than we did in the P-39. We also few a combat formation called the "squirrel cage." Unlike the Flying Tigers, we often escorted troopships and had to remain in their locale— we couldn't hit and run. When the top P-39 flight above 15,000 feet was forced by overhead attacks to dive, it was replaced by another flight that had time and fuel to climb above the current engagement and dive on the enemy. Meanwhile, the lowest flight immediately began climbing for height advantage again—hence the "squirrel cage." This rarely worked, because the combat was moving rapidly away by the time the slow-climbing P-39s were able to reach altitude again. However, as was true in World War I and in Korea and Vietnam, aerial combat rapidly lost the initial engagement altitude. The only situation in which the P-39 had a chance against the Zero was at 12,000 feet or below. Two of my victories were scored with the spray of the waves on my windshield partially obscuring my vision. I have seen both American and Japanese fighters clip the water in a tight turn and destroy themselves.

Now a few comments on my personal combat preferences. In aerial combat I never used the cannon, because its trajectory was much different from that of the six machine guns. I used the cannon while strafing ships or enemy land positions. It was highly effective against Japanese landing craft. One well-aimed cannon shot would not sink the landing craft but would clear the craft of soldiers because of the landing craft construction—a welded, round-bottom job similar to a bathtub. The ricochet effect of the cannon was devastating. In aerial combat I used only half the machine guns at one time to save ammo for the flight home; sometimes we had to fight 150 miles or more to get back, and woe to the pilot who didn't keep a reserve for that eventuality. Knowing the torque of the Zero engines, I anticipated the enemy to break up and to the right whenever I succeeded in getting on his tail. That gave me the fraction of a lead angle I needed to try to hit him. Because of the Zero's climb and turn ability, we got only one crack at him when he was aware we were behind him. If the Zero pilot dived with a P-39 behind him, he was a dead man; that was the

---

Opposite page: The P-39 Airacobra is in the background. In the foreground is the upgraded P-63 King Cobra, also manufactured by Bell.

one advantage we had, and most of the Japanese knew it. Some Japanese pilots were excellent flyers, and these were naturally the flight leaders. We would many times let the less capable wingmen get away just to try to down the leader. If we got him and had the fuel and ammo, the remainder were much easier pickings. However, I believe I'm safe in saying that most fighter pilots shot down by another aircraft never knew the enemy was near him until too late, if he knew at all.

I practiced gunnery every chance I had, because I felt that capability alone against the Zero helped reduce—not even—the odds a little in my favor. All we got against a Zero pilot who was aware we were in the area was a split-second, angle-off snap shot. If we missed, he would "get away to fight another day." I wanted that saying to apply to me, not the enemy.

Constant flying over the water made every pilot aware of his plane's crash-landing characteristics both on water and land. The P-39 was excellent in both instances because of its design; its fuselage was basically that used for the first jet aircraft of U.S. design. The convex belly of the P-39 enabled it to crash-land on the water with little shock to the pilot. Depending on speed, it skipped several times like a flat rock scaled on the water. That was the moment to roll out the door, for after several skips it dove straight for the bottom.

Our airstrip was parallel to the beach. One afternoon several of us were lying on the beach drying our flight suits after swimming in them (that was our way of doing our laundry) and watching several P-39 flights taking off on a mission. The engine of one of the P-39s quit as the pilot turned out to sea at about 500 feet. We watched him belly-land in the water about fifty feet offshore, roll out as the aircraft sank, and swim to shore directly in front of its. As he walked past on the way to the strip he remarked, "Thanks for your help, fellows. I hope I didn't disturb you." The only other remark was made by one of us: "You're welcome, Charlie, but don't come too close—you might drip on us." It was about three days before Charlie would speak to us again.

Early in the war, pilot experience upon arriving in the combat zone was extremely limited. My group had only thirty hours each in the P-39 and only two or three gunnery missions. Rear-area training was given when possible, but at that time this luxury was seldom attainable since the demand for combat pilots was too great or spare planes were too few. During lulls in activity a unique practice gunnery system was used. One plane flew in a varied and weaving pattern over a reef. A gunnery pattern was established with the pilots diving and firing at the aircraft shadow over the reef. It was dangerous, because some pilots in their target fixation dove into the reef; however, it was an invaluable aid in learning gunnery. That was how I determined the P-39 cannon could not be used in conjunction with the machine guns—its trajectory was too different and required an entirely different firing technique. From this gunnery practice and several subsequent aerial engagements, I also eliminated tracers in my guns. I felt that if I missed a Zero on the first squeeze, I wouldn't get a chance for another. Tracers just helped him get advance warning that he might be in deep trouble.

The finest angle-off shot and kill I ever witnessed occurred one afternoon as we were returning from a mission. Several flights of P-40s on a CAP over Guadalcanal were engaged by Zeros. One P-40 pilot at about 2,000 feet had a Zero on his tail and couldn't shake him. Our flight was letting down for landing and, as usual, had no fuel for a second pass at the strip. We were in widespread formation and had a clear view of the P-40 and the Zero below us and flying 90° to us. My No. 4 P-39 (who was the closest to the two) made a sharp bank, fired at about a 70° angle-off at the Zero who was less than a ship's length behind the P-40, and blew him up. Without changing course we proceeded straight for the field and landed. That night the happy P-40 pilot gave us some Australian beer he'd "borrowed" from some Seabees or Marines in the area and had hidden for a special occasion.

Many other tales could be told beyond the dry facts known to all fighter pilots; as such personal tales are published, they will provide important knowledge for future generations about the sometimes incredible events that took place during a very bleak period of World War II.

Lt. Col. Richard D. Kent flew the P-39 at Guadalcanal.

South Atlantic Express

Winton R. Close

It is April 1942, four months since Pearl Harbor. I am standing with the operations officer in the Headquarters of the South Atlantic Division of the Ferry Command, at Morrison Field, West Palm Beach, Florida. He points out the window to a Lockheed Lodestar sitting on the ramp and says, "That airplane has to be delivered to the American Military Mission in Tehran, Persia. Do you want to take it?"

"Yes, sir," I say, "Where is Persia?"

We walk over to the wall and look at the map of the world. We look at it for some time. I find Persia first.

"Here it is, sir," I say politely. "It's the pink one."

I also find the blue area between Natal, Brazil, and Monrovia, Liberia. Because Ascension Island is not yet open to air traffic, a non-stop flight between these two points is the only way to go. There seems to be a lot of blue. I say in a voice designed to be casual so that he won't think I am chicken, "I didn't realize a Lodestar had enough range to get across the South Atlantic."

"Yes, well, two large fuel tanks have been installed in the cabin, and it should make it all right. This is the first one we have tried."

While I am digesting this interesting information, he adds, "We would like you to leave as soon as possible."

This statement seems to require an answer. Because this is the first time I have ever seen a Lodestar except in pictures, I ask for a few hours in which to come up with an estimated date of departure. He generously agrees, and I go out to the ramp to look at the airplane. The Lodestar is good looking. It has a low, raked-back windshield, twin tails, and short wings. Good looking though it is, it still seems to me a little small to get across the South Atlantic, cabin tanks or no cabin tanks.

Opposite page: The Lockheed Lodestar.

Two months ago, I had made the South Atlantic crossing as a co-pilot on a B-24. That aircraft had plenty of range, so there was no fuel problem—only those of weather and navigation.

The weather problem is the equatorial front. It is not a nice front. This time of the year it squats on the coast of Liberia, looks ugly, and has low ceilings, rain, and poor visibility. It can close down your destination airport and make you wish you were elsewhere when there is no elsewhere.

The navigation problem is that we have to navigate by dead reckoning and celestial observation for about eleven hours, hit the equatorial front about an hour after dawn so that we can see what we are doing, get beneath its overcast immediately, stay in visual contact with the ocean until we pick up the coast, determine if we are north or south, of course, turn the appropriate direction, and follow the coast until we pick up the river that leads to the airfield. There is alleged to be a low-powered radio homing beacon at the field, but I know about these things and do not count on it.

A good fuel reserve can go a long way toward mitigating the problems of weather and navigation. But I do not know the fuel consumption of this plane and thus have no way of estimating the reserve. I must find out, so I tell the ops officer that before I leave I would like to fill all the fuel tanks and test fly the aircraft a distance comparable to the South Atlantic leg. Besides, I add with appealing logic, it will serve as a sort of shake-down cruise for the crew, the airplane, and me.

This idea becomes irresistibly attractive when I find out that there is no one available with experience on the aircraft to check me out. That is, there is no one to tell me about the hydraulic, electrical, and fuel systems; to fly around the traffic pattern with me and give me tips on how best to land it—and interesting things like that. So now I will have to get this information from the operating manual, if I can find it, and try to learn the rest as we go along.

Later in the day, my new crew reports in. The good news is that the navigator, Arnie, is a friend of mine and, for these days, a really experienced navigator. He has flown the South Atlantic twice before. The crew chief, who seems to weigh about 290 pounds, is the rest of the good news. Although he has never seen a Lodestar before either, he is an experienced C-45 crew chief, and I know by looking at him that he is a good, reliable, old-time knuckle buster.

Then there is a little bad news. The copilot has just graduated from flying school, and the radio operator looks like he is eleven years old.

And there is a little more bad news; I haven't found the operating manual yet.

That night we fly from West Palm Beach to Washington, D.C., and back non-stop, a distance roughly equivalent to the distance between Natal, Brazil, and Roberts Field, Liberia.

I learn some interesting things on the trip. The co-pilot cannot fly instruments—at least not well enough to provide a stable platform for the navigator. Because the plane does not have an automatic pilot, I will have to hand fly it all night across the ocean. I also learn that the nose of the plane pitches up quite abruptly as the landing gear is retracted after takeoff—at least with the cabin tanks full. This action must be corrected rapidly by means of the elevator trim control, which is a small coffee grinder-like handle that rotates in a plane perpendicular to the longitudinal axis of the aircraft. The pitch is very sensitive to small movements of the handle. This is different from what I am used to. I am used to a trim wheel. You want the nose down, you roll the wheel forward. You want the nose up, you roll the wheel back.

We also note that there is no astrodome through which the navigator can take his shots. This means that he must sight his octant through the windows or the windshield. As a result, the stars overhead will not be available to him. However, I consider all these things to be minor shortcomings to be worked around.

But when we land back at Morrison Field, dipstick the tanks and calculate the fuel consumption, we find more than a minor shortcoming. The fuel consumption is such that unless we can improve it, we will arrive at our destination with less than an hour's fuel reserve. And this assumes that we will not run into stronger headwinds than predicted, that our navigation will be right on the nose, and that the weather at our destination will not delay our landing. These are shaky assumptions. If one were inclined toward pessimism, he might say that they render suspect the entire enterprise.

I don't like the odds. I ponder the problem. I suppose I could tell the ops officer that I really do not care to make the trip. But if I do that, I will lose face, and he will get some other idiot to fly it and I will miss all the fun.

Besides, I want to see if Persia is really pink.

So I decide we will leave the next morning. After I have given this decision to the crew, the crew chief says, "Captain, some of the C-47s flying this route are taking along extra gas in five-gallon cans and emptying them into the cabin tanks as the gas from those tanks is used up. Why don't we do that?"

I tell him it's a good idea and to rustle some up—and to keep look-ing for the operating manual.

The next morning when we depart for Borinquen Field, Puerto Rico, we have on board fifteen five-gallon cans. They are empty but when filled will give us at least another hour's flying time. They also will increase our takeoff weight by about 460 pounds. I am not surprised when I find that the chief has stashed a large amount of canned food and other edibles in the lavatory in the tail of the plane. Apparently he believes it is his responsibility not only to make sure we have enough gas, but also enough to eat, and that it is my responsibility to get the airplane off the ground, and keep it off until we get where we want to go. Within certain limitations, these are not unreasonable job descriptions.

The trip to Natal is, with one exception, easy and uneventful. We take it in short hops, from West Palm Beach to Puerto Rico, to Trinidad, to Belem, to Brazil, and into Natal.

The one exception occurs about two hours out of West Palm. The radio operator comes forward and says, "Sir, I just sent my first message."

I assume that he means that he has sent the first of several position reports we are required to make. But a bell rings and I say, "What do you mean, your first message?"

"That's the first message I ever sent from an airplane," he says, with a pleased-looking grin on his eleven-year-old-looking face.

I know from my prior trip that radio communications, particularly around the Cairo area, are very important and somewhat complicated. Cairo is in a war zone. Communications are operated by the British in a style much different from ours, and understandably they are very touchy about the air traffic in their neighborhood. We need a good experienced operator to keep us out of trouble. But we don't have one, so I tell the one we've got to keep up the good work.

I find something good. I can lean out the mixture controls a little more than I had thought. This, plus the five-gallon cans may make the difference.

We arrive in Natal in the late afternoon and plan to depart the night of the following day.

We set the takeoff time to provide us with the darkness we need for celestial navigation and to cause us to arrive at the equatorial front just after daylight. I have to see the front before I get to it so that I can slip underneath it and stay in visual contact with the ocean. I do not want to have to let down through the overcast when I may not know exactly where I am. I might be over land instead of water, and in letting down through the overcast, I might hit a cloud with a solid center. That would really render suspect the enterprise. It could even make a shambles of the whole day.

The next morning, we double check the aircraft with great thoroughness and enthusiasm. The chief refuels the tanks, including the fifteen five-gallon cans which are securely lashed down as close to the center of gravity as possible. Everything is in good order by noon, so we all knock off for lunch and a nap.

At seven o'clock that night, when I walk over to the operations shack to file my departure clearance, it is raining. I am wet when I check in with the weather forecaster. The reason pilots check in with the forecaster is not what you may think. It is because the ops officer will not clear you for takeoff unless the forecaster has indicated on the clearance form that he has briefed you on the weather. We don't really care what the forecaster says, because we don't believe him anyway; we just want his initials on the form so that we can get on about our business.

Most weather men know this and resent it, and are prone to retali- . ate. They do this by talking at great length about isobars, a high pressure area over Lake Baikal, Russia, a low pressure ridge over the Hudson Bay area, and the cumulative effect of these things upon the movement of the Bermuda High. They know you have to stay there and listen. If you don't, they won't initial your clearance. This one is no exception. I know he doesn't have enough data to give us a good briefing on the en route weather, so I am not surprised when what he gives me is just a synopsis of the general weather to be generally expected along that general route that general time of the year. But he doesn't present it that way. He presents it as specific fact for our specific crossing this specific night.

I wait until he initials the clearance. I hate myself for what I do next. I say, "What are you calling the local weather right now?"

He steps right into it. It's delightful. He says, "Ceiling and visibility unlimited."

I walk over to one of his weather maps on the table, lean over it, and squeeze the rainwater out of my shirt right onto his isobars and depart.

When I get out to the aircraft, all the crew is there. At this point I really only care what the crew chief says, and he says everything is ready to go; and I believe him because that's the kind of crew chief he is.

The thunderstorm is still over the field. We wait for about fifteen minutes until it passes, then crank up the engines and taxi out to a position just short of the runway. I run the engines up and check the mags and the props. Everything checks out. I try really hard, but I cannot think of any good reason for staying there so I call the control tower and get clearance for takeoff.

I taxi out and line up on the runway. This is the blackest night I have ever seen. No stars are visible, and beyond the far end of the runway there is not one light. I know that immediately upon being airborne, I must rely exclusively upon the flight instruments for spatial orientation. I am now trying to prepare myself mentally to accommodate to that critical transition from the runway lights to the flight instruments. I am experienced enough to know that our longevity depends upon my ability to do this successfully but not experienced enough to be completely confident that I can do it.

On this comforting thought about spatial orientation, I open the throttles, release the brakes, and we start to roll. The takeoff is good. We get off the ground with two or three feet of runway to spare. Now I am so completely without outside visual reference that it is like flying inside an inkwell. But it's all right; I have made a good transition and am solidly locked on the flight instruments.

"Gear up," I say in a voice that comes out in a frequency higher than I am used to.

Now something happens. As the gear retracts, the nose pitches up sharply. This happened during our heavyweight takeoff on our shakedown flight, but that was in the daylight, and I was in visual contact with the ground. There is a big difference.

I cannot overcome this pitch-up with the control column alone, so I grab for the elevator trim tab control—the coffee grinder handle—and give it a substantial twist in—I cannot believe it—the wrong direction. The nose now pitches up more sharply. The airspeed is bleeding off rapidly to where we are in imminent danger of stalling, and I've only got 400 feet of altitude. I fight to get the control wheel forward with one hand while I turn the trim tab control with the other—this time in the right direction.

The airspeed is still decreasing and as it passes through ninety, I feel the right wing tip start to stall. Instinctively I kick hard left rudder to raise the right wing as the nose drops in response to the controls. Now I've got the wings level and the nose down, and I've averted a stall. We are still flying but I'm not out of trouble. I've got to keep the nose down until I can get some airspeed, but I'm almost out of altitude.

As the altimeter approaches 100 feet, I start to level off. The airspeed reads 100. I bottom out at eighty feet and hold it until the airspeed reads 115 and then start a slow climb. When I get to 300 feet, it feels like 3,000, and I start to breathe. At 6,000 we break out of the overcast into a beautiful star-lit night. I covertly clear my throat two or three times and say, "Arnie, give me the heading to Africa."

I have to say Africa. If I don't say Africa, he might think I want to go to Chicago, or something.

We level off at 9,000 feet. I throttle back to cruising power and lean out the mixture controls as far as I dare. My breathing is nice and regular. The chief switches the fuel valves so that we are feeding from the cabin tanks.

Arnie, who is six-feet-four, now finds that the only way he can shoot the stars is through the windshield. This gets a little clumsy. I am flying the plane manually, of course, and trying to maintain a stable platform for him. In the effort to get close to the windshield, he frequently sticks his elbow in my eye, hits the throttles and prop controls with his knees, and generally clutters up the cockpit. If I were not so sympathetic with his objectives, I would send him back into the cabin.

And there seems to be another complication that makes it difficult for me to fly straight and level. Every time I get the aircraft stabilized, the nose wants to pitch up. When I trim that out and again get stabilized, the nose pitches down. This happens several times. I wait for it to happen again. As the nose pitches down, I look over my shoulder back into the cabin just in time to see the crew chief seating himself. In one hand he has a large sandwich and in the other a bottle of coke. Now I see it all. This 290-pound man has been making frequent trips to the tail of the plane to his personal pantry. Every time I get stabilized, he gets hungry and goes to the back, making the nose pitch up. About the time I get that corrected, he comes forward to his seat, and down goes the nose.

I motion him to come up to the cockpit. I explain the problem and tell him he can have one more trip to the back. This time he had better bring forward all the goodies he needs until we land in Africa, because this is the last trip he is making. He understands this. The airplane and I feel his last trip to and fro. I look back. He is sitting in his seat surrounded by about twelve pounds of snacks, and my pitch problem is solved.

We have been airborne now for two hours, and it is time to pour the gas from the five-gallon cans into the cabin tanks, for enough gas has been consumed from them so that they can accommodate the seventy-five gallons. I know that strong gas fumes will permeate the airplane during this fuel transfer. Although I turn off all the electrical equipment, the possibility of a random electrical spark and consequent explosion still exists. The chief cracks open the main entry door—no mean trick against the slipstream—and we open the side windows in the cockpit. This produces a breeze of about forty knots through the aircraft.

But it all goes smoothly. The chief empties the fifteen cans in less than ten minutes, and as far as I know, never spills a drop. Another fifteen minutes and the gas fumes have dissipated, and we close the door and windows. I look back into the cabin and see the chief relaxed in his seat, eating a large sandwich. Thus reassured, I settle in to grind out the time—about ten hours to go now.

And so the night passes. The weather is perfect, the engines are running smoothly in spite of the extra lean mixture, and Arnie keeps plotting fixes. That he is able to do this under these conditions is amazing. And he never complains about the conditions. He just appears in the cockpit from time to time, wraps himself around my neck, kicks all the levers and switches within reach, takes a shot through the windshield and leaves.

He doesn't volunteer any information, but when I ask him how we are doing, he always replies that we are on course and are making a good ground speed. Of course I don't believe this.

I mean that I believe that he believes it; I just don't believe that what he thinks is an accurate reflection of the facts. But he is all I've got, so when he says these things, I always nod as though I do believe him for I don't want to worry him.

We have been out for hours now, and I am beginning to see the first signs of dawn. Short of land itself, there is no sight more welcome to a pilot flying the ocean. The appearance of dawn seems to reaffirm the order of things. If the sun really is coming up from the right direction, and on time, just like it is supposed to, why then, maybe there really is land out there about where the geographers advertise it to be.

Anyway, dawn makes us feel good, and in this case it means that we are not too far from our destination.

Our fuel situation is good. There is enough in the tanks to get us on the runway with a comfortable reserve. This assumes Arnie's estimated ground speed is somewhere near correct. It also assumes that we will hit the part of Africa we have been aiming for, and that the weather at the terminal airfield will be workable.

Soon I pick up the equatorial front. It is a solid cloud bank lying perpendicular to our flight path. It stretches north and south as far as I can see, and it seems to extend from the water to up to about 7,000 feet.

I begin to let down as I have planned so that I can get under the ceiling and remain in visual contact with the water in order to spot the coast as we approach it. I have to go down to 500 feet to get underneath it. I am in light rain but the visibility is not too bad. If it holds like this, we've got it made.

But in a few minutes, in accordance with that mystic law known to all airmen, the ceiling slowly starts to lower. Naturally the visibility also starts to decrease. Decrease in visibility is covered by a sub-paragraph to the basic mystic law, and works exactly the same way. Now I am down to 400 feet. At least that is what the altimeter says, but I have no current altimeter setting, so I don't know what my actual altitude is.

I have to face the possibility that the ceiling will go so low that I will not be able to stay underneath it. If that were to occur, I would have to climb up into or above the overcast to a safe altitude and take a chance on finding a hole to let down through, or hope the homing beacon at the field is in operation which would allow me to make a primitive letdown. In any case, I need an accurate altimeter setting. I let down until the propellers are almost clipping the top of the waves and set the altimeter to zero and climb back to the base of the overcast. The altimeter had been reading about 100 feet too high. That is, it said I was 100 feet higher than I really was. At the altitudes I am working, this is important information.

The ceiling and visibility continue to decrease, until I am down to about 200 feet with a forward visibility I estimate to be about one-half mile. Just as I am getting really nervous, it gets worse. I start to run through lower scud which occasionally cuts the visibility to zero. At this altitude and this close to land, this is no good. I mean this is worse than being nervous; this is downright dangerous. I am beginning to wonder what I am doing here, a couple of feet above a surly looking ocean, sloshing around in this dumb rain and these dumb clouds, with Africa out in front of me—God knows where—when with just a little planning and a little good judgment I could be back in Palm Beach at Ted Stone's Taboo with a pretty girl having a couple of martinis and a charcoal broiled New York strip sirloin. But no, I had to act smart. I had to say, "Yes, sir, where's Persia?" and "Here it is, sir, it's the pink one."

The situation is too dangerous to tolerate. Much as I hate to, I decide I have to climb up into the overcast. I advance the throttles to climb power. Just as I do, a white line of breakers passes underneath me. It's the coast. There is no doubt. A stretch of sandy beach and the dark line of trees whip by and confirm it. My adrenalin squirts from every pore. I rack the airplane up in a 180° turn to get back to the beach and yell, "Arnie, we just coasted in. Which way do I turn?"

This is a critical juncture. Arnie has to know if we are north or south of the airfield. There is no way to tell from the appearance of the coast which we have hardly seen anyway. I have had the radio compass tuned to the airfield homing beacon frequency, but naturally am receiving no signal. This is in accordance with another sub-paragraph of the mystic law; to wit: radio navigation aids only operate properly when you don't need them.

Arnie's reply is prompt and beautiful. He says, "Ah, yes, this must be Africa. We are about five miles south. Follow the coast north and we should hit the river leading to the airfield in about two minutes."

I can't believe this. I can believe that he is fairly sure whether we are north or south of course, but how, after eleven hours of celestial navigation based on observation taken through a windshield on an unstable platform, can he say with such aplomb that we are five miles south?

I sight the beach again and turn north up the coast, following the line of surf. Almost exactly two minutes later, in heavy rain, I pick up the mouth of the river that leads to the airfield. I turn up the river. I do not spot the airfield until I am almost directly over it. I make the tightest turn I can around the field so that I will not lose sight of it in the rain, make a close-in approach and put the wheels on the runway. I have made better landings, but none that ever felt so good.

I taxi to the parking area, kiss Arnie, and shut down those great engines. Just as I do, the homing beacon signal comes in loud and clear. This is in exact accordance with the provisions of the mystic law.

After the cockpit is secure, I remain in the seat for a moment and consider how lucky I am that some other idiot did not get this trip. I would have missed all the fun.

Early the next morning we take off. Four days later we land in Tehran. We are met on the ramp by an administrative officer from the American Military Mission. He is a nice young man in a clean uniform, and he says, "Welcome to Tehran. How was your trip?"

"Routine," I say, and get into the car to go to town.

Winton R. Close spent his entire military career, with a few exceptions, in heavy bombardment. His flying career started in B-18s, ended with B-52s, and included almost every bomber in between, particularly the B-29, which he flew in World War II.

P-40 Kittyhawk

Donald M. Marks

Doubtless, many military aircraft of the United States could qualify, in one sense or another, for the appellation "winged institution." But for being a breakthrough aircraft in its time, for being on hand and delivering in an unavoidable world conflict, for numbers produced, for pilots trained, and for theaters in which it served, few U.S. military aircraft can compete with the record of the Curtiss P-40. Tomahawk, Kittyhawk, Warhawk—call it what you will, this schooner of the sky entered full-scale production in the summer of 1939 and continued (although always under modification) until late in 1944. Over 15,000 P-40s were eventually produced, and although it was both praised and damned, it served in virtually every theater of World War II and, of course, gained an almost histrionic fame as the shark-toothed aerial weapon of Gen. Claire Chennault's China-based Flying Tigers.

I first met the P-40 in the summer of 1944 at Napier Field, Dothan, Alabama. Having just graduated from advanced flying school and feeling myself lord and master of the AT-6, I was elated to learn that I was one of a small group to undergo transition training in the P-40E. Of course, checking out in a new aircraft in those days did not entail the highly formalized training programs we have today, which employ much ground school, large dosages of simulator time, and dual-seated aircraft. Ground school we had, but it was fairly casual and even superficial by today's standards. The Pilot's Aircraft Handbook was certainly abridged in comparison with the Dash Ones for today's aircraft, and instructor pilots (IPs) always seemed to have other duties and/or concerns. In my case, my IP's wife was pregnant and his anxiety concerning her condition far exceeded his interest in teaching me some of the mysteries of the seemingly awesome P-40.

Opposite page: American and Chinese pilots return from P-40 flights over India.

Being familiar with only radial-engine aircraft, the pointed spinner and long nose of the P-40 gave each of us a bit of a start. Then, too, we had heard many rumors about the Allison V-1710 in-line engine; its vaunted horsepower coupled to the huge, three-bladed Curtiss electric propeller gave us fledglings a weak-in-the-knees feeling. Finally, weight and size were eye-catching, in that the P-40 weighed some 5,500 pounds empty and had a wingspan of thirty-seven feet, length of thirty-two feet, and stood almost eleven feet.

I recall that the preflight inspection was stressed by my IP and he graphically proved his point on a number of aircraft parked on the ramp. There were usually several loose Zeus fasteners; a myriad of leaks from coolant, water, fuel, oil, and hydraulic fluids; rust and corrosion; trim tabs out of alignment; and, due to humidity and summer thunderstorms, excessive condensation in the fuel tanks making it necessary to drain the fuel strainers prior to each flight. Also, a very hot Alabama sun shining on exposed metal surfaces could render those same surfaces absolutely untouchable.

If just viewing the P-40 from the ramp was small cause for consternation, climbing up the left wing root, throwing the seatpack parachute into the seat, and easing oneself into the cockpit was indeed real cause for dismay. First, you were forced to wend your way through an ingenious control-lock arrangement only to find that the wing itself substantially formed the shallow pilot's seat. Being short of arm and leg, I found the control stick much too far forward, as were the rudder pedals and instrument panel. Consequently, I immediately became probably the only "four cushion man" in the AAF. But once buckled in, and with my somewhat distraught IP standing on the wing root, I was privileged to attempt starting the elongated Allison. This procedure was not too complex. Battery switch was turned to "on," proper fuel tank selected, and mixture turned to idle cutoff. You then depressed the heel of the starter pedal to energize, the toe to engage, and once the Allison caught, vigorously primed until moving the mixture control forward sustained combustion. Once warmed up to where the coolant needle registered in the green, one was reasonably ready for the headier demands still awaiting him.

It is difficult for a flyer attuned to a radial engine to adequately describe the sinister harmony of the Allison engine, for once warmed up it had the snarl and purr of a giant tomcat. But it had its demands, too, in that you had to constantly address positioning the manual coolant shutters. In flight, many a new P-40 pilot learned this requirement the hard way because in moving the coolant shutter-control lever it was easy

---

Opposite page: Inside the P-40's cockpit.

not to position it in the proper indent position. Airflow on the shutters forced the lever sharply back, and the unwary pilot had barked knuckles for a souvenir. This quirk of the P-40 forced many pilots to wear gloves, a custom still adhered to in today's USAF.

I can still remember mechanics wincing from the Allison's snarl as they pulled chocks. And taxiing out did nothing to increase confidence as the long, black-striped nose looked more like the runway than part of the aircraft itself. With such poor visibility, it was necessary to continually "S" the aircraft, and a fair share of the unwary were guilty of running into mobile fire carts. Then, too, there was an interconnect between the rudder and the tail wheel which sometimes resulted in almost wild rudder kickings—especially when we were forced off taxiways onto natural turf. It was also apparent during early taxiing that the throttle control was uncomfortably close to the side of the fuselage. This engineering aberration was especially maddening during formation flying, as a tightly clenched fist around the throttle would rub against the fuselage wall during throttle movements.

In our training situation, we tended to bunch up during taxiing out to take off, and a common occurrence was to have the engine overheat, percolate, and thoroughly splatter the windscreen. In fact, the P-40 could be depended upon to bathe the pilot in at least one of the aircraft's vital fluids. At Napier, in an effort to combat the overheating, fire trucks would position themselves near the takeoff point and hose down the engine areas as the P-40s approached number one—not too effective really, but it was an effort to keep the Allisons cool and the aircraft mission worthy.

Taking the active runway for the first time in a new and more challenging aircraft is always an adrenalin-producing experience. With aircraft behind you and the brusque urgings of the tower, there is scarcely time to savor the unreality of the situation. On opening the throttle of the P-40, two factors were immediately apparent: I forgot that there was no automatic boost control and I blissfully exceeded the designed manifold pressure—even though the throttle gate was purportedly designed to thwart such violations; more frightening was the pronounced torque I encountered which necessitated tapping the right brake pedal to stay within the general runway dimensions. With over fifty inches of manifold pressure and some 3,000 revolutions per minute, we were airborne in about 1,000 feet.

Thrill followed thrill. The Rube Goldberg gear design required moving the gear handle up and then depressing a button on the stick which actuated an electric hydraulic motor. About thirty seconds were required for this cycle, and I came to believe that every P-40 pilot ought to have a third hand. Moreover, the gear rotated 90° as it retracted, and because it was not always symmetrical during the process, the long nose took some fright-inducing wanderings before the gear nestled into the wing wells.

With a little altitude and growling along about 300 miles per hour, one experienced a sudden sense of euphoria and, for a moment, actually felt as though he were master of the aircraft. I could not help but remember my IP's parting words as he had waved me out of the chocks: "If you get confused, climb it in the red and cruise it in the green!"

Trying to trim the aircraft gave me an opportunity to wax profane and as I experimented with various speeds and altitudes, I found myself literally a slave to the rudder trim. The elevator trim knob was especially difficult to deal with in that it was small and awkwardly positioned directly beneath the rudder trim tab. Thus, a moderate amount of digital dexterity was needed simply to trim the bird.

The need to constantly monitor the rudder trim produced its share of victims. Toward the end of the course, and while flying in a three-ship formation, the number two man apparently attempted to reset rudder trim while in normal formation. With his head in the cockpit, he fell back but drifted into the lead ship so that lead's empennage suddenly became a flapping, shredded mass of metal and canvas. Amazingly enough, lead managed some degree of control, but elevator action was virtually nonexistent. A hasty airborne conversation resulted in the lead pilot electing to bail out—which he did. I remember him slowing the aircraft down, sliding back the canopy, carefully stowing the Form #1 in his flight suit, crawling out on the wing root, and sliding down the trailing edge to blossom just before entering a thin, partial undercast. And for what seemed like an eternity, that pilotless P-40 continued in flight before the left wing finally drooped and the machine eventually entered a steep, pseudospiral before vigorously merging with an Alabama peanut field. Thereafter, our lead pilot was, for days, the hero of the base and a man who commanded much awe and respect.

The most noteworthy in-flight characteristic I can recall about the P-40 was its slight, effective, and agile ailerons. With the long nose, sharp spinner, and highly responsive ailerons, slow rolls or barrel rolls were pure delight. Indeed, the T-38 of today has astounding roll characteristics, but it is a jet and the controls are boosted. That old P-40, however, in many of its aerobatic maneuvers, reminds me today of similar aerial antics in the T-38. Also, as I recall, stalls in the P-40 came on with celerity but no real deceit; however, the aircraft would roll to the left with an accompanying sharp dip of the nose. The aircraft also had a pronounced tendency to be somewhat tail heavy.

At medium altitudes the P-40 was reasonably fast, as it had a maximum true airspeed of around 330 at 15,000 feet. And for those more adventurous souls who like really "creative" flying, the Bendix-Stromberg injection carburetor system allowed rather sustained periods of negative Gs; however, after about 15-20 seconds, the oil pressure began to waver, signifying that it was time to right oneself.

Loops commenced around 250 miles per hour at 5,000 feet and would gain about 3,000 feet in the ensuing arc—much better than the AT-6 and no need at all to play back pressure at the top and backside as demanded by the Texan. But much rudder was needed—all the way around.

Snap rolls were fun in the AT-6, but the few I did in the P-40 always seemed to be harbingers of some forthcoming structural failure, as I would hear strange murmurs throughout the airframe. The aircraft seemed to resent the maneuver.

I never spun the P-40, although it was a common adventurism in the AT-6. Also, in mock dogfights, I found the P-40 to be fairly good on acceleration, somewhat lagging in climbs "back on the perch," and reasonably responsive in heavy-G maneuvers. The normally light ailerons became quite heavy in a high-speed dive.

As with any reasonably successful flight, there must be a landing. My return to the field the first time was concerned more with doing just that than with the problem of inserting myself into a mixed pattern of floundering P-40s and AT-6s.

The lengthy nose of the P-40 still bothered me, and, of course, there were higher traffic pattern airspeeds to consider as well as the unsettling memory of tales about how difficult it was to three-point the aircraft. Notwithstanding these nagging doubts, I was committed to merging with the landscape in some fashion, and I fervently hoped that the aircraft shared the same concern.

Weaving my way down through Alabama cumulous buildups and attempting to dodge other P-40 and AT-6 aircraft, I went through a hurried prelanding check consisting of advancing the mixture and revolutions plus selecting for proper fuel tank, slowed the aircraft to about 220 miles per hour, and entered a 45' leg to the downwind. Turning on base was around 180 miles per hour, and I initiated a reverse of the gear-up procedure previously accomplished after takeoff. The gear indicator, although graphic, really didn't give the assurance that the gear was down and locked, so a crosscheck was accomplished by attempting to actuate the emergency hand pump on the right side. Of course, there was a horn check when throttle power was sufficiently reduced. Lowering flaps was a pleasure; you could move the flap selector to the "down" position and then just squirt down the desired amount of flaps by depressing the button on the control stick.

Naturally, I overshot final while mumbling "gear check" and performed an erratic "S" turn to line up with the runway. Final airspeed was around 110, and as I crossed the fence and began groping for the ground the whalelike nose blotted out the entire airfield—and there I hung. I have a formula for such moments in flying. When inordinate stress is upon you, simply commit your soul to God, consign your better judgment to the devil, and comfort yourself with a tight shoulder harness and a fervent soliloquy that you are indeed in control of the aircraft. With these matters arranged in a sequence of importance, your mind is suddenly unfettered to contemplate such trivia as airspeed, drift, lineup, height above runway, gear down, touchdown point, etc. In this case, touchdown was around 80 miles per hour and, predictably, a bit long. Because I could not see the runway's end, it passed my mind how nice it would be if someone were in front of me spreading concrete. Subsequently, I learned there was less heartburn in making wheel landings and then judiciously using the brakes once the tail wheel lowered to the runway.

Turning off the active, I manually opened the cowl flaps, raised the wing flaps (how close that handle was to the gear handle!), and began to "S" my way back to the ramp. Understandably, the crew chief was surprised to see me, my IP was nowhere in sight, and I shared my uncommon elation with myself. As the huge prop spun to a stop and the noisy, metallic murmur of the Allison ended, I could not help but feel a genuine sense of accomplishment. There have been many airplanes since the P-40, but for me it was a love affair I never really erased from memory—nor wanted to.

Unfortunately, or so it seems, when fighter pilots convene and converse, the talk revolves around the joys, thrills, and dangers of a particular flight; seldom do the aircraft actually receive their due. But candidly, what is it that makes any aircraft great? Such a question spontaneously and understandably triggers several responses. Aircraft are great because they are truly superior flying machines; others achieve stature in the hands of skilled pilots or superb tacticians; others simply have a good press—the P-40 probably falls in the last two categories. It was inferior to the Zero, but in the hands of AVG pilots, it compiled an enviable record. And its colorful air intake, plus its AVG role, produced for it the stuff that projects legends. I have flown a number of different conventional fighters and whistled about the sky in a few jets, but in the recesses of my memory there remains that long-nosed demon that gave me my share of anxious moments—and pleasurable thrills.

Unavoidably, the P-40 gave way to the Mustang, the Thunderbolt, and the Lightning. The latter aircraft all achieved eminence in the aerial battles of World War II but they were not even on the horizon in 1940. The P-40 was present for duty and it met challenges and tests until giving way to the new breed. In a sense, it was the mother fighter for the future USAF, for it spawned new fighter versions and trained countless pilots in the rudiments of flying a genuine fighter plane. Unequivocally, it was, and remains, a winged institution.

Col. David M. Marks flew the P-40 at Napier Field, Alabama, after graduating from flight training in the summer of 1944.

B-26 Invader

William Carigan

The Douglas B-26 got to me about the way Juliet got to Romeo. When we met, I dwelt in the house of the heavy bomber and so could only admire those lines from afar.

Shortly after World War II, on a day when I was Airdrome Officer at old Smyrna Army Air Field, Tennessee, Gen. Elwood "Pete" Quesada, then commander of the Tactical Air Command, landed and taxied his B-26 (then A-26) up to the ramp in front of operations. Before he disappeared with the base commander, he told me to prepare him a clearance for Langley. "Make it two hours," he instructed. Inbound, he had filed to cruise at a true air speed (TAS) of 300 miles per hour, and he'd made 300. When he got back, he found I'd made his clearance for 300 TAS, but the 600 miles to Langley against a 55-mile-per-hour headwind came out at two hours and twenty-seven minutes. I added three minutes for him to touch down. He shook off my estimated time en route the way a star pitcher shakes off the signal of a rookie catcher. Grimly, I moved his indicated airspeed up enough to make the ETA two hours. The general flashed his magnificent smile, climbed the side of the bird, and departed. I didn't; I sat there at operations until air traffic control closed his flight plan upon his landing at Langley, exactly two hours later.

A few months later, reporting to the personnel office at Langley for assignment, I learned I had a choice—base supply or duty pilot in the 363rd Reconnaissance Group. I made a show of thinking it over, and two days later I was following Instructor Pilot Roger Rhodarmer's directions about which foot to put on the ladder and which hand to put in which handhold; then and there I was on my first real date with the love machine. I felt the willingness of her exciting skin, and from there things just got better.

Opposite page: A B-26 Invader testing its machine guns prior to a night mission.

Looking at the B-26 was like looking at a classy lassie: good-better-best as you got closer. In 1947, the 363rd had the 162nd Night Photo Squadron, and to suit the night mission the birds were painted glossy lacquer black. Gleaming, exciting black made those birds interesting to everyone on the base, though climbing up the side and onto the wing pretty much excluded the social-security set from the cockpit—which, by the way, you drop into from above, stepping down squarely into the seat, staying off the canopy.

Once in the seat and strapped in, I nearly always set the parking brakes. That item was omitted from the checklists we had in that outfit, and one day I had a ground crew man running alongside waving his arms and pleading with me to stop before something untoward occurred. Brake-setting then became a prechecklist item with me.

No airplane ever had a more convenient cockpit. Everything was within easy reach, except perhaps a stewardess. The airplane was easy to start (but when the engines were hot you could really blow a stack, so looking at the stacks was a common preflight routine on the outside walk-around) and easy to taxi (except that idling revolutions would make taxiing too fast, lowering them sometimes caused the engine to die, and a very little braking heated the drums up too much).

With those early airplanes it was a good idea to pull up the ladder before taking off, because it wouldn't come up once the airplane was in flight. (Later versions had handholds and foot holes up the left side of the nosewheel door and fuselage; earlier models had a ladder on the right side, and this was to be retracted into the fuselage by the navigator or crew chief. But the method of entering the plane was continually being modified.) Warm-up and run-up were the same as for any other reciprocating-engine airplane. On a cold day you might have to wait a minute or two for the R-2800 engines—cylinder-head and oil temperatures—to get warmed up enough for the power check. The operating-limits markings on the instruments are clear and standard. You could stay out of trouble even if you'd never seen the tech order.

Everything is so simple and easy that before you know it you are ready for that big jingle you always get when you mash the throttles forward.

But wait; I forgot to warn you about one little thing. The rear gunner's compartment, usually fitted with two or four passenger seats, for normal operation is isolated from the front end. When you call aft on interphone to see if your passengers are ready for takeoff, they should give you an affirmative. If you get a negative, there are usually too many briefing items, so it's back to the ramp for shutdown and careful rebriefing. The person (or persons) back there is totally dependent on radio and the emergency bell. He has to know how to run that interphone, how to keep up with the flight on command radio, how to reply to the pilot, and how to behave in emergencies. Nearly every twenty-six driver has had one trip back to the ramp to get the procedures straight with that stupid ground-pounder back there. You're lucky when you park, shut down, go back, and open the door if you aren't greeted by a compartment full of white nylon parachute cloth. All he knew was to pull the ripcord. After that you are always careful in your briefing to see that your passenger understands. And brief *courteously*, because that guy back there is all too frequently a VIP. I've hauled a lot of stars and politicians and also tucked the lap robe carefully around some pretty WAFs and nurses.

But careful briefing and all, when you call back and ask if the passenger is ready for takeoff and get no reply, all you can imagine is the guy bouncing along the ramp behind you, interphone cord tangled around his leg.

The best A/B-26 story I know is about a passenger in the gunner's compartment whom the pilot didn't check out thoroughly on communication. The pilot took off and climbed through the overcast. As soon as he was on top, he had an engine start backfiring and smoking heavily. He turned back and advised the tower; then he saw a nice big hole which he dived through, coming out under the overcast and heading for the base. Back on the ramp, he shut down and went aft where, to his consternation, he found that the door had been jettisoned and that his passenger was missing.

Soon base operations got a call from the passenger who requested transportation to the base. When the passenger arrived, he reported on his adventure, which began when the engine started misbehaving. He called the pilot on interphone and got no response (naturally, the pilot was on the command radio). Alone and out of communication, the passenger got nervous. Then the airplane rolled over and pointed down. Deciding that they were crashing, he jettisoned the door and bailed out. Then the airplane leveled out and flew away toward the base.

The 162nd had a couple of dual-control airplanes (except that there were no brakes on the right side). Because it is easy to overheat the brake drums, the IP (instructor pilot) usually puts the student in the right seat for the first ride. Thereafter, the apt student sits on the left. Roger Rhodarmer put me on the right, and I followed through on everything. Every minute I liked the bird better. Cleared to line up and hold on the takeoff runway, we completed the checklist and closed up the

cockpit. The tower cleared us to go, and Roger mashed the throttles. That airplane sucked me back in the seat harder than I'd thought possible, and in ziptime the airspeed was at ninety. He had the nosewheel slightly up and power stabilized at fifty-two inches of manifold pressure and 2,700 revolutions per minute.

In another few seconds the airspeed was reading 130 and the wheels were off. Roger moved the gear lever to the "up" position and held the nose down for maybe five seconds until we were above safe single-engine speed. Then he backed the power off to forty-two inches and 2,500. At 160 he let the nose rise and the bird started climbing at 1,500 feet per minute. He pulled up the flaps, letting the bird assume its new attitude, set the power at thirty-seven inches and 2,300, then let the airspeed rise to 230, still maintaining the rate of climb above 1,500 feet per minute. Climbing at low airspeed (160–200) keeps the nose so high that you have no forward visibility. Naturally you are soon at cruising altitude, where you let the airspeed rise to 260 or 265, reduce power to thirty-three inches and 2,100 revolutions, and pull the mixture controls to "auto lean."

At this speed the airplane takes a good, tight, level sit in the air, and the controls respond immediately. If you want to cruise at higher speed, the best way to get it is to go above cruising altitude and build up the airspeed in descent to altitude. If, for example, you want to maintain 400 or 500 indicated airspeed for a bombing run, you can't do it in auto lean. And power will probably be up around thirty-eight inches and 2,400 revolutions. In the early-model airplanes you weren't supposed to open the bomb-bay doors above 240 indicated. Later models were equipped with bomb-door spoilers which changed this airspeed limitation to 425. The spoilers were three heavy, flat fingers about 3 inches wide and perhaps a foot long that extended from the underfuselage just forward of the bomb bay.

Cruising at thirty-three inches and 2,100 and indicating 260 consumes roughly 175 gallons of high-grade aviation fuel per hour. The bird holds 925 gallons in the wing tanks and bomb-bay tank, but the bomb-bay tank is only filled to 100 gallons; high-cruise endurance is just more than five hours. By reducing the power to thirty inches and, say, 1,900 revolutions, one can extend endurance by about three hours. I don't like to fly this spirited bird at airspeeds below about 230 because the controls really loosen up and feel sickeningly sloppy. In fact, at 200 the nose rises and the controls feel mushy (in reality that is still more than sixty miles above single-engine speed). I even like to fly single-engine well above 200. Bomb-bay ferry tanks, tip tanks, and external tanks extend ranges significantly.

Opposite page: B-26s in formation.

This airplane gets its fifty-two-inch takeoff kick from two Pratt & Whitney R-2800 engines and two-speed two-stage interval gear-driven superchargers—no turbo, so manifold pressure drops off at standard rate as you climb to altitude.

The highest altitude at which I ever flew the 26 was 27,500 feet; at that altitude operating at maximum continuous power, the nose sat quite high, and I couldn't get more than 170 on the airspeed indicator. I don't stay above 17,000 feet if I can help it. The airplane is cold, even though that glass canopy has you in the bright sunlight, and the oxygen mask bugs me. (I had my nose broken once and the mask shuts off the air on the side of my deflected septum.) I hate to be cold. One winter night at McClellan, I walked from operations to the airplane in a heavy downpour, getting totally soaked. Now, I don't have to tell any flyer how cold it is above the high Sierras in winter or how I felt a few minutes after pointing east.

So if you ever buy a 26 for sport flying, plan for fair days at altitudes below 12,000 feet. You'll get that deep suntan.

The airplane is restricted from aerobatics and I never tried any, but I did investigate a fatal after the driver tried to make a loop. Stalls are clean, never vicious, and you have to stand the airplane straight on its tail practically to get a power-on stall. There is plenty of warning, and the airplane almost recovers itself unless you are taking a nap.

Fuel management is simple because you can feed either engine from any tank. Usual management is to use up the bomb-bay tank as soon as you settle into cruise. To speed the consumption and to keep the left and right tanks in balance, I used to run both engines on that tank. In about thirty minutes the tank will empty. If you're sightseeing, you get momentary cardiac arrest when both engines quit. You're sitting there between those two noisy Pratt-Whitney R-2800s when suddenly they both quit at the same time. Because you are in normal cruise there is no problem getting back on tank-to-engine on each side. You soon realize what has happened; that silent moment will bring you back to reality. The navigator is no help about this—a crew chief is better—but someone has to sit watching the fuel-quantity and fuel-pressure gauges. When they start fluctuating, simply turn on the fuel booster pumps and switch the fuel selector valves to tank-to-engine on each side. But look away, think of something else, and there's that jarring moment of silence.

The airplane has no dirty tricks. You're almost as safe as if you were in God's pocket. But wait. One time I declared an emergency. I was instructing a student on a clear day, flying at about 10,000 feet over the

Great Salt Lake. Suddenly the airplane controls came all over queer—and I mean queer. The airplane didn't respond properly to the controls. I asked the tower at Hill to clear me in because I had a strange creature on my hands. I went over everything, could find nothing. When I pointed down at the field, pulled the power back and slowed down, the controls began to respond normally. Trouble again. This stable airplane behaved as if it were a ball trying to fall off a pointed stick—weird and frightening. Another search and this time I found the landing-light switches in the extended position. When I retracted the landing lights, the trouble disappeared and the airplane was a 26 again. The tech order warns you not to extend the landing lights above 190, but doesn't say why. Now I know why. With the student doing things and me doing things, I never figured how the lights got extended. But I repeat: Don't extend landing lights at airspeeds above 190.

The chief problem with engine failure is keeping airspeed above 140 so that directional control can be maintained. On takeoff, the bird passes through that speed very rapidly and the problem is largely academic. Fortunately, engine failure is very infrequent. But if you ever lose two engines, there will be no time for pondering through the tech order. That's a time for psalms and prayer and a long runway right under you.

Emergencies are rare, but one fine day I lost an engine while in the landing pattern. I was in the right seat checking out a pilot who was catching on fast, and—would you believe—I was ready to give him a simulated single-engine landing. On the downwind, as I reviewed the procedure with the student pilot, I noticed oil-pressure fluctuation. Behind me in the jump seat, the crew chief began to punch me and point over my shoulder at the warning instrument. The engine was also suggesting heavy loss of oil. On the base leg, the chief shouted in my ear that if I didn't feather the engine it might freeze (I didn't and it did, but not until we'd touched down). I told the student to keep following his simulated single-engine procedure, but that it was real. As we turned final I told the tower we were losing the engine. The student performed perfectly, and when we touched down and slowed down, the engine froze. Off on the taxiway we turned, but that was as far as we could taxi. When we climbed out of the plane, I told the student he'd passed the test; but from the way the crew chief was shaking his head, I assumed I'd failed mine.

The normal way to bring the B-26 in starts with a 1,000-foot overhead approach. If cleared, you can complete the preliminary checklist: mixtures rich, props 2,400, fuel on the main tanks, fuel boosters on, and throttle back to kill off airspeed. When the cat dies to about 220, start a smart 180° turn to downwind, rolling out, still slowing. Drop flaps 15° at this point to further slow the airspeed. As the airspeed slows to 160, lower the gear and push up the power to maintain airspeed at 160.

On base, establish 150 IAS, set props full high, and maintain 1,000 feet; turn final, dropping the nose and reducing the power. When level on final approach, reduce airspeed to 140 and start the flaps down to 38° (or, in the 363rd, 52°). The easiest landing is 38°; 52° is not quite so easy: it is more difficult to keep the nosewheel from popping onto the runway. This sweet bird of my youth drills straight down the runway on the landing roll, requiring very little effort on the driver's part. But stay off the brakes until you're way down the runway and well slowed down. Those brakes heat up fast if you're heavy footed, and you must have brakes to stop the aircraft safely. There are emergency air brakes, but they simply go full on and lock the wheels. They can be released, but there are only about four applications in the system. And remember to save the last one for the full stop, or else be prepared to field some embarrassing questions.

If you don't manage to stay off the brakes, normal or emergency system either, you'll have smoking wheels when you stop and you'll get contemptuous looks from every ground-crew man in sight, as well as from iron-butted commanders who chance to be in the area.

Always use the simple checklist. It's not hard to follow; and reading it off makes the crew chief feel important. If that man can also read maps, manage radios, and give position reports, you have an important gem. That's the kind of a guy who'll also learn to handle the plane and provide you with a chance to relax during the mission. In my travels I have seen many bad crew chiefs (or flight engineers if you wish): lazy, dull, afraid of the airplane, natural slobs, alcoholics, and the like. But I don't remember ever seeing a bad B-26 crew chief. Maybe it's because nearly everyone loves the bird. Anyway, I always had expert and enthusiastic help with the B-26.

I never bailed out of the Invader, and came close only once, at night, when I was in the aft compartment. The pilot planned too long a night VFR flight that wound up at destination in a thunderstorm, without fuel to go to another base. Fortunately, we landed on fumes. But I thought over the bailout procedures. From aft you can go out the righthand side door, or out through the bomb bay, if the pilot opens the doors for you. The pilot and the crew man in the right seat go out the top after jettisoning the canopy (being careful to duck because the windstream tends to make the canopy dish in slightly). Each man goes out on his side of the

---

Opposite page: B-26s in flight.

plane, face down and headfirst back over the wing. But—a testimonial to the reliability of the airplane—I never knew a pilot who bailed out.

I did manage a midair collision over Biggs Field at El Paso. Nobody was hurt, but the other pilot was practically in shock for a couple of hours. My right prop cut off his one and only prop. Flight safety people absolved me completely because of my attempts to avoid the cluster of light planes in the area. But one of them came up almost from under my belly and flew into my right propeller while I was in a steep turn away and to the left. The strength of the B-26 made it, for me, merely an incident.

Before concluding this reminiscence, I must mention a modification that seemed somewhat hastily engineered. I refer to the FA-26, a photo modification that was mounted under the tail and included a parabolic flash reflector about four feet in diameter. It also boasted a bomb bay full of high-voltage generators to make the huge flash work. I went west to Sacramento to pick up the first of these FA-26 models, and upon my ground walk-around inspection, I kept thinking of Rube Goldberg. I won't tell how many volts that bay full of generators cranked up to run that flash unit because you'd never believe me. I will say that normal power settings left airspeed about thirty below usual. I flew that plane back to Langley at 230 and the operation pulled out rivets all around the area under the tail, an event that was not confidence-inspiring. Tolerance and decency demand that we say no more of the FA-26.

Recently I had occasion to look at the Flight Manual for the last model of the 26, the B-26A aircraft, which was used in Southeast Asia, and was impressed with the differences the modification embodied. The early 26s had no wing de-icers, no heater props, no tip tanks, no drop tanks, no ADI (antidetonant) system, no reversing props, no antiskid brake system, no copilot brakes, no flight instruments, nor anything like as many restrictions and injunctions as the A-26 has. The old airplane wasn't as heavy; everything was computed in miles per hour and the redline speed was higher. Manifold pressures and rpm are higher in the A-26A. There is still some seat-of-the-pants flying in the A-26A but, I believe, more fun to be had from the old love machine.

I approached the Invader the right way, coming from the B-24 through the B-25 to the B-26. The B-24 is the heaviest, of course, and the slowest. The B-25 is lighter, faster, and easier to handle. The 26 feels so good in the hand, is so fast and so much fun that it shouldn't be compared to the 24 and 25. But the landing approach, the handling, and the touchdown are alike for all three (provided you use 38° flaps).

Weather and instrument-navigation techniques were somewhat sporty on the early 26. Lack of wing-de-icing equipment posed something of a problem, but the bird would carry a lot of ice and burn it off rapidly once you got below the icing level. Instrument navigation was dicey in the 1940s—the only aids were a radio compass and a low-frequency receiver (the old coffee grinder that didn't have frying pan reception until there was heavy weather, but that was when the listening became interesting). Sometime in the 1950s, omni receivers were retrofitted, a modification that took the sweat out of instrument navigation. When I was assigned to the Pentagon to work for the Chief of the Air National Guard, I found their deluxe stable contained 26s with two omnis, autopilots, comfortable aft sections for VIP passengers, and super-qualified crew chiefs, among other refinements—not the least of which was superior maintenance.

I was always looking for a reason to visit an Air Guard base and managed to visit forty states the first year in that assignment. I retired following my tour there, so the B-26 Invader was the last aircraft I ever flew for pay. I had my darkest days with the B-24 and perversely came to love that sweet old beast; but I had my brightest days with the B-26 and will never forget that blithe spirit.

William Carigan flew B-24s in the Fifteenth Air Force during World War II. He flew the A-26 Invader in 1947–1948 and the B-26 Invader from 1954 to his retirement.

C-46 Commando

William S. Woznek

The 58th Squadron of the 375th Troop Carrier Group flew C-47s under adverse conditions in the battle for the Pacific during World War II. We had moved from Port Moresby to Dobodura to Nadzab and now we were on Biak Island, Dutch New Guinea. The C-47 Skytrain had served us faithfully in our missions to advance bases over enemy-held positions. Our cargo included almost anything that could be moved through the large cargo doors—from pigeons and silverware to observation planes, prefabricated outhouses, jeeps, troops, bombs, gasoline, and miscellaneous supplies. Sometimes the supplies were dropped, but usually we landed on quickly improvised landing strips cut from the jungle. Unfortunately some of the return trips included both wounded and dead troops.

The 2nd Combat Cargo Group joined us on Biak. Our roles were the same even if our names seemed to indicate a difference. We flew the same kinds of cargo to and from the same jungle flight strips; the difference was in the aircraft we flew. Theirs were the new and much larger C-46 Curtiss Commandos.

We had grown to know our C-47s like a comfortable pair of old shoes, and some of us owed our lives to the aircraft's capabilities in times of stress. Many of us were saddened by the news that the 47 was being replaced by the 46—a beast of unknown quality and questionable reputation. But it was inevitable, and in December 1944 another flight commander and I were assigned to a crew and plane from the 2nd Combat Cargo Group for a flight check prior to delivery of new C-46 aircraft to the 375th Group.

The passing of almost thirty years has faded the finite technicalities, but the gross impressions remain. The transition in size seemed greater from C-47 to C-46 than had been the move from trainer to C-47. The

---

Opposite page: The C-46 Commando.

engines appeared to be massive but in proportion to their four-bladed props. The Boeing Stratocruiser type of double fuselage could be entered only with a ladder—a task which awed some who entered for the first time.

Those of us who had been fortunate enough to have flown the AT-9 found a familiar cockpit arrangement. Both planes had been built by Curtiss, and it appeared that the very functional cockpit of the AT-9 had been transposed to the C-46. This familiarity proved to be an asset, since no handbooks were available or briefings provided before our first and only transition flight. The check pilot seemed a bit embarrassed at having to check ride individuals whose overseas time and combat experience were so much greater than his own. His teaching technique was to answer questions; if no questions were asked, no information was volunteered.

A brief familiarization with the controls and switches and their operation was followed by starting both engines and taxiing to the flight strip. It was fortunate that the wind was calm, because the massive fin and rudder provided a surface that in a strong wind turned the plane into a weathervane. The use of throttle to taxi seemed to add to taxi speed without sufficient directional control—a situation which made reliable brakes a necessity not always available. Brake systems on the C-46 seemed adequate only when new, and "new" appeared to be for only the first day of use, with the result that one always assumed that brakes were at the point of failure. The problem was exaggerated because the brakes never seemed to work evenly, and frequent loss of hydraulic fluid could be anticipated.

The transition training lasted a total of two hours. We each did two touch-and-go landings and an engine-out procedure. We were now considered qualified C-46 pilots, expected to provide training and experience for other flight commanders and the pilots and copilots in our individual flights. To say that we were ill-equipped for the task would be a gross understatement, and the difficulty was compounded by the lack of an airplane for training purposes.

It was January 1945, more than a month since our first and only flight in the C-46, when we were assigned our first aircraft. Supplies were needed in the Philippines, and here was a perfect opportunity for on-the-job training. A bit of cockpit time would have been desirable, but we had to be off if we were to meet any kind of schedule. Fortunately the crew chief was familiar with starting procedures, and with his help we got under way. I am sure he would have preferred to abandon ship at the revetment. The radio operator was muttering with a grim look and clenched teeth. The copilot at this point was little more than an observer, since this was his first experience with the Commando. (The name was indeed impressive!)

We were cleared for takeoff and started our roll. The initial acceleration seemed a bit ponderous, but the roar of the 4,000 horsepower was reassuring as the airspeed indicator needle climbed slowly. The hydraulic boost control system had little palpable effect on the plane's flight characteristics, and the plane did not appear to be hasty about becoming airborne. A little more nose-up trim was added as we entered the last fourth of a 4,000-foot strip.

Biak is less than a hundred miles from the equator, and the sun beat down on the coral strip and the lumbering C-46. I could feel the strained presence of the crew chief standing between the pilot seats. The copilot was puzzled that this powerful machine was not airborne as quickly as a 47. Back pressure was gently applied and increased. It wanted to fly—it better fly—we were approaching the end of the strip. A bit more back pressure and it came off the ground, not much more than a couple of hundred feet from the end of the runway.

Fortunately we did not need to gain altitude rapidly. After liftoff the plane went into malarian chills as it shook and shuddered until it seemed every rivet would pop and all the instruments would fall out. The control column trembled as if possessed by some native witch doctor. This I assumed to be the indication of a power-on stall and quickly called for "gear up" as I dropped the nose slightly to assume nearly level flight. The symptoms disappeared.

Three months of squadron operations passed without incident, but there was a common complaint that the airplane did not want to fly in a loaded configuration. Each of us experienced stall tendencies on takeoff, and we wondered about our operating procedures. Weight and balance on the C-47 were no problem—load about 5,000 pounds and keep it well forward. The same procedure was used on the C-46, only the figure was 10,000 pounds.

We decided to recheck our information that the C-46 would carry 10,000 pounds, and we found that the original information was correct but the interpretation was different. We had been operating on the basis of weight loaded into the cabin, without including the normal operating elements of full tanks, crew, and auxiliary rescue equipment. The results had been that under ideal conditions we were operating with a 2,000-pound overload off short strips at tropical temperatures. This news

gave us new respect for the airplane, and a change in loading weights improved flight characteristics remarkably.

Landing at full gross weight was not recommended, but we often wondered about the possible consequences should the occasion arise. The Commando proved, at least in one instance, to be equal to the task. We had a full load of fuel in the tanks, a complete airborne 6 x 6 truck, two passengers, and miscellaneous cargo on board. The estimated weight of the cargo was 11,500 pounds, which was 1,500–3,300 pounds over our normal load.

Everything was checked, and the takeoff roll and liftoff with the now-accepted stall vibration were normal. The copilot was given the "gear up" signal as we crossed the end of the strip. Almost simultaneously a resounding explosion was heard from the starboard engine, and it immediately began to shake in sympathy with the rest of the airplane. There was a loss of rpm and manifold pressure but no other indication of our problem.

I could hear the crew chief almost screaming in my ear, "Feather it! Feather it!" I didn't believe the plane would stay in the air with only one engine with our load, and I could visualize the 6 x 6 coming through the cockpit in a forced landing. We decided to utilize what power we had, hoping that the vibration would not tear the engine from its mount and possibly take the wing with it, and try to land.

We leveled off at 200 feet and started a gentle left turn over the water. The tower was notified of our problem, and we were cleared for landing. Fire equipment was moved to the strip and a harbor unit was alerted for a possible water landing. Nearly maximum power was used on the good engine, and only enough power to maintain our speed and altitude was demanded of the ailing engine in order to minimize the vibration. I am positive we could not have survived in this overloaded configuration had the starboard engine been feathered. I must hasten to mention that the C-46 would perform exceptionally well with a full legal load on a single engine.

The pattern was unorthodox, but we managed a good approach leg to the strip. If there was ever to be a good landing, this had to be it. The combination of our gross weight and a hard landing brought visions of the landing gear struts protruding through the wing.

The low altitude gave little time to trim the plane after closing the throttles. Touchdown at the beginning of the strip seemed imperative, since I wasn't too happy about stopping the momentum of this load and

---

Opposite page: A C-46 over "The Hump" in India.

judged the prospects of a controlled ground loop and its effects on the gear.

Touchdown was at the very near end of the strip and feather light. The coral pebbles began to turn the wheels before the shocks took up the weight of the aircraft. Deceleration without brakes was such that power was necessary to taxi to the far end of the strip. The color began to come back into our cheeks by the time we had returned the plane to its repair area, where close examination indicated a blown cylinder in the starboard engine.

Many more incidents could be mentioned as to the marvelous capabilities of this aircraft, but it continued to have a bad image, especially on single engine. A visiting civilian factory representative appeared deathly afraid of the airplane. He would not relinquish the left seat in a flight demonstration and permitted us to fly only momentarily from the right seat. When asked to demonstrate a full-feathered single-engine landing, he refused. When asked to observe my procedures for a full-feathered single-engine landing, he said he would watch from the ground.

In my opinion, the C-46 had the potential to become a great airplane. The mechanical deficiencies were a result of hurried production for a wartime effort, exaggerated by the experiences of inadequately prepared crews. C-46 casualties were emphasized, but there was no mention that they were often caused by tremendously exceeding the operational limits. It is unfortunate that the Commando was replaced by more modern cargo aircraft before it had the recognition it truly deserved.

Dr. William S. Woznek began his flying career in 1938 at age sixteen. He spent more than two years flying troop carrier missions in the southwest Pacific theater during World War II.

Spitfire VIII vs P-51 Mustang

Charles M. McCorkle

Which was the best Allied fighter of World War II? What's your favorite? If you spell it "favourite," it has to be the Spitfire—no doubt about it. But if you're American, particularly an American fighter pilot, you'll probably be one of a clique of supporters of the P-51, the P-47, the P-38, or possibly some navy fighter. There are other candidates, but their supporters lean on emotion rather than logic.

The Spitfire was the Allied symbol of victory in the Battle of Britain, but it was relatively low in power, service ceiling, and firepower in those critical days of 1940. It had already been tested in the United States before we entered the war but didn't create any sensation. Its speed was only average—368 miles per hour at 19,000 feet—and its service ceiling was only about 33,000 feet with a combat load. What the Spit had going for it was its margin of superb maneuverability, and that seems to be what accounted for its earlier successes. Its great disadvantage lay in its meager fuel supply—sufficient for battling within a hundred or so miles from home but far short of U.S. standards. The Spit carried only eighty-five Imperial gallons (106 U.S. gallons) internally—far less than contemporary American fighters.

Long range and endurance weren't serious needs for Europe in late 1941, but they soon would be. When our B-17s first arrived in England and Eighth Air Force leaders were planning daylight bombing of Germany, U.S. commanders asked for RAF fighter escort as deep as possible—even all the way to Berlin. The RAF answer was, "But our fighters haven't the range." So Wright Field's Engineering Division was given the job: "Build enough range into the Spitfire so it can fly to Berlin and back to England."

Opposite page: A Spitfire XIV.

When in 1940 North American offered the XP-51 to Wright Field, it was a good airplane but not yet great. It was flown and liked by the pilots of the Pursuit Project Office. It was not only faster than the others—particularly at a low altitude—but maneuverable and had plenty of range. Its test reports were forwarded to headquarters with favorable comments. Headquarters' reply stated that there was no requirement for an additional fighter; Bell, Curtiss, Lockheed, and Republic as well as navy contractors were all building fighters. Also, we couldn't afford to dilute North American's B-25 effort. The British took on the XP-51 as a low-altitude fighter and photoreconnaissance aircraft because of their serious need for almost any quality aircraft and also because they discerned its talents.

Was it better than the Spitfire at this stage? The British never would have agreed that it was, although it was somewhat faster and had far greater range. The Spit could outturn and outclimb it and thus could defeat it in conventional dogfighting combat. Both airplanes were plagued by low horsepower at high altitude and had lower service ceilings than the Me-109s, which were still diving on the RAF at will. It should be pointed out in comparing these fighters that when the prototype Spitfire flew in 1936, it was an extension of several years' development, while the Mustang wasn't conceived until 1940. Thus in many ways they were of different generations, if we consider the acceleration of technical developments during wartime.

In 1942 came the achievement that brought both the Spit and the P-51 into the truly superior fighter category. This was the Merlin 61, an advanced Rolls-Royce engine with the new big second-stage blower. It was rated at 1,650 horsepower for takeoff; its high blower cut in automatically at about 20,000 feet, providing good performance on through the 30,000s and service ceilings in the 40,000s, outperforming all German engines in the upper regimes.

Spitfire squadrons began looking downward at any Germans they could find, and those became scarcer by the day as Spit VIIIs and IXs took to the air in 1943. Since Vs were not too distinguishable from VIIIs and IXs except at fairly close range, any formation of Spitfires had to be taken very seriously.

The P-51, meanwhile, was popular with RAF pilots. But its performance restricted it to low-altitude work, its additional weight making it inferior to the Spitfire V and many others at altitudes over 20,000 feet. Through the cooperation of its British ties, North American Aviation arranged to get two of the new Merlins to Wright Field for installation in two P-51s. North American agreed to pay for the modifications and the

---

Opposite page: A P-51 Mustang over France.

flight test work to be done. A mock-up board met and gave its recommendations, and work began on the new airplanes—the XP-51Bs. In late 1942 they were completed and testing began, closely monitored by Washington. A series of speed points was flown, and the top speed of the P-51B peaked out at 442 at 24,000 feet, a full 50 miles per hour higher than that of the Allison-powered P-51A. The vastly improved ceiling of the aircraft also was apparent. When the magic number 442 was cabled to Washington in code, North American received an immediate order for 400 airplanes.

In the spring of 1943 the 54th Fighter Group, recalled with its P-39s from the Aleutians, was moved to Bartow, Florida, and reequipped with P-51A Mustangs. We became the first P-51 group in the States and were assigned to the 3rd Air Force as an RTU to train replacement fighter pilots. The Mustang was a delight to fly. It was a pilot's airplane—comfortable and relatively roomy, everything where it was needed, plenty of speed and range, and (to the gratification of former P-39 pilots) a cockpit heater that worked. It had a "laminarflow wing" which reduced drag and allowed the modest Allison horsepower to zip us along at airspeeds we'd hardly ever seen. It was delightful, tractable, easy to fly; and our accident rate was quite low.

In the summer of 1943, I joined the stream of graduate replacement fighter pilots going overseas. Arriving in Sicily via Trinidad, Natal, Dakar, Marrakech, and Tunis, I was assigned to the 31st Fighter Group, now stationed at Termine. And of all aircraft to have as its equipment—Spitfires! It had mostly Vs but was beginning to receive IXs and a few VIIIs, these latter with the pointed wings for high-altitude performance. The IXs looked like Vs should, but the Vs were equipped with large, ugly Vokes chin filters, and looked very dowdy compared to the glamorous machines that had defended Britain. But there they were—the world's best fighters, or so some claimed. I had some doubts but felt highly honored to be given command of the 31st and privileged to try out the Spitfire.

The 31st was preparing for the invasion of Italy, including the landing on the Salerno beaches of the ground elements of one squadron, so I had the opportunity of training in the Spit and worked from the rear ranks forward. Leaving the IXs to the experienced Spit pilots, who could use them to greatest advantage, I started in the Vs. The Spitfire V was no dream fighter, I discovered. It was light, delicate, easy to fly (a P-26—P-40 combination?) but showed little performance other than beautiful handling and very high maneuverability. The wing loading was about twenty-eight pounds per square foot, compared to about fifty for the P-38s and

P-40s and forty or so for the P-51s. This gave the Vs unbounded maneu-verability—the kind the United States no longer produced because it was provided at the expense of speed and range. Although the Spitfire V is claimed to have had a top speed of 369, those we had—equipped for the desert—were much slower. The 31st had been fighting superior-perform-ance Luftwaffe fighters with them, and its record over the previous year was good but not impressive. They were truly a delight to fly, however, and great for aerobatics.

By now each squadron had several of the newer aircraft, and replace-ments of VIIIs and IXs trickled in slowly but steadily. While almost as maneuverable, they had greatly improved performance. They were pow-erful—they seemed to leap from our dirt runways and had starting rates of climb of nearly 6,000 feet per minute. The Spit IX reached 43,000 feet faster than had the P-51, but it really didn't want to climb much higher.

Despite the beautiful performance of these airplanes, their short range was a real headache to us. They carried internally (the V and IX) eighty-five Imperial gallons, equal to about 106 U.S. gallons. We carried for day-to-day missions an external blister tank of thirty Imperial gallons (thirty-seven U.S. gallons) for a total of 143 gallons. At consumptions of sixty gallons per hour and more, this was an appallingly small supply of fuel. It permitted a sweep of 200 miles or more in radius but for covering a beachhead from Sicily allowed us only a few minutes on station. So larger tanks were provided (blister tanks of somewhere near sixty Imper-ial gallons) so that two-and-a-half-hour missions were feasible, of which a full hour could be on patrol over the beachhead. (Such missions had become customary in the Mediterranean, where beachhead patrol was flown over the beaches of Sicily, then Salerno, Anzio, and so on. Any air action of consequence necessarily converged on the landing beaches, so these were more than just routine missions.)

Even so, the range and duration of the Spit was sadly lacking. One means of making up this deficiency was to station the Spits as near to the front lines as possible. Of course that provided poor living conditions, even with our tents, but the excitement of occasional strafings kept every-one interested. No Spit mechanic had to be told to dig a slit trench beside his sleeping area—he usually dug it before he pitched his tent. Up there within sight and sound (and sometimes range) of the cannon fire you felt you were part of the war. As late as early 1944 we lost num-bers of Spitfires to cannon fire—a dozen or so at Nettuno on the Anzio beachhead—a direct result of trying to station the aircraft as near as pos-sible to the action.

The fall and winter of 1943, once the Salerno invasion was con-cluded, provided dull air action for Italy-based Spits. Now equipped almost entirely with VIIIs and IXs, the 31st had trouble finding a fight. Battle area patrol became usual; occasional sweeps were permitted, and some escort missions with B-25s or A-20s which never were molested from the air. Their direct opposition consisted of FW-190As as either fighters or dive-bombers, protected by Me-109Gs. Victories for Spits were steady but far from numerous. The Luftwaffe tactical air force played its game cautiously and well, considering that it was heavily outnumbered. It chose odd times for hit-and-run dive-bombing attacks in the battle area and struck with little warning; any lucky defenders who were in position to pursue were likely to be confronted by Messerschmitts following through at a higher altitude. Yet the 31st victory-to-loss ratio moved near three to one—far better than its record with Spitfire Vs.

With late winter came Anzio, plenty of action, and a flurry of victo-ries, along with orders to move to the Fifteenth Air Force and be reequipped with P-51s. The P-51B already had been introduced into England in the Eighth Air Force, where it was serving as escort fighter. This was to be the role of the 31st in the Fifteenth Air Force. The first two P-51s soon were reported available at Oran in Algiers and were fer-ried to Italy where the 31st was still located at Castel Volturno, on the beach north of Naples, with one squadron on the Anzio beachhead at Nettuno.

Now we could see which was the better aircraft. Needless to say, the subject had received plenty of attention since the conversion had been announced. During a year-and-a-half of Spit operations both the pilots and the ground crewmen had become extremely partial to the Spitfire. Now came this new bird with great recommendations, but the 31st had believed and proved that the Spit could lick anything it encountered. Although a few weeks of flying a new aircraft nearly always makes it pop-ular, here was a case where a test had to come first. After several pilots had become familiar with it, a Mustang and a Spit took off for scheduled "combat," flown by two top young flight commanders. Their approxi-mate takeoff statistics were: Spit IX—horsepower 1,650, wing area 242, weight (optional) 7,300, wing loading 30; P-51B—horsepower 1,650, wing area 233, weight (optional) 10,000 (near), wing loading 43.

When the fighters returned, the pilots had to agree that the Spitfire had won the joust. The Spit could easily outclimb, outaccelerate, and outmaneuver its opponent; the P-51 could outdive and outrun the Spit. That sounds like faint praise for the P-51, but we must remember that

---

Opposite page: A Spitfire Mark IX.

our opponents were not Spits but Me-109s and that the P-51's climb and maneuverability actually were quite good—nearly as good as the Spit's. More important, the fuel capacity of the P-51 was so superior to the Spit's that an entirely different dimension was added to the combat capability comparison range. Range didn't come into play in this particular encounter, though its integration in the P-51 made the aircraft relatively heavy compared with the Spitfire, which thus had better maneuverability and climb. However, it could and did assure the emergence of the P-51 as the best of a new breed—the direly needed long-range escort fighter.

The former Spit leaders now had to plan a different mode of combat, based on these differences. More Mustangs came, and the 31st and other groups received there as they moved to the Fifteenth Air Force—the strategic arm of the Mediterranean Allied Air Forces. After a short period of reequipping and training the P-51s were ready to go. The mission was different, the environment changed radically, and even the enemy—still the German Me-109s and FW-190s—changed.

Instead of the one- or two-hour sorties in the Spits, missions became five, six, and seven hours long—tied to the bomber stream of the Fifteenth, with one fighter group protecting each bomber wing. It was difficult to do this job well—a bomber wing usually stretched for many miles—but that's where the action was. The same pilots who had been unable to find a fight in the tactical war now were sometimes returning out of ammunition. In a fighter group results weren't assessed by survival or losses or munitions expended; they were assessed by victories and, to a degree, by victories versus losses. In both these measures this particular group excelled and went on to become the highest-scoring fighter group in the Mediterranean Theater.

The incorporation of long range into the P-51 gave U.S. forces a fighter escort without peer. It could transport offensive forces so far that most of the enemy defensive units with their limited range could not join the fight that unlimited numbers of U.S. bombers and fighters had brought to a place of our choosing. This example of concentration at maximum range to attack enemy units piecemeal has the ring of classic military history studies.

How did the demands of war affect our fighters? The P-39, an interceptor by design, became a tank-buster. The P-47, a great high-altitude fighter and our strategic escort star, lost its role to the 51 and became a great fighter-bomber. And the P-51, which started as a low-altitude fighter, got the starring role of all. The Spitfire kept its missions the same throughout.

Opposite page: A P-51 in flight.

The answer to the basic question of which was the number one fighter of World War II: the Spitfire was best for the interceptor mission, while the P-51 was best for its work as an escort fighter, and each was a real pleasure to fly.

Maj. Gen. Charles M. McCorkle is one of the few pilots who flew both Spitfires and Mustangs; in fact, he became an ace in both.

B-29 Superfortress

Haywood S. Hansell, Jr.

For the pilots and crews who flew the Superfortress in 1945 there was a word that described her simply and well—the same word that would have come immediately to the mind of an old line cavalryman: she was a thoroughbred. Like her smaller sister the B-17, she could take an astonishing amount of punishment and still keep flying till she brought you home. No mean quirks. No faltering at the hurdles. Whatever the obstacle ahead, you knew without question she would have a go at it. She was big and lithe and beautiful and very powerful. And like the old line cavalryman, the pilot came to be a part of his mount. Maybe it was a matter of smooth vibration from her four powerful engines when you had them synchronized. I don't know whether other pilots of multiengine aircraft got the same message that engine drone carried to me, but I had only to think of a song to have it picked up and sung to me by the rhythm of the engines. It was pleasant but likely to be dangerous, because it became a lullaby that put me comfortably to sleep.

General Arnold had taken the most daring and farsighted logistics decision of the war. Before the B-29 had even had her first flight he had authorized enormous factories for mass production. She was all new: four new engines of unprecedented power (Wright R-3350 with 2,200 horsepower each), a pressurized cabin, remotely controlled guns, cruising altitude and speed and range far higher than her predecessors. And to cap it all she was to operate unescorted, in spite of the European experience with bombers versus fighters, against the Japanese homelands. She faced a tight strategic schedule to operate from bases not yet captured but 1,500 miles away from her targets.

Opposite page: Bombs speckle the sky over Rangoon, Burma, as they spew from the yawning bomb bays of Superfortresses based in India.

She was initially conceived as an all-weather bomber, operating preferably at night and in cloud cover, using a new radar bombsight. She did operate in this mode from bases in China and later from the Marianas. But the task initially assigned her from the Marianas called for destruction of small targets not easily identified by radar, so it became necessary to rely on visual precision bombing in daylight, at least in the initial phase.

This of course had all kinds of effects upon her as a bomber. The first was a radical change in her armament. The first B-29s had twin .50-caliber guns in the top forward turret. But experience with daylight bombing in Europe indicated that the most vulnerable quarter of attack from fighters was from the front. I cringe to confess that I chaired a committee that insisted on changing the forward top turret from two to four .50-caliber guns. The change ruined a beautiful cockpit by installing a large ammunition drum which took up all the room and blocked movement in all directions. The navigator-radar operator could barely squeeze by to reach his station. The weight went up considerably too, although the four-gun turret was near enough to the center of lift not to cause serious problems in longitudinal balance.

I shall never forget my introduction to the B-29. I was Chief of Staff of the Twentieth Air Force when General Arnold, its Commander in Chief, sent me to a modification center at Birmingham, Alabama, to try to straighten out a production jam. There were many B-29s on the field waiting for installation of armament not yet available. Meanwhile the Training Command was screaming for B-29s for crew training. I arranged to release some B-29s, with incomplete armament, to the Training Command and was about to return to Washington when it occurred to me that this was a good chance to get in a little B-29 flight time. I mentioned this, and presently a young captain taxied one up to the operations office. He tried his best to get me to sit in the airplane commander's seat, on the left, but I firmly declined. I suggested that we go over to an auxiliary field and perhaps I'd swap seats with him there.

The pilot's compartment was a new and strange environment for me. In the B-17 you sat in a comfortable seat and looked forward through a nearly vertical windshield just up front of you and along the nose of the fuselage. You had a reference point to adjust to the horizon. But in the B-29 you sat down in the curved nose of the airplane and there was no nearly vertical curved shield—only a series of small planes stretching out in front of you. Furthermore, there was no nose of the

fuselage along which you could look as a reference. After a while you adjusted to this, but initially it was confusing and uncomfortable, and there was a tendency to fly on instruments even in clear weather.

We went over to the auxiliary field and made a few landings and swapped seats. I tried a couple of landings, with indifferent success, and suggested that we go back to Birmingham, where I had a stripped-down B-17 staff plane. He suggested that I fly back to Birmingham, but I objected. Birmingham has pretty good sized hills around it, and I didn't relish finding a cloud with rocks in it. Besides I wasn't at all sure I could get the airplane down successfully. But he kept insisting that I could do it, and I was ashamed to admit that I couldn't, so I gave it a try. I got down all right, with no greater damage than chagrin over the trail of blue smoke hovering over the runway, produced by burning rubber when I used all the brakes she had to keep from running beyond the end of the strip. After taxiing back I rose to get out while the captain was filling out the Form-1. He turned to me and asked, "General, how much time have you got in B-29s?" I said, "I don't know. Whatever it is, you just got it." He turned pale and said in a shaken voice, "My God, General! I'm not fully checked out on this airplane."

One effect of this experience was to convince me not to take any more foolish chances. I got permission to take a "crash" checkout course at Roswell, New Mexico. In five days, during which I put in what seemed like 150 hours of work both in ground school and in flying, I learned a lot of things I hadn't known. In the first place I learned that the B-29 was a military command—not just an airplane. It was something like a naval ship, in which many people had to work as a team. Maybe Jimmy Doolittle could have flown it alone, but not us lesser mortals. The pilot, the copilot, and the flight engineers all had specific, coordinated functions in flying the airplane. The airplane commander called for power settings and wing flap settings and cowl flap settings and landing gear settings, much as the captain of a ship calls for engine performance and wheel corrections. The gunners had flight functions as lookouts, since the pilots could not see toward the rear quarters. And of course they had responsibilities for their remotely controlled guns, which had to be properly stowed for takeoff. The idea of ship command was deliberately fostered. The crew lined up at the left front position of the airplane for formal inspection by the airplane commander prior to entering the aircraft. Inspection checks and responses by intercoms were precisely prescribed and precisely performed.

The checklist dialogue between pilot and copilot was extensive: sixteen questions, checks, and answers before entering the airplane; twenty-five before starting the engines; nine before taxiing; twelve before takeoff; thirteen before landing. The flight engineer responded in like manner: twenty-eight questions and answers before starting engines; five as the engines were started; two before taxiing; eight before takeoff; four after takeoff; ten before landing; fifteen after landing. The bombardiers had a checklist of twenty-three items before the engines were started and eleven as the airplane approached its bombing run. The navigator had a total of nineteen points to check. The radio operator had thirty-two. In the final analysis the airplane commander was responsible for the entire performance of his crew.

This transition from individual pilot to airplane commander marked the end of an era that had begun in World War I. The last vestiges of "the daring young man in the flying machine" finally disappeared. Gone were the black silk stocking fastened to the leather helmet and the white strip of parachute silk worn as a scarf. Gone were the jaunty leather coat and the boots and breeches that had lasted into the thirties. In their place was a very determined and rather serious young man in a prosaic cloth flying suit; his swagger stick had given way to a slide rule, and he carried a book of charts and diagrams which clearly showed that the art of seat-of-the-pants flying had changed to the science of computed flight control. The only carry-over was the battered and still jaunty fifty-mission cap.

The plane had an optimum set of manifold pressures, throttle settings, gross cowl flap settings, and rpm for every altitude airspeed; weight changed constantly with expenditure of fuel—and abruptly with release of bombs. Fuel load was carefully computed before takeoff, and since the margin of safety was kept as low as prudence would permit, every effort had to be made to achieve maximum fuel efficiency.

The manual which described the use of the "Composite Cruising Control Chart" contained an example which indicates the relationship of vital factors:

To find instrument air speed and power conditions for optimum attainment of a desired true cruising airspeed
Conditions (illustrative)
    Outside temperature—10° C
    Observed pressure altitude—10,000 ft.

Gross weight (calculated)—90,000 lb.

Desired true airspeed—292 mph

Enter the curves at outside temperature: 10° C.

Follow the projections and intersections through seven steps as illustrated and read:

RPM—2300

Manifold pressure—39 inches of mercury

Cowl flap gap—1 inch

Fuel consumption—775 gallons per hour

Instrument airspeed—253 mph

Computations and power settings were normally made and changed every two hours or with change of altitude.

Even the landing approach speed was computed in relation to the gross weight. The airplane was initially kept at about 160 miles per hour with flaps at 25° in the approach pattern, and speed was decreased to a final approach at about 30 miles per hour above computed power-off stalling speed for the existing gross weight.

The B-29 was reliable in her responses to power settings and control movements. But when she was straining to carry just as many bombs as possible under conditions of maximum performance, there was not too much room for error by the crew. In the early days of operation out of Saipan and Guam, before we had acquired an emergency landing field on Iwo Jima, some B-29s just didn't make it home from targets 1,500 miles away.

This scientific approach to flying large airplanes has become routine, but in 1944 it seemed unnatural—and somehow not quite in the right tradition for combat pilots who considered that their natural talents put them in a class apart.

The B-29 had a flying characteristic that was new to most of us. As soon as possible after takeoff it was necessary to get her "up-on-the-step" and flying slightly nose down till she reached 195 miles per hour. You didn't go to a climb-out attitude immediately, as you could with a B-17. If you did, you simply mushed along at low speed consuming enormous quantities of gasoline. After reaching 195 you could climb all right, but after reaching cruising altitude it was again necessary to nose her down, get up on the step, and then set the controls for long-range cruise. This presented real problems if you were trying to maintain some sort of cruising formation.

Opposite page: Flight engineer's compartment aboard a B-29.

It took a long time to learn to get maximum range from her. The final solution was very high manifold pressure coupled with very low rpm. This went counter to all our instincts. The big props were geared, and by the time you had cut engine rpm to the prescribed rate, you felt you could hear each labored cylinder explosion and count the propeller blades as they went by. To those of us who were accustomed to the smooth roar of high revolutions, it seemed unnatural and uncomfortable. But it cut fuel consumption way down.

On the last day of my crash course, I went through another experience that stayed with me. We were flying over some very rugged terrain in New Mexico, a few thousand feet above the mountains. The instruction crew—who got pretty bored with these checkout rides—was engaged in a spirited game of gin rummy when one of them turned around, cut both throttles and mixtures on the right side, and feathered those props. He then went back to his gin rummy game. I struggled and worked myself into a lather. The control surfaces of the B-29 were large and didn't have much power-assist. Extreme left rudder could be held at the expense of a broken leg or a permanent malformation of the knee and ankle. Even with full power in the left engines I couldn't seem to hold altitude while I struggled to adjust trim tabs. After perhaps ten minutes, while I lost several thousand feet of altitude and several years of my life, the crew interrupted their game long enough to restore power on the right side. Yes, you could fly the B-29 with two engines out on the same side.

Like any fine steeplechase hunter the B-29 had a pace and cadence of her own, and the crew was well advised to observe it. You could roll easily and smoothly into a turn without excessive pressure on the controls, and she responded willingly without a break in stride. But if you tried to crowd her, to force her, she resisted and felt more like a Percheron on a beer wagon.

The engines overheated quickly on the ground. When we began operations in the tropical climate of Saipan we found that we could not afford the luxury of engine run-up and ignition check before takeoff. As a consequence we tested the engines and checked ignition on the actual takeoff run. A marker was placed along the runway, and if you were still having trouble by the time you reached it you cut the throttles and abandoned the takeoff. The engine characteristics were greatly improved with the later introduction of fuel injection.

When I took command of the Twenty-first Bomber Command, with headquarters at Peterson Field, Colorado Springs, we began simulated training attacks for the Mariana operations. We first had to adopt a standard formation and then laid out missions that were analogous to a run from Saipan to Tokyo. Most of the B-29 groups were training on bases in Nebraska, Kansas, and Colorado; and we chose Havana, Cuba, as a representation of Tokyo. The first few missions were a ghastly disappointment to us. We hadn't learned the secrets of cruise control, and we wound up with airplanes down all over the southeastern part of the United States. This was in late August 1944. We had contracted to launch attacks from Saipan against Tokyo in November, yet we couldn't fly squadron formations the equivalent distance even *without bomb loads*—although we enjoyed all the benefits of weather information and communications and no enemy opposition. It was truly a shoestring operation that took off from Kansas for a still incomplete airstrip on Saipan. The 73rd Wing began the movement in October.

We had two mechanical difficulties that threatened disaster but were cleared up literally at the eleventh hour. The exhaust valves of the top rear cylinders were not getting enough cooling air and were burning out. This often caused engine fires, and the crankcases were cast magnesium which burned like a flare. This problem was finally solved by running in a gooseneck pipe which sprayed cool air directly on that valve housing, and putting cuffs on the props which pumped more air through the engine cowling. The other problem was frosting of panes in the cockpit and plastic bubbles at gunners' scanning stations. Wright Field found a cure for this by increasing the output of the heaters and running flexible hose lines to the panes of the cockpit windows and to the Plexiglas scanning bubbles. Fortunately there were no accidents resulting from frosting.

Toward the end of September, I took the first B-29 to the Marianas. I joined one of the top crews of the 73rd Wing, and we started the flow which ultimately became massive. The crew was commanded by a very bright and capable young major named Jack Catton (who later became a four-star general, commanded the worldwide Military Airlift Command, and in 1973 was Commanding General Air Logistics Command). I'm sure he viewed my arrival with dismay, perhaps apprehension. I took a most unfair advantage of him by virtue of rank: I became the airplane commander and he the copilot. But if he had reservations and felt disappointment, he concealed them well and accepted his temporary role with good grace.

We took off from Mather Field near Sacramento. The design gross weight of the B-29 was 120,000 pounds, but Wright Field reluctantly per-

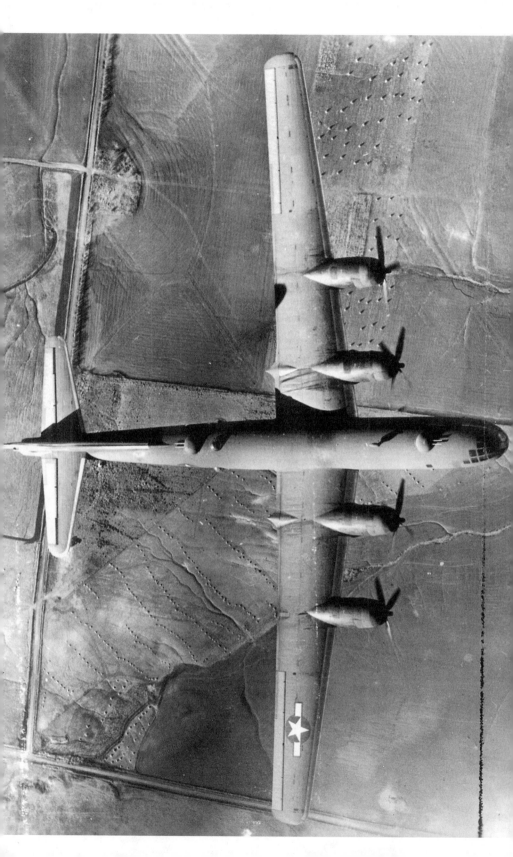

mitted an overload weight to 128,000. With our spare engine in the
bomb bay and the various kits we carried, we weighed in at about 130,000
pounds. On the takeoff run I finally felt the weight lift from the landing
gear and I made a cardinal mistake. I snubbed the brakes. This in itself
was not bad; it was standard procedure after the wheels left the ground in
order to stop their high-speed spinning as the gear was retracted. But
when I hit the brakes we were not yet fully airborne. The braking action
felt as if some giant hand had shoved us in the nose. Fortunately we got
off all right, but we hugged the surface of the ground for a long time
before we reached climbing speed. I don't know whether Jack Catton had
been prematurely gray, but by the time he reached Saipan he was. If he
had had time to look at me, he might have noticed a pale green cast of
countenance.

On the leg from Honolulu to Kwajalein, I swapped with Jack Catton,
and he functioned as pilot. There was no snubbing of the brakes. But I
was back in the left-hand seat, as we were about to start engines for the
last leg of the trip to Saipan, when a young Navy lieutenant came up and
asked if we would lead him as far as Eniwetok, about 300 miles pretty
much on our course. I made another mistake. I got a little flippant with
the young man, asking him what kind of airplane he had; he replied with
evident pride that he had a brand new Navy fighter. I asked him what
speed he wanted to fly and assured him that we would be glad to slow
down for him; we could easily make up the lost time after we had
dropped him off. He told me, and I had to bend the throttles just a bit to
make it, but I was feeling pretty smug when I called him on the radio to
say that that was Eniwetok just ahead. His response was instantaneous:
"OK, General. Sure appreciate this. Good luck. From here on you're on
your own." He laughs best who laughs last.

The 73rd Wing was ready for takeoff on its first mission on November
14, right on time. Engines were running with airplanes loaded to an illegal 140,000 pounds when a typhoon hit us and blotted out everything on
the island. It was ten days before it was possible to undertake the mission,
but on November 23, 1944, the Twenty-first Bomber Command attacked
aircraft factories outside Tokyo and launched the beginning of what was
soon to be the end.

The B-29, like the B-17 before her, had more staying power than
her crews. Fifteen hours in the air in the face of a desperate enemy and
plowing through terrible weather took its toll even on the magnificent
crews. But they would never have been able to stick it out at all if they

---

Opposite page: A B-29 Superfortress in flight.

hadn't known they were riding the Grand National with a champion thoroughbred.

Maj. Gen. Haywood S. Hansell Jr. was flying pursuit planes and bombers long before World War II. During the war he served as commanding general of the 3rd and then the 1st Bomb Wing, Eighth Air Force, and subsequently as commanding general of the XXIst Bomber Command, Twentieth Air Force in 1944–45.

Index

Page numbers in italics indicate illustrations.

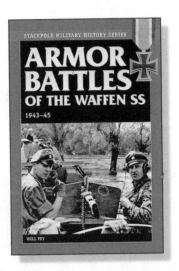

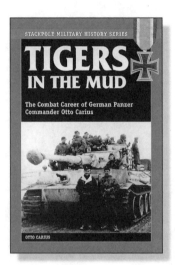